# CULT HEROES

## RANGERS FC

# CULT HEROES

## RANGERS FC

Paul Smith

KNOW THE SCORE

Published by **Know the Score Books**

**Know The Score Books** is an imprint of **Pitch Publishing**

Pitch Publishing
A2 Yeoman Gate
YeomanWay
Durrington
BN13 3QZ

www.pitchpublishing.co.uk
www.knowthescorebooks.com

Text © Paul Smith 2007, 2010

Paul Smith asserts the moral right to be identified as the author of this work.

A CIP catalogue record for this book is available from the British Library.

First published in hardback 2007
Published in paperback 2010
Reprinted 2017

ISBN: 978-1-84818-110-6 paperback edition
(ISBN: 978-1-90544-907-1 hardback edition)

Printed and bound in India by Replika Press Pvt. Ltd.

# CONTENTS

# DEDICATION

To Coral, Finlay and Mia
– my heroes

# ACKNOWLEDGEMENTS

I HAVE many people to thank for taking me along an intriguing and educational journey, not least the supporters who argued so forcefully and eloquently for the inclusion of their own particular heroes. Not every recommendation made the final cut, but every opinion was welcome and indeed the memories of Tommy Malcolm, Jim Templeton, Colin Glass, Stephen Pollock, David Dowling, Jim Jack and John Macmillan form the backbone of this book. Thank you all.

Professionally I had the valuable input of Archie Macpherson and David Francey, two of the Scottish game's most famous and authoritative voices, as well as the insight of photographer Eric McCowat, not to mention the benefit of the army of journalists, broadcasters and authors behind the cuttings, audio clips and publications which provided such a rich source of information and comment for me to research. Simon Lowe and his team at Know the Score Books deserve enormous credit for their drive and attention to detail.

Personally those nearest and dearest know by now the part they have played in each and every piece of work I produce, not least my wife Coral and children Finlay and Mia for another year filled with love, laughter and happiness.

Paul Smith
August 2007

# INTRODUCTION

WRITING AN introduction isn't so much laying the foundations for a book but more of a topping out ceremony, a chance to stand back and admire the fruits of months of hard labour. At least it should be.

On this occasion you find a writer on the defensive before a page in the first chapter has even been turned. The reason is simple: public opinion.

Usually criticism follows the release but this time it began before the book was even written. At the heart of the debate is the definition of cult hero.

Just as the finishing touches were being applied the Rangers support was sparked into life after a glimpse of the front cover. The messageboards became the forum for debate. How could Willie Johnston or Ally McCoist be considered a cult hero? How could I get it so, so wrong? Where's the line in the sand that separates the legends from heroes? Can one man wear both caps? The answer to the last question, in my opinion at least, is yes if those two caps fit.

*It is better to debate a question without settling it than to settle a question without debating it.*

**Joseph Joubert**

Willie Johnston is a legend because of his double in the European Cup Winners' Cup final but a hero for so many different reasons. Ally McCoist will forever be a legend, with records unlikely ever to be matched, but the adulation heaped upon Super Ally also ensured cult status.

John Greig a cult hero? Surely not, surely the man voted the greatest ever Ranger is outwith that niche. Unless you delve back into the archives and find the cult moments that for supporters of a certain age will tick all the boxes.

For a touch of moral support I turned to the Cult Heroes series back catalogue. If Alan Shearer is a Newcastle cult hero then Ally McCoist is a fitting Rangers equivalent. If Gianfranco Zola gets the vote at Chelsea then Paul Gascoigne can fill his boots on the Rangers list. In fact, in a BBC viewer's poll the top three Rangers cult heroes came out as Ally McCoist, Davie Cooper and Paul Gascoigne – so there is form for some of the selections.

Every supporter will have their own cult hero and there's every chance they won't be in this book. That's the beauty of football, if you could please all of the people all of the time there wouldn't be winners and every game would end in a draw.

Other clubs boast cult heroes both weird and wonderful but Rangers is a different proposition. The true heroes at Ibrox have, and always will be, the winners.

At the time the book was first released, late in 2007, there was a clamour for Filip Sebo to be recognised as the cult hero of the moment. At the time of writing, late in 2010, Sebo is but a fading memory and Maurice Edu is the man of the moment.

The men who did get this author's vote each won the hearts of the Rangers support for different reasons, whether attitude and appearance or character and controversy.

Some will forever remain cult heroes, for others the affection has cooled. Yet each in their own time was an idol.

The journey from the early days of Rangers Football Club to the present day charts the rise and fall of the shooting star of Light Blue stardom, examining the factors that influenced adulation then and now.

The remit on paper was simple. Pick 20 heroes, do the research and interview those who survive to tell the wonderful tales of life as a Rangers star. Half way through the process it all changed. Deep in conversation with some of the most loyal supporters in the Ibrox ranks – the realisation that the fans and not the players understand better than anyone what makes a hero.

The process has been long and winding, taking me down avenues I would never have imagined. The result, I hope, is entertaining because the journey for me certainly was.

The 20 players chosen all had an impact on the lives of the fans who followed their fortunes week in and week out and from speaking to so many supporters from different generations a common theme emerged.

What makes a hero is a performer who, for whatever reason, burns the image of himself in the Rangers jersey into the subconscious of Joe Public.

In truth 20 is a grave restriction. There's no room for Sammy English, a man so many of his contemporaries considered to be the greatest Rangers striker ever, or for Jock Tiger Shaw and so many of the greats of his era. Winding forward a few decades, there's no room for John Bomber Brown, for the conductor Graham Roberts or for Croatian braveheart Dado Prso.

Instead of labouring on those who did not make it, celebrate those who did and the triumphs and occasional tribulations that made them stand out.

Certainly those who shared their finest moments will raise a glass to them and in turn I toast those who passed on the recollections and experiences that made this such a joy of a project to work on.

Whether colleagues in the media or dedicated fans, the enthusiasm of everyone I encountered along the way bowled me over.

I can understand the passion, if I delve deep into my own memory bank. As a journalist, dealing with football players day in day out can deaden the normal sensitivities, the men who stand apart as heroes to the fans become colleagues in a sense – and have you ever idolised a colleague? But every journalist has been a supporter and had their hero. I spent hours trying to perfect the double shuffle so expertly imported to Scotland by Mark Walters and just as long trying to tackle like Ian Ferguson. But I only ever had a poster of one player on my wall and that was Paul Gascoigne, pre-Rangers in his Spurs kit. In those days, when he was on the way to the highest highs before anyone could have imagined the lowest lows that would follow, he was the player whose feints and turns left a lasting impression on an impressionable young football fan. When he finally wound up in Scotland, ageing physically if not mentally, his mesmerizing performances did not disappoint but his off-field antics soured the memories for this former Gazza aficionado.

That is worth bearing in mind when you flick through the 20 chapters that follow. Just because a player is viewed one way now doesn't mean he always was, some who were heroes in their day have seen their halo fade in more recent times. This isn't about how players are regarded now, more about how they touched the lives of the fans who had posters on their wall when they were at their peak.

**MAGIC MOMENT:** The coolest man on the park took the penalty nobody else wanted to and put Rangers on course for the club's first Scottish Cup success in 25 years .

# DAVID MEIKLEJOHN
## *'MEEK'* **1919-1936**

### GERS CAREER: Games 563; Goals 46; Caps 15

COMETH THE hour, cometh the man. The most cliched of sporting maxims but it is one worth dusting down and re-using when it comes to grappling for an explanation for the elevation of one of Rangers' first real heroes to cult status.

In David Meiklejohn's era the type of adulation and god-like reverie was reserved, quite simply, for God and not mere footballers. Fast forward the best part of a century and more people worship at the temple of football than the altars of Christianity but in the 1920s and 30s a reputation, a haircut or a celebrity wife didn't cut the mustard with the fan on the terraces. Judgements from the flat-capped brigade were made purely on substance, and Meiklejohn was a man who offered that in spades.

In a pulse-stopping moment he cemented his place in the hearts and minds of the Ibrox faithful and indelibly penned a place in the early annals of his burgeoning club.

That moment came in April, 1928 as part of a Rangers side aiming to end a quarter century of cup heartache by taking the Scottish Cup back to Ibrox for the first time since 1903.

Celtic were the opponents, Hampden was the setting, the crowd of 118,115 was a British record and despite the league dominance Rangers enjoyed in that period it meant everything to the Govan masses crammed into a national stadium which creaked and swayed with every cheer and groan.

The game was 55 minutes old and poised at 0-0 when the search for a Rangers hero was launched after a blatant hand ball on the line by Hoops captain Willie McStay had kept out Jimmy Fleming's net bound effort . The Light Blues had a penalty and there was one man with the iron will and steely nerve to shoulder the responsibility; his name was Meiklejohn.

*Nothing gives a person so much advantage over another as to always remain cool and unruffled under all circumstances.*

**Thomas Jefferson**

Hard as it is to believe, legend has it that a stadium packed to capacity, and beyond, actually fell silent as two sets of supporters anxiously awaited the moment of truth. Bob McPhail, the regular penalty taker, was restricted to a watching brief. This was Meiklejohn's time.

The defender stepped up, took a few short strides forward and hammered an unstoppable shot past John Thomson to score . His beloved side were on their way to the winning post and a strike from McPhail coupled with a double from Sandy Archibald cemented a 4-0 win to ensure the famous trophy was bedecked in red, white and blue once again.

At the time, he said: "I saw in a flash, the whole picture of our striving to win the cup. I saw the dire flicks of fortune which had beaten us when we should have won. That ball should have been in the net. It was on the penalty spot instead. If I scored we would win; if I failed we could be beaten. It was a moment of agony."

As poetic as it was accurate, Meiklejohn was not the type to hide behind his team-mates. On the day in question he also carried the burden, not that he saw it that way, of captaining Rangers in the absence of regular skipper Tommy Muirhead. It was a role he would grow into and make his own following Muirhead's retiral two years later and nobody would argue there was a better candidate.

In the 1920s Meiklejohn and his team-mates were the kings of the old First Division, lording it over their fierce city rivals with eight championship wins from a possible 10. The cup, however, had been a painful competition for the men from Edmiston Drive and Meiklejohn in particular.

Up to that point he had played a part in cup defeats at the hands of Albion Rovers after two semi-final replays, Partick Thistle in the final of 1921, Morton in the following year's final, Ayr United and Hibs in the early rounds, the humiliation of a 5-0 reverse at the hands of Celtic in the 1925 semi-final at Hampden, a last four defeat by St Mirren and last eight heartache imposed by Falkirk in 1927.

In between he had collected championship medal after championship medal but Meiklejohn craved a matching cup badge and in 1928 he would leave nothing to chance with that inspiring penalty.

At the post match celebration banquet, the uncompromising defender proved himself to be an uncompromising speaker as he stood up to hush from the gathered revellers and declared: "We have won it at last – we can do it again." Sure enough, he was a man of his word and he went on to earn four further cup winner's medals in his remaining eight years wearing the jersey he took so much pride in.

Football is a global industry bridging continental gaps today but in the era of Meiklejohn it was played by locals for locals. Govan had become home to the famous Rangers Football Club at a time when its rise mirrored that of its adopted club.

Meiklejohn himself was a Govan boy, growing up in what had just decades before been a village of 9,000 people but by 1907 had exploded to become what could be classed as a city in its own right, with a population of 95,000. That number would grow to 125,000 in the years that followed.

That expansion justified the conscious decision by the Rangers founders to move the club west, having been born at Fleshers Haugh in 1873 before moving on to Burnbank on the city's Great Western Road then Kinning Park before coming to rest in Govan in 1887, settling on the current Ibrox site two years later.

Only in 1912, seven years before Meiklejohn fulfilled the dream of every boy around him by becoming a Ranger, did the burgh of Govan fall into line and become part of the rapidly expanding Glasgow.

Govan's rise to prominence had an industrial foundation, home to a prospering shipbuilding industry and supporting cast of trades at the turn of the century. T. C. F. Brotchie, one of Glasgow's most esteemed historians and prolific authors of the time, described Govan as: "One of the great workshops of the world. Within its boundaries, it is impossible to get beyond the sound of the hammer. From early morn till late at night, we hear the continuous hum of industry."

Sir Alex Ferguson, like Meiklejohn, was Govan born and bred. In fact, his Cheshire home bears the name Fairfields in tribute to the shipyard his father worked at and one of his stables for racehorses, Queensland Star, was named in honour of one of the ships Ferguson senior had worked on.

Writing for the *Scotsman* newspaper, Ferguson observed: "I remember going down to Fairfields to see my father on some of those mornings when the wind howling up the river would have frozen the marrow and seeing men up aloft, working as hard and as effectively as if they were in shirt sleeves on a fine summer's day. They were made of some stuff. For anyone from Govan, the yards were the very fabric of life. And what people should realise about communities like that is the extent to which the main industry reaches out and affects every other aspect of life in the area. The dependency element was absolutely crucial."

It was from that working class and earthy backdrop that Rangers drew the core of its support, Ibrox providing an escape from the yards for the tens of thousands of men who spent their working week embedded in an unforgiving environment in which the conditions were treacherous, the hours long and the rewards far from lucrative.

The men in light blue provided the entertainment in the early days of Meiklejohn's era, which coincided with the beginnings of radio and the cinema in Glasgow. There were no film stars yet, there were no pop stars in music. But there were footballers and they had a captive audience.

In fact it was an obsessive following. One *Weekly Record* journalist, after witnessing the Rangers support at a Hampden semi-final against Hearts in the Scottish Cup in 1930, wrote: "Never in all my experience have I heard such a yell of exultation greeting a football team. It was terrific, awe-inspiring, ear splitting, unforgettable."

As Meiklejohn's time with the club progressed, the stars of football not only provided entertainment but something to cling to as the industrial decline began to bite. In the decade following that Scottish Cup win in 1928, unemployment across Glasgow doubled.

Despite the hardships of life in a country with no benefit system (that would not follow until the 1940s), the popularity of Rangers failed to dwindle. When Meek, as he was known to his team-mates and terracing fans alike, first came into the team in 1920 he played to an audience capped at 25,000 on safety grounds and by the time of his swansong in 1936 the support continued to fill Ibrox to capacity in the face of the potential drain created by the leaking of the area's economic lifeblood.

Together with their Old Firm rivals, Rangers have become Scotland's undisputed governors of the Scottish game.

The overwhelming support, which in the present days dwarfs the following of clubs in the capital Edinburgh, can be traced back to the mean streets of Glasgow in the early 1900s. Despite being smaller in mass than Edinburgh, Birmingham, Liverpool or Manchester it far outweighed those cities in population. In Edinburgh in 1921 there were 32 residents for every hectare – in Glasgow the figure was 133. It was from that shadow of overcrowding Meiklejohn emerged, although his playing career coincided with a rapid building programme designed to combat the problem.

Population was not the only factor in the mushrooming popularity of the Old Firm, a phrase only coined in 1904 by a cartoonist in *The Scottish Referee*. Religion was becoming a factor. Bill Murray, author of The Old Firm, notes of the Meiklejohn era: "It was apparent that the two clubs were attracting people to their games who didn't otherwise show much interest in football. This was in part because they played the best football but it was also because they drew on deeper passions than the spectacle of a thrilling encounter tightly contested. A game of football between Celtic and Rangers reflected the religious and almost racial divisions that scarred community life in many parts of Scotland."

The sectarian element was never hidden but in truth nobody can decisively trace the root of the popularity Rangers were beginning to enjoy. What can be determined is that the arrival of supporters in their droves was promoting the players to a new level of fame, although professional football was still in a relative state of infancy and riches had not yet followed.

It would be wrong to try and paint the icons of the day as cult heroes in the modern mould. There was none of the hysteria and blind adulation between them and the Ibrox loyal, more of a bond borne from respect.

Meiklejohn was a star on the pitch but there was no superstar status, he was a working man living among the working class at a time when Govan was Govan. He would still enjoy a quiet drink with his neighbours, at least when he could escape from the prying eyes of the army of amateur spies employed by his manager to ensure none of his trusted troops overindulged.

The difference for this working man was his yard was Ibrox and, for the second half of his career at least, he was the foreman and the one who demanded more respect than most.

It took one of the most tragic events in Scottish football history to highlight the esteem Meiklejohn was held in by the paying public. In September 1931 the talented young Celtic keeper John Thomson fell to the ground after diving at the feet of Rangers striker Sam English to thwart a Light Blues attack. English limped away, Thomson remained prone on the ground suffering from a depressed fracture of the skull which hours later claimed his life. The Rangers support, unaware of the severity of the situation, began to chant from behind Thomson's goal. The imposing figure of Meiklejohn, relatively small in size but huge in stature, ran to the touchline to silence the crowd. His request was granted, the boisterous Ibrox faithful fell silent.

Meiklejohn and his Rangers peers, alongside the likes of Patsy Gallacher at Celtic, were the sporting stars but the heroes of the time also numbered the staunch left wing politicians, the Red Clydesiders, who shared the same audience. Substance once again favoured over celebrity.

The only other rivals were the entertainers of the music halls – the likes of Tommy Lorne, Tommy Morgan and Dave Willis – but they could not match the pulling power of their ball playing contemporaries.

In 1928 Meiklejohn and his team-mates moved into the luxurious new main stand at Ibrox, complete with the surviving red brick façade and famous marble entrance hall lined with wood panelling which had been earmarked for fitting out the good ship *Queen Mary*. The 10,000 capacity grandstand was the largest in Britain and its interior the most lavish, blue was most certainly the colour.

Rangers and Ibrox was developing star quality but the contradiction was that Rangers, as a club, did not encourage superstars. Meiklejohn's time on the playing staff coincided with the beginning of Bill Struth's tenure as manager at Ibrox.

Taking pride of place on Struth's desk was a sign reminding visitors 'The club is bigger than the man'. For visitors, read any player who dared to overstep the boundaries of his strict disciplinary code.

From the time the club was founded under the Argyle name in 1873 by brothers Moses and Peter McNeil, Peter Campbell and Wiliam McBeath, the emphasis had been on teamwork and togetherness. From day one, there was no room for individualism.

What Struth did was take that ethic to a whole new level. He was obsessive in his approach to preparation, from the training he put his team through to his choice of tailored suits for his squad. He ensured his team travelled first class and were treated to the finest food, but in return he expected total commitment and compliance.

In one speech, Struth claimed: "To be a Ranger is to sense the sacred trust of upholding all that such a name means in this shrine of football. They must be true in their conception of what the Ibrox tradition seeks of them."

Considered eccentric by some, Struth himself would always keep at least one fresh suit hanging in his office at the shrine of football, a stone's throw from where he made his home on the Copland Road. The kit hung next to the cage of a canary he, according to legend, kept on side with a regular nip of whisky. Outside the office was a light and only when it was lit could a player enter for the type of dressing down the top man was becoming infamous.

That wrath was not reserved for the players, even the fans got both barrels from time to time. Struth used the press in the 1920s to appeal to the Rangers fans to clean up their act, stating: "Ever since their inception, the club have always had very high ideals – ideals which sometimes have been difficult to live up to, and all must make a determined effort to eradicate this bad language during our matches so that the good name of the club shall remain unsullied."

Meiklejohn was a perfect role model for his manager and became a key man for Struth both on and off the park, indeed McPhail, while reflecting on his career, claimed: "While Davie Meiklejohn was the club captain, I was the unofficial vice-captain. Struth relied heavily on us to make sure the team played the way he wanted. He would have Meek upstairs in his office for a chat before most matches. What was said then was not for general consumption, but it was obvious to me that Meek would probably be telling Struth how the game should be tackled and where our advantages would be. Struth was a fair man, but he was cute. If he (Struth) didn't know too much about football, he knew how to handle men."

McPhail was not being disparaging by questioning a legendary manager's insight into the finer nuances of the beautiful game. Struth did not come from a football background and was proud of his roots in athletics, a stonemason by trade who topped up his wage packet by running in lucrative races during the season. Before being appointed to the top job at Ibrox in 1920 he had served on the coaching staff at Hearts and been trainer at Clyde, the sum total of his football career to that point. Inexperience did not count against him and Struth remains one of the finest managers in the long and distinguished history of what he made *his* club, from top to bottom using the ethos of the founders.

Even in more modern times, the Struth-inspired yearning for the spirit of the early days was not ignored. Graeme Souness, as manager, said: "All of us at Ibrox must always remember what being a part of Rangers Football Club means – that is something I insist upon and anyone who forgets will get no sympathy from me."

Whether Meiklejohn was fortunate to be found by Struth or Struth was lucky to have Meek, we will never know. What is clear is the partnership coincided with a rich vein of form for the club.

Described in Rangers' official history as a "marvellous defender" and one of the club's "greatest ever captains", the club's Complete Record penned by Bob Ferrier and Robert McElroy adds: "As a player he was resolute, skilful, uncompromising, vigorous and, above all, a man for the hour".

The Govan boy's professional relationship with his local club began in 1919.

Meiklejohn was just 19 when he was plucked from the man's world of Scottish junior football, one tier below the professional game. He had been turning out for Maryhill across the city when William Wilton, Struth's predecessor, lured him home to Ibrox.

Wilton was the first manager Rangers ever had and the man credited with setting the standards in discipline, appearance and values which Struth continued. John Allan, author of *The Story of Rangers*, said: "The ideals for which he strove are still sought after by those who are left in custody of the cherished traditions of the club."

Under Wilton, Meiklejohn made the first of 635 appearances in Light Blue on March 20, 1920, on the north-east coast at Pittodrie.

Meiklejohn wore the No.4 jersey and helped his side to a 2-0 victory on their way to the Scottish league championship. The manager, Wilton, tragically died when a yacht he was a guest upon overturned in rough seas as he marked the end of a triumphant season by accepting an invitation from a Rangers director to take to the water.

Meiklejohn, who scored his first Rangers goal in a 1-1 draw with Hibs at Easter Road just a month after his debut, made 11 appearances under Wilton but it was as a Struth player he became established as the rock on which the success of a generation was built upon.

He played in 41 league and cup games under Struth in the 1920-21 season as his side swept to another title, increasing the margin of victory over increasingly bitter city rivals Celtic from three points in 1920 to ten in 1921.

Celtic gained revenge by taking the top honour the following year but Meiklejohn and Rangers were back on top of the pile by 1923, the first of a hat-trick of consecutive championship successes.

Celtic toiled to match the league consistency displayed by the team from the south side of the city, breaking the dominance in 1926 before the mantle was handed back to Rangers for an imperious five season league winning run only broken by Mother-well in 1932.

Meiklejohn collected a further three First Division winner's medals (1933, 1934 and 1935), to sit beside the five Scottish Cup gongs he amassed, before retiring as a one club man at the end of the 1935-36 season. One of his final duties was to hold the Scottish Cup aloft after a 1-0 win over Third Lanark, then Glasgow's third football force, in front of 88,859 supporters at Hampden on April 19, 1936. The captaincy was passed to Jimmy Simpson.

European football was not a factor in the Meiklejohn era but Struth was a great believer in letting his men see the world, touring Canada and the US in the aftermath of the 1928 hoodoo busting Scottish Cup win and repeating the exercise two years later as a reward for a momentous season. Just as they did on home soil, the team from Glasgow showed no mercy and racked up a series of victories on their travels.

The 1929-30 campaign was Meiklejohn's finest as a Ranger. He helped his team achieve the unthinkable, with the Clean Sweep. The league championship, Glasgow Cup, Charity Cup, Second Eleven

Cup and Alliance Championship trophy joined the Scottish Cup in the Ibrox trophy cabinet. It was the finest year in the history of the club and Meek was in the thick of it with 31 appearances in the league as Rangers held off the challenge of a Motherwell side in the ascendancy and an ever-present run of eight Scottish Cup games including the 2-1 final replay win over Partick Thistle.

Meiklejohn's career with Scotland was less fruitful than his honour-laden spell on the Ibrox payroll but no less worthy of note. A renowned leader of men at club level, he also captained his country.

Meek made his debut in the dark blue of his country in 1922 during a 2-1 defeat at the hands of Wales in Wrexham, in good company beside Ibrox team-mates Alex Archibald and Alan Morton.

He went on to make 15 appearances in an international career spanning 11 years.

The first of three goals for Scotland came in a 3-1 win at home to Wales in 1925, a game which marked his first taste of victory for a team restricted to competing in the British International Championship. Not that it was viewed as a restriction of trade, with the home series considered the pinnacle of representative football.

Success against the Auld Enemy was the target and Meiklejohn savoured that experience on three occasions, in 1925 and 1929 as well as skippering his charges to another win against England in front of 129,810 fervent fans at Hampden in 1931.

The captaincy had first passed to the Rangers stalwart in 1930, inherited from James McMullan, and he would go on to lead the Scotland team out half a dozen times. His one and only taste of European action came as captain in a 2-2 draw against Austria on home soil in 1933.

That game also marked the end of Meiklejohn's international career and he signed off in style, scoring the opening goal in front of his Glasgow public.

As captain of Scotland and Rangers, Meiklejohn's standing in the game was never in question. A fine defender and a legendary leader, those qualities could not overshadow his talent as a sublime ball player.

Willie Thornton, himself a legend in the old fashioned Rangers mould, described Meiklejohn, who retired just as his own Ibrox adventure was beginning, quite simply as: "The greatest player I ever saw."

Bob McPhail, in his memoirs penned by Allan Herron, went a step further. McPhail said: "The best skipper I ever played under, anywhere, was Davie Meiklejohn, his influence on Rangers was incalculable. I've never seen a better centre-half in my lifetime, and I've been around for a wee bit. Meek was such a complete footballer he could have played anywhere on the field. He was no taller than I, five feet ten inches, yet he could get himself up to meet those cross balls with brilliant timing to beat players much taller than himself.

"Like all the great players I've seen, he always seemed to have time and space to do the things he wanted to do with the ball. He was a brilliant passer, with both feet, and when he cleared with his head he invariably found a team-mate. When Davie played at centre-half, before the arrival of Jimmy Simpson, he would nod the ball with considerable grace to either of his half-backs or else send it further to myself or whoever was at inside-right. His timing was quite brilliant. He never looked under pressure, always seemed in control of the ball, and in the days when he would play at right-half he would come up and have a pop at goal along with the rest of us.

"As a captain Meiklejohn was simply the best. His influence on the players around him, and his encouragement to younger players, was a responsibility he accepted without a worry. Struth knew he had a genius in his defence and knew he was a lucky man to have him. Rangers have never had a greater servant."

Meiklejohn's reputation lived on, even beyond his death in 1958. John Greig, recalling the day he realised he would follow in the bootsteps by claiming the honour of the Rangers captaincy, recalled: "When Scott Symon approached me one day after training with the news that I was to follow in the footsteps of such Rangers legends as David Meiklejohn, Jock 'Tiger' Shaw and George Young there was no fanfare of trumpets. He said simply, 'I want you to be captain'. That was it. The manager clearly didn't feel that any other words were necessary when bestowing such an honour on me."

Alan Morton, a contemporary and team-mate at Rangers, led the tributes at Meiklejohn's funeral, which drew more than 2,000 mourners to Craigton cemetery in Govan, when he said: "No cause was ever lost when Davie was behind you. He will go down in history as one of the greatest Rangers ever to wear the colours." These weren't platitudes to fit the occasion, they were heartfelt observations shared by everyone who crossed paths with Meiklejohn.

The great man died far too young, at the age of 58, after collapsing in the directors' box at Airdrie's Broomfield ground. After calling time on his playing career Meiklejohn crossed to the other side of the fence, launching into a career as a journalist with the *Daily Record*. Indeed, one of his first assignments was to pass judgement on a young Struth protégé by the name of Willie Waddell as he made his debut against the all-stars of Arsenal – the 17-year-old announced his arrival by scoring the winner. Meiklejohn took to his new role as critic like a duck to water, writing: "He paid his way. If I have one fault against him, it is in not using his speed when left with a clear field. However, it was a big match for the youngster and he did exceedingly well." Waddell of course would go on to propel himself into the echelons of the Ibrox legends, alongside the newest recruit to the press box. The switch from player to reporter was not at all rare to that generation.

Meiklejohn and his colleagues who made the move were deemed consummate professionals despite the obvious potential for a conflict of interest while working in the most partisan football city on the planet.

For Tom Campbell, author of 'Celtic's Paranoia... All In The Mind?' it is a subject close to his heart. Campbell wrote in the Celtic fanzine Not the View: "I would suggest that the distrust of the Celtic supporters for journalists is a relatively new development. The pre-1980 journalists were generally a credit to their profession, although some, like Tommy Muirhead, David Meiklejohn and Willie Waddell (former Rangers stars) must have had a soft spot for their old club."

Despite a talent for writing, Meiklejohn was not absent from the frontline of football for too long, being appointed manager of Partick Thistle in 1947.

Eleven years later Meiklejohn's death stunned Scottish football, the news breaking down the Old Firm boundaries as supporters from both sides stopped to remember the man known as Meek.

The legend lives on, with the Govan boy one of the first inductees to the Rangers' Hall of Fame, and the name will never be forgotten.

And there's the crux of the matter. He did not earn a fortune and nor did he enjoy fame as we know it now, but he was the pin-up for a generation of supporters charmed by his skills with a ball at his feet and his passion for the cause. He could turn defence into attack with a deft header or an incisive pass and for a man who spent his career in the back line he knew the way to goal, making a habit of scoring in high pressure situations and demonstrating his ability to remain composed while others would have crumbled.

Perhaps more than that, they loved everything Meiklejohn stood for. He was a winner – as his haul of top class honours bore testament to – but he was a winner in keeping with the Rangers' traditions, a team player who put his club before personal glories. He was dignified in victory and defeat, respected by the team-mates he captained and the opposition he crossed swords with.

In essence he was everything a Rangers cult hero should be, the personification of the type who deserves the adoration of the masses. As it would transpire, he was very much a man of his time.

Future generations would find new heroes, perhaps more adventurous and exuberant but also less disciplined and conscious of what the values their club were founded upon, but for the flat cap generation Meiklejohn fitted the bill. And who could blame them?

MAGIC MOMENT: Three moments of devilment and the
Auld Enemy were undone. Morton put Scotland and
Rangers on the world football map in 1928.

# ALAN MORTON
## 'THE WEE BLUE DEVIL' 1920-1933

### GERS CAREER: Games 440; Goals 105; Caps 31

A S A cult hero Alan Morton had it all: the nickname, the trademark move, the song and an appearance which made him well and truly stand out from the crowd in the hustle and bustle of Scottish top flight football. The Wee Blue Devil, as he was christened, could quite easily be lauded as the first pin-up in the club's history, his career going virtually hand in glove with that of David Meiklejohn. He arrived just months after Meek and the pair spent 13 years together in the Ibrox dressing room.

Most teams have room for only one hero but for the Rangers side of the 1920s and 1930s there was more than enough space for two. Meiklejohn and Morton worked in different quarters and served different purposes but both shared the ability to satisfy the demands of one of the most demanding sets of supporters in the game.

The Wee Blue Devil blazed a trail wherever he played with his own brand of wing play and it was not only the Rangers' supporters who grew to love him.

The nickname itself was invented not for his exploits in the light blue of his club but after one memorable day in the dark blue of his country.

The day of Alan Lauder Morton's baptism as the Wee Blue Devil was March 31, 1928. The church for the occasion was Wembley Stadium, London, and beneath the twin towers of the famous old ground a star was named.

The Auld Enemy clashed in the British International Championship and the outcome was emphatic, Scotland recording a famous 5-1 victory against their oldest rivals to send the bulk of the 80,868 home to think again.

Morton provided that food for thought with a starring role in the demolition, even if it was Alex Jackson's hat-trick and a double from Alex James that served as the wrecking ball. It was Morton who provided the momentum and the direction.

For each of Jackson's three goals it was Morton who sent over one of his legendary crosses, but more on that later.

The first came in two minutes, the second just a minute before the interval and the third in the 65th minute as the Morton and Jackson show shone from start to finish.

With the dust barely settled, the Wee Blue Devil label had been applied and it stuck for the remainder of his career and indeed the remainder of his life. There are conflicting reports about who was responsible for the spark of imagination, with some crediting it to an English journalist and others to an English fan in the Wembley crowd.

Regardless, it suited the man down to the ground. He was small in stature, blue through and through with the ability to put defences through hell each and every time he took to the turf.

The nickname captured the distinguising feature in a nutshell. Morton was wee, there was no doubt about that. At 5ft 4inches he did not cut the type of figure who would strike terror into the heart of an opposition player but his tiny frame, tipping the scales at just nine stone, carried a player whose strength was in his head.

Morton's intelligence on and off the ball gave him the ability to tear defences to shreds and while he could take the knocks when they were delivered his way, it also kept him out of trouble more often than not.

Reports from the Wee Blue Devil's hey day make note of his ability to kill a ball stone dead with a single touch, the type of balance which would put a ballerina to shame and ability to turn on a whim, leaving defenders in knots. His dribbling prowess was the stuff of legend but the key was an uncanny knack of knowing when to release the ball, so often the failing of a great winger. Despite playing on the left flank, Morton favoured his right foot and packed a powerful shot and deadly accurate pass. That said, he worked and worked on his left foot until it came close to becoming an equally valuable tool.

His dimunitive standing never held Morton back, if anything it made him all the more endearing to those on the terraces. The underdog in every challenge, towered over by every defender yet more often than not it was the Wee Blue Devil who came out on top.

*Talent hits a target no one else can hit. Genius hits a target no one else can see.*

**Arthur Schopenhauer**

The wing wizardry and trickery left home fans cheering for more and the visitors gasping in amazement, but that was not the real killer weapon in Morton's substantial armoury.

The trademark move was in fact his 'floating lob'. Whether passing, crossing or shooting it proved to be incisive and capable of catching out defenders and goalkeepers alike. Those who witnessed it claim Morton had the ability to make the ball stall mid-flight. It proved impossible to defend, just ask England's class of 28.

The name and legend live on in the 'Ballad of Alan Morton'. Proof positive, surely, that Alan Morton established himself as a real cult hero at Ibrox.

> He was a proud young Airdrie lad,
> Alan Morton was his name
> He played for Glasgow Rangers,
> the left wing was his game
> The Ibrox crowd, they loved him so,
> they crowned him King of all
> And every time he scored a goal,
> they sang him 'Follow on'.
>
> Now Alan played his heart away
> in Rangers' Royal Blue
> And then one famous Saturday
> in Scotland's darker hue

Young Alan laid the English low,
the legend it was born
And every time he scored a goal,
we sang him 'Follow on'.

And so that is the story
my father said to me
He said 'Now son when you're a man,
will you do one thing for me
Each Saturday down Ibrox way,
though Alan's dead and gone
Every time the Glasgow Rangers score,
will you sing them Follow on'.

He didn't have just one tune adapted in his honour. Oh no, there was more for the Little Blue Song Book of the 1920s. To the strains of Keep the Red Flag Flying High, the Ibrox faithful revelled in another catchy ditty:

Oh Charlie Shaw,
He never saw,
Where Alan Morton pit the baw,
He pit the baw into the net and scored a goal for Rangers.

Morton's uncanny habit for getting the better of Celtic keeper Charlie Shaw clearly went down well with his friends in the Light Blue masses. The Gers fans of the era may have been more beige than blue in their Tweed bunnets but they knew a thing or two about carrying a tune. Morton was the subject of their affections more often than not and his cult status has been transported across the generations in the lyrics passed down through generations of Rangers aficionados. They may not be sung any longer but the songs remain as a quirky link to the days of Morton and Meiklejohn.

Greatness came from humble beginnings. Morton's birthplace, in a cottage on Skaterigg Farm in Glasgow, no longer stands. It is now the home of Glasgow High School's games hall, a facility more used to honing skills in the oval ball game than Morton's beloved football.

He moved from Old Anniesland with his family to Airdrie and was overlooked by the Diamonds of his adopted home town, failing in a trial with Airdrieonians. Their loss would be the gain of Queen's Park, Rangers and Scotland.

Morton was already at his peak when he joined Rangers in 1920, at the age of 27. He was an international player at that point having served his apprenticeship with Queen's Park alongside his brother Bob Morton and caught the eye of the Scotland selectors. He linked up with the Spiders as a teenager and the amateur status at Queen's fitted perfectly with Morton's career as a mining engineer. Football and mining were the two loves of this bachelor.

Even as a star with Rangers, Morton had the foresight and dedication to continue his profession outside of the game and continued to operate in the field long after his boots had been pegged up for the final time.

The son of a coalmaster, Morton was at the heart of an industry crucial to Scotland's prosperity in the first half of the 20th century. An act of parliament was established in 1872 as the government got to grips with the issue of mine safety and the engineers had a key part to play in limiting the risks posed to pit workers. Morton was employed in the proud mining community of Airdrie, travelling through the 16-miles to Ibrox to train and play as a part-timer.

Morton thrived in his working environment, every ounce the professional. That approach spilled over into football, the bowler hat he sported around Ibrox marking him out as an upwardly mobile man. The briefcase he carried was the finishing touch, earning him the tag of the 'wee society man' or 'wee insurance man'. Not a patch on the Wee Blue Devil

Morton was involved in the coal industry at a difficult time, when mine owners were arguing pay was too high and hours too short. His unionist beliefs stemmed from that background.

His work commitments tell an intriguing story about the state of play in Scottish football in that era. Morton, a hero to tens of thousands, thought nothing of going out to graft during the days leading up to Old Firm games.

Flick through the generations to the current period of highly rewarded stars and it is a very different tale. In 2007 Livingston owner Pearse Flynn caused outrage among the squad at the struggling First Division when he dared to suggest they go out into the real world.

Flynn wanted to open the eyes of his 'heroes' by pressing them into action at one of his Scottish call centres. Only a fly on the wall of the Livi dressing room could vouch for what followed but, whatever the reaction, the outcome was that the plan was hastily re-arranged to become an extra training session. The irony is the Livingston players could quite comfortably have slotted anonymously into an office environment.

Could a player of Morton's standing do that in the current climate without spending the day fighting off autograph hunters and fawning fans with camera phones? Probably not.

It's difficult to imagine Kenny Miller rolling up for a shift at Tesco but that is exactly what Morton did at the mines most days and he did it unhindered by the trappings of fame we've come to expect. No paparazzi, no fuss.

Undoubtedly the work-football combination gave Morton a far greater connection with the paying punters than any professional in the modern era could boast. During the week he worked side by side with those who paid through the gates to watch him entertain as part of his weekend hobby. The office banter must have been interesting.

It was another man's professional ambitions that opened the Ibrox door for Morton, taken to Govan to replace Dr Jim Paterson on the left wing when he moved to London to further his medical career. Paterson had previously replaced Alec Smith, another Rangers legend, and the baton passed with ease between the three men in a seamless stream of talent.

It was in June, 1920, that Bill Struth made Morton his first signing as manager of Rangers. What a signing it proved to be.

The Rangers fans would soon learn Morton's value to their team but the Glaswegian, an intelligent man, was confident of his own ability and his manager shared that faith. Struth made the Wee Blue Devil the highest paid player in Scottish football when he plucked him from Queen's Park, the star quality matched by a star's wage packet – at least in the relative terms of the time.

Morton was a forward thinker on and off the park, to the point of removing a single stud from each of his boots in an attempt to give himself greater mobility and aid his ability to weave his way past line after line of defenders.

When he retired from the game in 1932, with his 40th birthday approaching, he continued to work in the mining industry and also lent himself to the unionist cause in a life as busy as it had been while he had been embedded in top class football.

He was also invited on to the Rangers board and served as a director until his death in 1971 having given more than half a century of sterling service to the club.

The role as a director gave Morton a powerful position in Scottish football, one he relished. It was not a decision taken lightly by the normally closed shop of the Light Blues boardroom but in appointing Morton they had recruited a man of wisdom as well as a figurehead to which the fans could relate, in fact a board with Morton on it could do little wrong. Willie Waddell followed suit and in more recent times John Greig has also been elevated to director level but it remains a select band of men who have carried out both roles.

The contribution of the man many of his peers noted down as the finest player ever to grace the Ibrox stage is remembered today by an oil portrait of Morton resplendent in Scotland colours, hanging at the head of the stairs leading from the famous entrance hall to the Blue Room. Chairman David Murray may have moved the picture from pride of place in the hall but even a man of his power would not attempt to wipe Morton completely from the modern day club.

In fact, Murray, prompted by a fan and shareholder, admitted in 2006 at the club's annual general meeting that part of the ground could be named in Morton's honour after Bill Struth was imortalised in the same way earlier in the year when the main stand was renamed to mark the 50th anniversary of his death. The Wee Blue Devil Stand to sit opposite the Bill Struth Stand? It does have a certain ring to it.

Murray was publicly cautious when pressed on the issue of naming a stand in Morton's honour, no doubt wary that his every cough and splutter at the annual general meeting would be chewed over for weeks to come. Privately he will be aware that no fan would argue against the move despite the fact few survivors ever saw the great man kick a ball in anger.

With stadium naming rights selling for millions it can only be assumed Rangers have not been devoid of offers. Emirates spent £90million on their tie-up with Arsenal and the revenue prospects for Rangers in a similar deal must be tempting.

Yet, even in the cash strapped times and budget conscious era, tradition is the one thing Murray knows his supporters value more than most. The day when Ibrox is known as anything different is not looming and the ties to the heritage of the club look set to grow stronger.

Struth's name has already been adopted for the main stand, the idea of a Morton stand has been floated and David Meiklejohn has been suggested as another tag fit to adorn the walls of the famous old ground.

Meiklejohn and Morton are two of the finest players in the history of the club but it is impossible to quantify exactly where they rank on the hypothetical pecking order. There is no accurate gauge but the names linger on, proof positive of cult status for the legendary duo.

Morton's death in 1971 did not bring an end to the honours. He forms part of the backbone of the Rangers hall of fame and in 2005 his name was added to the Scottish Football Museum's own roll of honour. Fittingly, he joined along with his Wembley partner-in-crime Alex Jackson.

That accolade was as much for his contribution to the club game as it was for his international achievements, lofty as those were.

With Rangers he could not have predicted the glory which lay ahead when he stepped out on to the pitch at Ibrox on the summer afternoon of August 17, 1920, to play his first league match in light blue.

The result was positive, with Rangers winning 4-1 comfortably. Morton wore the No.11 shirt for the first time but it was far from the last, with the jersey seldom off his back for the next decade and beyond.

His first goal came in a 5-2 win at Dumbarton less than two months later and the flying machine was well and truly off the ground. He chipped in with six league goals from 39 appearances that season as Rangers romped to a 10 point title success, leaving Celtic trailing in their wake.

Morton, an ever present in the Scottish Cup run that season, tasted defeat in the final when Partick Thistle ran out winners but he would set that record straight in later years with a succession of cup triumphs.

He seldom missed matches through injury, his part-time training regime rigorous enough to ensure he could withstand the heavy domestic programme and keep pace with his full-time colleagues.

League championship wins followed in 1923, 1924 and 1925 before the sequence was broken by the Hoops. The Govan dominance was revived in 1927, 1928, 1929, 1930, 1931 and of course the Scottish Cup was landed, famously, in 1928 as well as 1930 and 1932.

Renowned as a provider rather than a goalscorer, Morton was still sharp in front of goal. His best haul came in the 1928-29 season when he bagged 18, including 14 in the league as his side obliterated the opposition. Celtic, 16 points behind, were the closest challengers. An 8-0 win over St Johnstone, featuring a Morton hat-trick, demonstrated the superiority Rangers enjoyed.

The 1931-32 season proved to be Morton's swansong and, now well and truly in the veteran phase of his career, a lifetime in the game was beginning to take its toll. He played 17 times that term, returning the following season to play six further games before deciding to bring the curtain down. The encore came in a 5-1 win over Airdrie at Ibrox, Morton signing off with the final goal and bidding farewell to the faithful who had backed him through so many good times.

All in all he played 495 appearances for Rangers and scored 115 goals.

Bob McPhail best summed up his team-mate when he said: "He was simply in a class by himself. What an entertainer. The wee man was simply a magician.

"Like myself he was a natural right-footed player and would work the ball with his right foot, though he could use his left foot to good advantage. He hated heading the ball. For a wee man he had an extremely long stride and always seemed to have his body half-bent over the ball. He would never beat his opponent the same way twice. Outside, inside or through his legs, he would torment the life out of full-backs. He was always shouting for the ball: 'right Bobby, out here' 'hey I hope you haven't forgotten me' or 'its getting cold out here'. He was easy to play with. He took all his corner kicks with his right foot to get that peculiar inswinging, hanging lob of his. It was like hitting a sand iron against an eight iron. You could see keepers hesitating as the famous Morton lob seemed to hang in the air. It got us many a goal. He wasn't particularly fast, but he was nimble of foot and thought and was always at the right place the right time."

For a club who over the years established a reputation for a team ethic and disciplined style of play, the characters to have graced the Ibrox turf tell an entirely different story.

Celtic may have won plaudits for a free-flowing cavalier philosophy but Govan's football theatre has not been devoid of entertainers. The relationship between the Light Blues fans and their wingers has always been a special one.

Morton was not the first but arguably he was the first to be elevated to cult status, imortalised in song and image.

Moses McNeil, the Rangers' founder, was himself a powerful right winger who went on to become the club's first Scotland international in 1876. Alex Smith was another of the Ibrox star wingers to turn out for his country in the days before Morton burst onto the scene. Post-Morton, the likes of Willie Henderson, Willie Johnston, Davie Cooper and even the awkward figure of Ted McMinn have had the fans on the edge of their seats. Mark Walters and Brian Laudrup continued that tradition more recently and the hunger for trickery on the flanks is as strong today as ever for a group of supporters reared on the tales of the illustrious men who have patrolled the left and right beats in Govan.

Organisation and structure have their place at Ibrox but more often than not it has been the flair players the fans have taken to heart and Morton falls decidedly into that category.

His talents were not lost on the international selectors. As a Scotland player, Morton was on his way to becoming established in dark blue when he switched to the Light Blues. His debut came as a Queen's Park player in 1920 when he played in a 1-1 draw against Wales in Cardiff.

His second cap, still as a Spiders player, brought a goal in a 3-0 win against Northern Ireland at Celtic Park.

A further 29 caps followed as a Rangers player and four further goals. Morton captained his country against Northern Ireland in 1931, a measure of the esteem he was held in by the selectors.

The undoubted highlight was the day the Wembley Wizards were born in 1928. That famous team were, and still remain, a true phenomenon. Their 5-1 demolition of the Auld Enemy in London in 1928 has been credited as the greatest attacking display of football has seen. Ever.

Writing in the *Athletic News*, player turned reporter Ivan Sharpe said:

"England were not merely beaten. They were bewildered – run to a standstill, made to appear utterly inferior by a team whose play was as cultured and beautiful as I ever expect to see."

And Morton, the Wee Blue Devil of Glasgow's Light Blues, was at the shuddering epicentre of that explosive performance. He skipped past his English opponents with the ease the Rangers' contingent within the travelling Tartan Army had come to expect.

Morton's crosses provided Alex Jackson, the Huddersfield striker who had been brought back to Britain from the US by Aberdeen just two seasons previously, with the ammunition he needed for a hat-trick and Alex James banged in a double to compound the misery of the hosts.

Morton's poise and precision on a slippery surface was exemplary, with the Scottish side mastering the conditions as the rivals foundered. The plan had gone like clockwork.

Pre-match, the team talk had been left to captain Jimmy McMullan in the days when players were left to go out and play without the hindrance of managerial meddling. Would a talent like Morton have flourished within the confines of the modern tactical maze? We will never know.

McMullan told his team-mates: "The SFA's president Robert Campbell wants us to discuss football but you all know what's expected of you tomorrow. All I've got to say is, go to your bed, put your head on your pillow and pray for rain."

The rain did fall and as McMullan predicted the fair-weather opponents could not cope. So the Scottish national team's first set of heroes were born on that damp but jubilant day in London.

Many of the players in the pages that follow have starred for Rangers and Scotland yet very few have earned cult status in both shades of blue. Morton and Jim Baxter, a member of the 'new' Wembley Wizards in 1967, are the two who succeeded more than any in transcending the traditional club barriers. Flair will overcome even the highest hurdle in the fickle world of football.

Scotland's tradition of celebrating glorious failure may have become legendary but the glorious successes of the past have never been forgotten. Archie Gemmill's goal in 1978 and the Wembley Wizards, old and new, are the memories deemed fit to be preserved. Indeed the Wizards' monitor lives on to this day, adopted by a Lanarkshire branch of the Tartan Army to provide a lasting reminder of Morton and his colleagues.

In typical Scottish fashion the Wizards MKI were very much the underdogs. When the team to face the English was announced – without the Rangers heroes David Meiklejohn and Bob McPhail – the *Daily Record*'s verdict was to the point: "It's not a great side."

On paper perhaps not, but on the greasy Wembley turf it worked a treat as the wee men did the business. Hat-trick hero Jackson stood at just 5ft 7inches but he and his fellow pint-sized attacker Morton struck fear into the hearts of the home side.

They became overnight legends in the eyes of the tens of thousands of Scotland fans who had journeyed south in hope rather than expectation but the pre-match preparations serve as an indication of just how much the football times have changed.

The Scotland Cult Heroes of 1928 spent the eve of their Wembley triumph in the lobby of the Regent Palace Hotel sitting side by side with the supporters.

Just as Meiklejohn drank side by side with the Rangers followers in Govan, Morton and his team-mates chewed the fat with the fans until well into the evening as they counted down to their moment of glory. He was a hero, a legend, an idol and an icon but not in the modern sense. Morton was not poles apart from the man in the street or on the terraces. He was not worshipped from afar but a living, breathing star in touching distance of the punter on the street.

Just like Meiklejohn his cult status was not akin to that of the modern superstar. Far more accessible, perhaps less revered but equally more real to the fans.

**MAGIC MOMENT:** When Bob McPhail pocketed his seventh Scottish Cup winner's medal he equalled a record that has never been beaten.

# BOB McPHAIL
## *'GREETIN BOAB'* 1927-1940

### GERS CAREER: Games 408; Goals 261; Caps 16

T HE FAN who pays money each week wants to be entertained. He wants to be excited. And there is nothing more exciting in this game of football than the goalmouth incident. The public want to see goals and more goals, not the square pass into oblivion.

That, in a nutshell, is the mantra of Mr Robert McPhail. It is the philosophy of one of the finest forwards Ibrox has ever seen and the approach to the game that made the man a Cult Hero and which keeps his name at the forefront of the minds of Rangers' supporters well after his departure to that stadium in the sky.

The Barrhead-born star's observations on the desires of the paying public were set to paper for the first time in his 1988 biography 'Legend – Sixty Years at Ibrox' amid some fascinating insights into his expert opinions on just what it takes to become a hit in front of one of the most demanding audiences in world football.

Contemporary players should sit up and take notice because McPhail did it all. He won trophy after trophy, scored goal after goal and vitally he did it at the same time as earning the adoration of his public.

The international star, who died in 2000, mused: "I've known since the day I kicked my first ball for Rangers back in 1927 that it takes a special kind of footballer to establish himself at Ibrox, as indeed it does at Parkhead. Even though I had won a Scottish Cup medal with Airdrie and had been capped against England while at Broomfield, there was no guarantee that I would fit into the Ibrox set-up. I had to work at it.

"Nothing has changed over the years. It is not just good enough to play well. You've got to be a winner. You've got to be consistent week in and week out, hail, rain or sunshine, month afer month, season after season. You've got to learn to take stick from the crowd and from your opponents, who will always try to raise their game because it's Rangers they are playing. There is no respite if you win a cup. You've got to go out and do it again the following season.

*One chance is all you need.*

*Jesse Owens*

"As a Rangers player you must convince yourself that you are better than your opponent and then you've got to prove it. You must have confidence in your own ability, display a little arrogance, and if the going gets tough then you've got to stand up and be counted. It is still a man's game. There is no hiding place for a player at Ibrox. You are public property and every game is a cup final. You play before big crowds every week and they expect nothing but the best.

"At Ibrox second best is unacceptable and the good players have to learn to live with this. I've seen them come and go at Ibrox for the past 60 years and you soon learn to pick out the ones who are going to make it and those who would be better with clubs that are not expected to win anything.

"Pressure? I never felt any when I was a player. I don't think any of us did. Under Bill Struth we just went into every match expecting to win it. And if we didn't, the dressing-room inquest was indescribable, without Struth having to say a word. It was really all about the pride in being a Rangers player.

"The players are very much actors in studded boots. They love the roar of the crowd, just as I did in those far-off years. But in those far-off years I always tried to earn my applause. I would try and be last man out when Rangers took to the field on a Saturday. The crowd would cheer you on to the field – but I always felt that I shouldn't be cheered until I had done something. Until I had earned it. It might have been some kind of superstition I suppose, or some strange quirk in my make-up. But I did feel that I wanted to work for my applause. A good goal, a good pass or a good tackle. As a player I respected my profession and I think the fans of Airdrie and Rangers, in particular, respected this in return. I have nothing but good memories from my career."

McPhail left the supporters with their own set of memories to cherish, recollections of a forward in full flow who struck fear into defences all over the country thanks to his ruthless approach to goalscoring.

Despite record breaking returns in front of goal, subsequently only beaten by Ally McCoist, McPhail was a traditional inside forward, not an out and out central striker, and shared in the defensive duties expected of him. That makes his phenomenal strike rate of 261 goals in 408 games for the Light Blues all the more remarkable. He could fetch and carry, chase and hassle but more importantly he knew the way to goal.

McPhail could also mix it physically when he wanted to, a factor that cannot be underplayed when it comes to winning over the supporters. The Ibrox crowd has always appreciated those who are willing to shed blood, sweat and tears for the cause as much as they have those blessed with a double shuffle or killer lob.

After one bruising encounter with Hibs goalkeeper Willie Robb, one sports writer wrote: "McPhail had all the makings of a rugby player in his dealings with Robb."

In his own words, McPhail said: "I was never really one for turning the other cheek" and added: "I don't think a good shoulder charge ever did anyone any harm." He could battle with the best but that did not always win favour with his disciplinarian manager.

McPhail recalled: "My problem was one of early retaliation. If someone kicked me, then I kicked them back. I believed in an eye for an eye, and opponents soon learned to their discomfort that if they kicked McPhail then they'd get a bloody sore on in return. Bill Struth did not like my philosophy. He would have me upstairs, give me that piercing look and tell me: 'What you are doing is not good for Rangers. All eyes are on you when you are wearing the jersey. If you are playing the man then you are not playing the ball, and that is what we are paying you to do. If you are fouled then leave things to the referee, do not retaliate.' I would promise, of course, to be a good boy but all of my good intentions would go out of the window when I was deliberately fouled by an opponent. They didn't call me 'Greetin Boab' for nothing."

He earned the nickname Greetin Boab for furiously berating team-mate Torry Gillick one afternoon. It stuck, and McPhail was quite proud of his reputation for being hard to please.

It was not his only tag in football. Clyde trainer Mattha Gemmell gave Greetin Boab his other nickname, Whistle, after one game between the two clubs. Spotting McPhail emerging from the Shawfield bath he claimed the lean Rangers star would look like a whistle if he bored a few holes in his body.

Despite a lack of bulk, at just over 5ft 10inches, he had a frame well suited to his role. McPhail had pace to match his power and precision, the sprint king of Ibrox and even quicker over a 100 yard dash than flying winger Sandy Archibald.

Despite making his name as an inside left, he was a naturally right footed player and he hit his shots with pace and precision married to a wicked spin that claimed a succession of goalkeeping victims.

After one match against English champions Arsenal, in an unofficial British championship play-off, a journalist compared McPhail to Arsenal record signing Bryn Jones when he said: "If Jones is worth £14,000 then McPhail is worth the Bank of England."

From an early age McPhail's talents were clear. It is doubtful if a football player can ever really have too much too young and McPhail had the winner's medal so many wait a lifetime for by the time he was just 18. But there was never a question of that early success curtailing his ambition or drive.

He broke into the Airdrie team instantly and as an 18 year-old he was a key part of the side which lifted the Scottish Cup in 1924, resplendent in the Diamonds No.10 shirt. Hibs were the beaten finalists as Airdrie triumphed. It proved to be the club's one and only success in the national competition.

McPhail and his side overcame Morton, St Johnstone, Lanarkshire rivals Motherwell, Ayr United and Falkirk en-route to the Ibrox showdown with the Leith side. Willie Russell was the real star with his double on the day but he had an admirable supporting cast featuring McPhail and the talents of the controversial yet inspirational Hughie Gallacher.

Each of the Diamonds' players earned a place in the history books but for McPhail it was just the first page of many in an amazing club career in which he won the affections of the Airdrie and Rangers' faithful.

Airdrie were far from underdogs during that era and the cup win came during a sequence of four consecutive second placed finishes in the league. McPhail had cut his teeth in a side capable of competing with the best, had experience of the big occasion following his Scottish Cup victory and was already a Scotland international. The next logical step was to join a club who could satisfy his appetite for the big stage year in and year out. Rangers provided that opportunity and fitted the bill perfectly. The marriage made in heaven never threatened anything other than a happy ending.

Carrying the weight of a hefty price tag has proved a delicate balancing act for a string of Rangers recruits. Tore Andre Flo could never justify his £12million billing while decades earlier Colin Stein had revelled in his role as the club and country's most expensive forward. It is difficult to envisage a day when the Flo figure will be beaten but if it happens the record busting man would be well advised to cast an eye over the archives and look to the life and times of McPhail for inspiration.

He was the first real big money buy and a player who provided one of the best returns despite the huge investment the club made.

When he signed from Airdrie for £5,000 in 1927 it was a fee big enough to buy 100 new build houses in Glasgow. That outlay, equating to millions of pounds in today's economy, came at the end of a long hard fight for the services of Scotland's brightest international prospect.

A long line of English clubs formed an orderly queue at Broomfield waving cheque books under the noses of the Diamonds directors. Derby County went to the extent of locking their target in a hotel room until he agreed to sign. He did agree to sign, but only in a successful attempt to evade his captors and later admitted he never had any intention of moving to the English Midlands.

The Airdrie board eventually decided to go to a closed bids system because of the strength of interest in their most valuable commodity but McPhail was not playing ball. He made his excuses and declined the opportunity to attend the ceremonial opening of the envelopes. He refused to be a pawn in their game and was patient, an approach which paid off when Rangers stepped in after the dust of the initial bidding war had settled and struck the deal to lure McPhail to Govan.

He arrived full of confidence despite his tender years. He and new Rangers team-mate Jock Buchanan, who had been an Airdrie colleague when the Scottish Cup was claimed just a few years earlier, perfected a well worn routine around the ground involving the winner's medals they wore on watch chains. The teasing of their team-mates ended with one fell swoop of David Meiklejohn's boot in the 1928 final of the Scottish Cup when Celtic were defeated.

McPhail was just 22 by the time he tucked the second cup winner's medal in his waistcoat pocket. Even Hoops' chairman Tom White greeted the victorious Rangers players with a smile after the triumph, apparently claiming it was "their turn" to lift the famous trophy.

McPhail, one of 10 children in the family brought up in Barrhead where his church-elder father served as a head gardener, had his vices. A smoker by the time he reached his early teens and a habit he continued in his playing days, it did not appear to do him any harm as he became a schoolboy international as his early promise became clear. There was good pedigree in the family, with elder brother Malcolm winning a Scottish Cup medal with Kilmarnock's victorious side of 1920.

The man who became a Rangers hero actually grew up idolising a Celtic star. The subject of McPhail's affection was Tommy McInally, another of Barrhead's finest. McPhail would pass him in the street and admit to being in awe of McInally before earning his own big break. The pair went on to become travel companions and great friends, making a mockery of the Old Firm divide.

That is not to say that the city rivalry did not get its teeth into McPhail, a player who had little time for Celtic icon Patsy Gallacher. The feelings stemmed from their first encounter, when a young Airdrie prospect by the name of McPhail nutmegged the Hoops star – and received three punches to the groin in return. The referee's suggestion to the stricken youngster? Quite simply: 'My advice to you, son, is to stay away from him. He's too old fashioned for you.'

Those incidents were few and far between, with McPhail admitting: "Though there was great rivalry between the two Glasgow clubs, there was no real enmity."

McPhail was Rangers through and through. As a favour to his brother Malcolm, who had gone from player to St Mirren director, he played on with the Paisley side after his exit from Ibrox in 1940 and his last game in a Buddies shirt was against the Light Blues in the

Scottish Cup semi-final soon after. He was accused of deliberately missing a goalscoring opportunity by sections of the media but McPhail later argued: "The truth was I felt that if I had scored I would have had my leg broken. The Rangers centre-half, Willie Woodburn, was coming in fast to make his tackle and looked to me like being a fraction late. Having played with Woodburn in my last season at Ibrox I knew there was no way he would pull back. So I chickened out. I threw the scoring chance away by deliberately hesitating."

Before his brief cameo with the Paisley Saints the Ibrox icon had amassed a staggering treasure trove. He became an instant hit following his arrival in 1927 when he bagged a double in a 4-1 battering of Celtic in the Charity Cup but the best was yet to come.

His record of seven Scottish Cup wins from eight final appearances, six victories with Rangers and one with Airdrie, is matched only by Celtic duo Billy McNeill and Jimmy McMenemy.

McPhail also won the league championship an incredible nine times with Rangers. His record of 261 goals in just 408 games was not beaten until Ally McCoist hit full flow. A veteran of 39 Old Firm games, he scored 70 times in just 106 league games for Airdrie before switching to Rangers and his total for both clubs in all competitons was 355 strikes. His most profitable season came in 1932/33 when his haul was 30 goals in 31 league games and three cup strikes in seven ties.

That wealth of know-how was not lost in the corridors of power at Ibrox and the legendary forward served under a succession of managers at Rangers after retiring from playing. He was utilised as a mentor to the Ibrox reserve side and continued in that role up to and including John Greig's tenure. He did not pick the team but did pass on decades of experience in the game. Something money simply could not buy.

McPhail was offered a seat on the Rangers board but declined, vociferous about his determination to avoid the politics of the game he adored. Instead he combined his part-time commitments with the second string with a burgeoning business in the electrical industry, Meikle and McPhail. Incidentally it wasn't a Rangers dream team, the first half of the company name was derived from his neighbour and founding partner Gordon Meikle rather than an abbreviation of former club-mate Davie Meiklejohn.

He continued with the company well past retirement age. McPhail's death in 2000 brought an impeccably respected minute's silence in a league game against Hearts at Ibrox from a set of supporters who in the main would not have been around to see the subject play but to a man were aware of the contribution he made to the club they follow. McPhail had many contemporaries who he would have argued made just as great an impact but it is his name that lives on and commands respect among a select band of heroes from the 1920s and 1930s. The reputation outlived the man and will forever be part of the fabric at Ibrox.

McPhail himself had no doubt that his era was a rich one for the club. He said: "I would argue as long as it takes that the greatest Rangers team from any period in the long and quite illustrious history of the club would come from my time at Ibrox in the Throbbing Thirties when thousands had to be turned away from games."

The demand for terracing space at Ibrox, stemming from the success on the pitch, made Rangers a cash rich club. The playing staff were not in the super-wealthy bracket of the modern day player but neither did they plead poverty.

When McPhail made his big money switch there was no entourage of representatives, no Gerry Maguire style agent to fight his corner. He didn't need it and didn't want it.

What Struth had thrust in front of him was a contract offering £6 per week over the summer, £8 per week in the weeks he played in the first team and bonuses of £1 for a draw and £2 for a win in league matches.

The last contract he signed, in 1939, showed exactly the same terms. Amazingly McPhail, despite his heroics in front of goal, never received a pay rise in his Ibrox career and he didn't go banging on Bill Struth's door seeking a millionaire's lifestyle.

Even the £8 basic wage stood McPhail and his colleagues in good stead, ahead of the average working man in salary stakes but not in the bracket of the super wealthy.

During Struth's reign every single player in the first team had the same terms, there was no disparity to breed egos and surely the spirit in the dressing room was better for that policy.

McPhail made great play of the fact that he felt well rewarded as a Rangers player, not just when it came to his weekly wage packet but equally in the five star treatment the squad received. From tailor made suits to luxury retreats on the west coast, he and his team-mates had it all. McPhail said: "We were well off and we knew it. So did Bill Struth."

In fact, the Rangers players of McPhail's generation were reputed to be the richest in British football by narrowly shading the earnings of their Celtic rivals. To put it in context, a labourer would earn less than £3 per week.

The win bonus for the Scottish Cup triumph in 1928 was £20, prompting McPhail's travel companion Tommy McInally, of Celtic fame, to quip: "You didnae win the cup, Bob, you bought it!"

Despite the apparent extravagance, Rangers was a well oiled commercial machine in those days. The thought of dropping into the red horrified the directors, who signed off a considerable profit of more than £6,000 in the wake of the 1928 cup win.

McPhail was not ignorant of the type of superstar wage packets that professional sport had to offer. During the 1928 tour of North America the Rangers players and McPhail took the chance to watch Babe Ruth in action, the baseball icon pocketing a cool $80,000 a year for his efforts with the bat, but they were not envious. They could still live in style in Glasgow.

When he got married in 1933, McPhail paid for his new marital home in cash – £650 in crisp new notes. He drove a Morris-Cowley bottle nosed sports car. McPhail was every inch the star.

Mind you, he was not always aware of the company he was keeping as his club treated him to stays in the world's most exclusive destinations. McPhail told a wonderful tale of one incident during a trip to New York by Rangers when he accompanied Hollywood star Greta Garbo in a hotel elevator. He didn't know who his travel companion was until he saw the jaws of his team-mates drop as she strolled out of the lift at her stop.

They did not look out of place among the Hollywood gliterazzi. Even in the 1920s, image was all for McPhail and his colleagues. Struth had them well drilled – from what to wear to how to walk, no stone was left unturned in the pursuit of perfection. Players were instructed to swing their arms on the walk from the train station to opposition ground, hands in the pocket was not an option for Struth the perfectionist.

Despite looking the part and rubbing shoulders with the showbiz elite, McPhail did admit in later life he was slightly bemused by the power football and footballers held over the public. He had witnessed the adulation heaped upon former Airdrie team-mate Hughie Gallacher by the Newcastle United fans. The Toon Army wept when Gallacher moved to Chelsea and McPhail wondered from afar, admitting he was taken aback by the esteem the man he had partnered at Broomfield was held in. Not because he wasn't a great player, but simply because McPhail and most of his generation did not seek that type of attention.

He did not search for a life in the limelight, something which would have sat uncomfortably with his upbringing. McPhail was a principled man who heeded the advice of those closest to him. He once refused to play for Bill Struth during an overseas tour because the game fell on the Sabbath. Struth, a man of great dignity himself, understood and respected the wish of his most potent attacker. He soon relented on the Sunday issue, but no doubt he earned the respect of his manager with his initial stand, a manager who did much to shape McPhail's life and build upon the virtues instilled in him by his church going parents.

Rangers under Struth made regular trips to Turnberry, staying in the lap of luxury, McPhail said: "We didn't realise it but we were being slowly and gradually educated in how to conduct ourselves in public, how to handle publicity, how to behave, good manners, how to dress and how one should conduct oneself at the dinner table."

Struth had influence on all aspects of his players' lives and careers. When the great man spoke, McPhail listened intently – even if it meant passing up the opportunity to play in one of the biggest fixtures in football. The prolific Rangers forward never played for Scotland against England at Wembley, rejecting a succession of opportunities after a gentle nudge from his wily manager.

McPhail revealed in his biography: "My love of Rangers proved to be greater than the chance to play in that famous game, which brings out the best and the worst in Scottish supporters. I found myself in a rather unique tug-o-war. The chance was there for me to play for Scotland at Wembley, at least twice, but I said 'no' for reasons which seemed important to me at the time.

"My priority was simply Rangers Football Club. And I found that the more I played in the light blue jersey, the more dedicated I became to the club.

"Of course I'm disappointed that I never played at Wembley. Regretful? I don't think so. I made my choice and all these years later I still think I did the right thing. It was the very success of Rangers which really prevented me from playing in the famous London ground."

Left out of the side for the famous Wembley Wizards win of 1928, two years later McPhail was carrying a knock when the rematch rolled around. With a Scottish Cup final just a week away, he opted out of the Wembley clash.

In 1932, with another cup final looming for Rangers, McPhail and team-mate Meiklejohn withdrew through injury under pressure from manager Bill Struth. The committed blues brothers needed little persuading.

In 1934 and 1936 it was the same story, injuries kept McPhail sidelined from the international show but he pulled through in time to turn out in the Scottish Cup finals which followed immediately after.

He added: "In a way Struth was making it abundantly clear he wanted me fit and well in his cup final team because he must have felt my experience and influence was vital, even though he released other players for the Wembley match. Now, never at any time did he tell me not to play at Wembley. The decision was always left to myself but the man knew me better than I knew myself. He knew that if I played at Wembley I'd give it 100 per cent because I tried to give this game I loved everything I had every time out. I was only interested in being a winner. So when Struth suggested I'd be none the worse for a week's rest before a final, he was suggesting he wanted a McPhail who was as fit as possible at that particular time of the season."

Every time McPhail pulled out of an international squad he found his pay packet boosted by £6, the match fee Scotland players received at that time.

Incredibly McPhail amassed just 17 caps despite being one of the most prolific strikers the Scottish club game has ever seen. He made his first appearance in the dark blue of his country while still an Airdrie player. His debut came in April, 1927, in a 2-1 defeat against England at Hampden.

In the 16 games that followed McPhail bagged a credible seven goals in Scotland colours, notably a double in a 3-1 victory against the Auld Enemy a full decade after his first tussle with the side from over the border.

His open willingness to put club before country was partly to blame for a cap haul that did not equate to the talents of one of the biggest Rangers heroes of all time. The wealth of talent washing around the Scottish game was another but whenever McPhail was utilised during his 10 years of international service he delivered.

In the days before the World Cup and European Championships there were no great global adventures for McPhail and Scotland. His only ventures from British soil for international fixtures were across the channel to France and a longer trek to Czechoslovakia for friendlies in the 1930s.

He did not have the type of European audience to play to as more recent Cult Heroes have enjoyed. The name of Ally McCoist reached parts that his illustrious striking predecessor simply couldn't, fame was very much confined to his home patch.

Did that lack of exposure dilute McPhail's status? In a word, no. The phenomenon of cult status is surely defined by its local nature. The appreciation of the home fans rather than mass market appeal, and McPhail certainly qualified on that score. The man who would have walked over hot coals to win a match for Rangers was most loved at Ibrox and for that he was eternally appreciative.

**MAGIC MOMENT:** Two cup final penalties in 1949 and Rangers were Scotland's first treble kings.

# GEORGE YOUNG
## 'CORKY' 1941-1957

### GERS CAREER: Games 428; Goals 56; Caps 53

G EORGE YOUNG was as far removed from the role of reluctant hero as you could possibly get. The illustrious defender was a giant of a man on and off the park who accepted his cult status, embraced it with a typical bear-like hug and ran with it.

While others before and after him struggled to cope with the demands of an adoring public and life under the microscope, Young was a consumate hero. While others have been derailed by the role of Rangers icon or given in to the many temptations elevated status brings, the Grangemouth boy never faltered.

His success on the pitch stands up to the closest scrutiny. Young, who joined the Ibrox club from the junior ranks in 1941, won the Scottish league championship six times and the Scottish Cup four times to add to the two League Cup victories he played a central role in.

In between he squeezed in a total of 53 caps for Scotland, skippering the national side in 48 of those matches and in all but title managed the men in dark blue. As captain his influence on all things Scotland was massive, a key ally to the selection committee in determining tactics and keeping his international colleagues in check.

Sir George Graham, the secretary of the Scottish Football association, was once asked if the asociation had considered appointing a manager in the days when selectors ruled the international roost. Graham retorted: "We don't need a manager, we've got George Young."

The cool and composed defender had the physical presence to fill his role as leader of club and country. At 6ft 2inches tall and tipping the scales at over 14-stone he stood out from football's crowd, even if it did cause his teams certain kit difficulties. Scotland's back-room team had to remember to pack a pair of 42-inch waist shorts to cater for their captain.

Young had height and bulk but he was a well tuned machine. He played 34 consecutive internationals during his 11 year career with Scotland and between 1948 and 1953 missed just five of 150 Rangers games.

He was as committed in training as he was in match situations and the approach carried over into his off pitch duties. Young took his role as an idol seriously.

In his 1951 biography *George Young – Captain of Rangers and Scotland* he made that perfectly clear. The Light Blues star, who holidayed in Aberdeenshire rather than far flung destinations and spent Sunday morning worshipping at Killermont Church, was well aware of his position as a role model.

He said: "I feel that all sportsmen should set young Britain a good example off as well as on the field. Thousands of youths try to ape their favourite footballers. If the word gets round he is a superb gentleman, that player can have a terrific influence upon those lads who follow his fortunes. I don't think it is carrying things too far to say it helps shape a youngster's whole outlook on sport."

*If a man has any greatness in him, it comes to light not in one flamboyant hour but in the ledger of his daily work.*

**Beryl Markham**

Young, unlike so many of those who followed in his stud-prints as a hero to the masses, was not uncomfortable on his pedestal. Slightly embarrassed, yes, but at the same time he held the role with his crushing grip and made the most of it.

Young, who died in 1997, enjoyed breaking preconceptions about a profession which had its share of rough and ready characters, giving up hundreds of hours every year speaking to everything from supporters clubs and youth organisations to pensioners gatherings. Nothing was too much trouble for the gentle giant who saw that commitment as part of his Ibrox job description.

He said: "Football fans in many parts of Britain, and Europe come to that, have frequently told me what they think of George Young. Sometimes they have been flattering, on other occasions fans have given me a vocal whipping which must have brought a flush to my cheeks. For all that I love the fellows who follow football, talk football and, of course, give me a living by reason of their enthusiasm for our great game.

"When one considers the authoritative manner in which so many specatators can talk about football, and the men who play the game, I am always puzzled by one thing. It is that so many of these knowledgeable spectators are astounded when we meet socially and they find shaking their hands ordinary men like themselves. On dozens of occasions, when either giving coaching demonstrations or talks to youth clubs, I have felt rather embarrassed when someone has walked up to me and remarked: 'You know Mr Young, you are entirely different to what I imagined a professional footballer would be!"

Far from rough or uncultured, Young was a devoted family man and businessman. While at his peak with Rangers he combined his playing duties with life as the owner of the Tillietudlem Hotel.

He described himself as: "An ordinary fellow who plays football for fun and a living and whose only dislike in life is people who cannot see any good in another fellow – and believe me, there are quite a number of such folk who follow the football game."

Ordinary is one word that nobody else in football would have chosen to describe Young. Aside from his size and standing, he possessed talent in abundance. The great and good of British football testified to that time and time again.

Young married power and intelligence on the field with a renowned sense of fair play. It made him a stand out for Rangers and a hero to the Ibrox faithful. He was part of the famous Iron Curtain, surely the only defensive unit in football's history to earn the type of reverie more normally reserved for flowing forward lines. Anchored by goalkeeper Bobby Brown, the Iron Curtain had Young and Jock Shaw as its full-backs sandwiching the trio of Ian McColl, Willie Woodurn and Sammy Cox. That illustrious group of six earned cult status and any one could have been pulled out and poured over as a hero in their own right.

It was a no-nonsense set-up, hard but fair thanks in no small part to the influence of Young. The late Hibs forward Willie Ormond recalls the lasting impression the Rangers skipper made on him in his first outing against the Light Blues. Ormond once said: "In my first game against Rangers at Easter Road, I was a cocky youngster. Willie Woodburn – the ferocious tackler and Rangers and Scotland centre- half in the early 1950s – yelled after I had gone past him with the ball: 'George, get that little bastard!' At the first moment, after the ball had next gone out of play, Young put his massive paw on my shoulder and said gently 'Never mind, son, what Woodburn says, I'll deal with you in my own way'. Which I knew was fair play."

Tom Finney, a man Young referred to as 'my friend the Preston plumber', once said: "He was like a giant octopus. You would beat him seven times in one move, and thought you were past him, then that eighth leg would come out to reclaim the ball."

England team mate Stanley Matthews added: "When I saw George in a Scotland line-up, I knew winning would not be easy."

He may have been known as the Octopus to Finney, but to his team-mates he answered to the name of Corky. Through the wonders of the internet, anyone searching for an explanation to that moniker will come up with several variations on the same theme but Young, in his biography, provided the original and genuine account. He said: "As is the custom when the Scottish Cup is won, at the banquet which followed our success over Morton in 1948 the trophy was filled with bubbly. After the first bottle of champagne had been opened, a waiter handed me the cork with a smile saying 'I hope this proves so good a luck-bringer you regain the International Championship'.

"I have never been a superstitious fellow. Good football, not good luck, is the essence of success, but somehow this cork, and its reputed fortune-bringing qualities, intrigued me. I decided to give it a trial. Scotland, after all, hadn't won a full international since the end of the war."

Before leading his side out against Wales, Young shot a glance at the lucky cork he had taken with him to Cardiff. Scotland won 3-1, the cork had done its trick and Young had a new tag.

That novelty was just a flashing moment in a magical international career. Young, who made his debut for the national side in a 0-0 home draw against Northern Ireland in November 1946, was the first player to pass the 50 cap barrier. In 2010, Darren Fletcher became the latest player to break that barrier and earn a place in the SFA's roll of honour. Denis Law, who began his career with Scotland a year after Young's ended in 1957, was the second to make it to 50 not out.

The only blot on Young's career with club and country was that his talents were not tested on the biggest platform of them all. Injury kept him out of the 1954 World Cup and by the time the 1958 tournament came round he was winding down his career and did not make the cut. That did not detract from his sterling service in national colours, both as a player and leader of men.

Young had the international credentials, the distinguished physical appearance and he had the nickname. All that was left in the classic Cult Hero repertoire was the song and the Rangers fans obliged with, amongst others, a verse of 'Have you seen the Glasgow Rangers?'

It's the home of famous heroes
And their praises have been sung
Willie Waddell, Torry Gillick
Alan Morton and George Young
So when all my life has ended
And when death has made its mark
May you scatter all my ashes
On the slopes of Ibrox Park."

Young was acutely aware of the sentiments of the Ibrox followers and admitted in his enlightening biography that, despite his best intentions, it was impossible to blank out the songs and chants from the crowd. Just as he accepted the good will of the Rangers fans he grew to appreciate the subtle nuances of the crowds he entertained.

Young said: "I always make a point of stressing to any young footballer that if he wishes to make progress in the game he must forget the crowd on the terraces and put everything he has into playing good football. To be honest I sometimes pass on this advice with my tongue in my cheek, for often it is the most difficult thing in the world to ignore the wisecracks, advice and sometimes hostile actions of the cash customers.

"Experience of playing on grounds all over Britain and the continent has taught me one important thing: no two crowds are alike. The people who pack every football ground have a mass personality and character one can only fully understand through playing before them."

Young always believed the Hampden crowd was a polite one, almost welcoming to opposition teams. He added: "How different it is at Ibrox and Parkhead. The fans who pass through the turnstiles want to see their favourites win – and who can blame them? The enthusiasm of the real supporter is the thing which keeps the game alive and whenever I set foot upon the park at either Ibrox or Parkhead I know what to expect – terrific vocal support for the home side.

"What is the fundamental difference between an Ibrox and a Parkhead crowd? Small thing, perhaps, to the spectator, but one you notice as a player. At Ibrox the crowd cheers. The fans at Parkhead roar their encouragement. I enjoy immensely playing at both grounds for another reason. It is that both sets of spectators are looking all the time for good football. Like actors on the stage, professional footballers appreciate performing in front of folk looking for the finer arts of the game.

"If it were not for the supporters, fellows such as myself would have to look around for another calling. This is a fact I never overlook, for the cash customers, who pay their shilling or so to pass through the turnstile, are the lifeblood of the game. Without their support, first class football, as we know it today, could never have grown into the magnificent spectacle which we accept as a matter of course."

George Lewis Young was born in Grangemouth in 1922, starting his career with Kirkintilloch Rob Roy before earning his move to Ibrox as a teenager in 1941. He went on to spend 18 years with the club as a centre-half and right-back.

He took his bow in a 3-2 league win at Hamilton on November 8, 1941, and played 10 further games as Rangers beat Hibs to the Southern League title by eight points. Rangers also topped their Southern League Cup section. It was not a bad rookie season by anyone's standards but Young had barely got his feet wet. Soon he would have waves of success washing over him at national level when the post-war First Division resumed in 1946/47.

Rangers won the title at the first time of asking following the resumption of full competitive football, pipping Hibs by just two points, and hammered Aberdeen 4-0 in the final of the League Cup.

In 1948 Young added a Scottish Cup medal to his collection but it was the 1948/49 campaign which brought rich rewards. Rangers, with Young pulling the strings, won the title by two points from Dundee and clinched the League Cup with a 2-0 victory against Raith Rovers.

The treble was on and Rangers could become the first team to complete the Scottish clean sweep. Clyde were the team standing in the way in the Scottish Cup final but two penalties from Young helped the Light Blues to a 4-1 win to clinch a historic trophy hat-trick.

The league and Scottish Cup double followed for the ever-present Corky in 1950 and 1952 and another championship in 1956 and 1957.

After leaving Ibrox in 1959, Young had a three year spell in charge of Third Lanark in the top flight, with Thirds finishing third behind Rangers and Kilmarnock in 1961, before retiring from football to concentrate on a career as a hotelier.

Even after his retirement from football his standing in the British game remained unquestioned. Indeed, he was one of the founding members of the all-powerful pools panel in 1963 along with England internationals Tom Finney, Ted Drake and Tommy Lawton.

Young had become one of the biggest personalities the sport in Scotland had ever seen, living through an era when media interest in football was growing with every passing season and the thirst for news from the Old Firm was unquenchable.

Young's shrewdness in his dealings with the newspaper reporters of his era cemented his place in the hierarchy of the professional game. He was always polite, accommodating and open with the press men who followed his team and a bond of mutual respect developed.

The routine for the Rangers side of the 1940s and 1950s was a relaxed one. After training for two hours in the morning, the players would head for the Ivy or Corn Exchange restaurants in the city centre for lunch early in the week.

The pattern changed towards the business end of the week, with the Ibrox squad encouraged to head for the golf course after Thursday's training session for a spot of rest and relaxation.

Friday, on the eve of a match, was a day off from football but Young took that as an opportunity to slip his business hat on and spend hours behind his desk at the hotel.

Post-match on a Saturday he would return home to sit by the fire with his wife and digest the evening match reports. He classed that as "night school", insisting reading newspaper reports was part of his education as a player.

Like so many players who have earned cult status, Young welcomed the media with open arms. Today there is a culture of cynicism among many plying their trade in Scotland's top flight. The media, it all too often feels, is the enemy in a perpetual game of them against us.

The more sensible operators, like Young and so many other personality players in the mould of Ally McCoist, realise that in fact newspapers can be a key ally.

Young definitely had two feet firmly planted in the latter camp. Like every player he endured uncomfortable criticism but he accepted the positives outweighed the negatives.

Young said: "I am one who has always got along splendidly with the football writers. At times they have slated me. On other occasions they have been most kind. Naturally, as a footballer who has always tried to keep both feet planted firmly on the ground, I have learnt to take the good with the bad.

"Not always do I agree with what they have written. There have been occasions when I have wondered if reporters have watched he match in which I have taken part, but never for one moment have I ever doubted the sincerity of any football writer.

"Journalists – at least those with whom I have come into contact – have never attempted to inquire into my private business. Never at any time have I been concerned in serious trouble with the writing fraternity."

In fact, Young would adopt the role of peacekeeper when some of his less media savvy colleagues were on the warpath.

He added: "Football needs the press. The sporting press needs football. Both sides must appreciate this fact. By mutual trust and understanding we can do a tremendous amount to further this great game."

In many ways he was ahead of his time, not just when it came to his appreciation of the the fine detail of positive public relations. Top clubs now spend tens of thousands of pounds employing media minders for their stars but for Young those dealings were a matter of common sense.

Just as he considered his duties as a star of football's big stage to include public appearances he realised he had to do his bit to communicate with the paying customers through the media.

He was a high profile player, a national personality and in demand. Yet he did not find himself in the same financial league as others of similar stature in different showbusiness genres.

It was a matter of huge frustration for a man who basically held down two jobs, just as fellow Ibrox hero Alan Morton had done before him.

The maximum wage still applied to football during the defender's career and he led the calls for that outdated ruling to be capped as he demonstrated a perceptive grasp of the way the game he loved was heading.

Young, well before the first paperazzi flash bulb had shone, made comparisons between his football colleagues and the big names from the equally well exposed worlds of comedy, music and theatre.

Young was unbashful when it came to acknowledging his own standing as a cult hero to the Rangers masses. It was not a case of arrogance, simply realism.

That place in society was not commensurate with the rewards Young had bestowed upon him. While Bob McPhail lavished praise on the way he and his generation were reimbursed, the game and society had moved on by the time Young led the club.

While Meiklejohn, Morton and McPhail were ordinary men doing an extraordinary job the men in the upper echelons of the game moving into the 1950s began to realise their role had evolved into something altogether different.

While Morton and the Wembley Wizards would spend the eve of matches socialising with supporters, Young's generation were beginning to find themselves being set apart. Restaurants would set aside private dining rooms to protect their star customers from autograph hunting fans: a touch of Hollywood had come to Glasgow.

There was never any question that Young did not relish the role of acting as an ambassador for his beloved club but that loyalty and devotion did not prevent him from questioning what he was gaining in return.

He said: "One who has thoughts of entering professional football in the hopes of making a fortune, my advice is 'don't!' The professional in my honest opinion is the most underpaid of all public entertainers. Do not get the impression I'm a Bolshie because I hold these views, for they are shared by hundres of other fellows, and by folk who like me have given the matter serious thought.

"Just think what a star footballer, a man who might by reason of his skill and personality attract thousands of spectators, usually receives as the maximum for his services: £14 a week during the playing season, plus a bonus of £2 for a win or £1 for a draw. Do you think this is fair? Sit in judgement upon the question and I feel you will side with me and agree that soccer stars are grossly underpaid and the time has arrived for the whole question to be delved into most deeply."

A year prior to those public statements in his biography, Young had shocked the fans who idolised him by refusing to re-sign for Rangers. Young had been a boyhood Rangers fan and had rejected a string of clubs to join the club he worshipped. But it was not blind loyalty. It became a matter of national importance and the story everyone was following with intensity.

Young said: "In the street I found myself hailed by perfect strangers who, after some innocuous remarks, would bring the subject round to my row with Rangers. At lunch I have even had fellows interrupt me to ask the same question. My telephone at home rang at all hours of the night and day with inquiries from folk who seemed to be most anxious that the Rangers and I should come to an agreement."

Young found himself at a crossroads in his life and shellshocked Ibrox supporters had to get used to the idea that their rock could be unearthed from his place at the heart of their club.

The likeable big defender found himself in the uncomfortable position of lobbying for a higher wage while balancing that desire with his humble nature. Young was desperate to retain the dignity he prized above all else and, not surprisingly, he succeeded. The man on the street could surely relate to a powerful argument.

Young explained: "I love association football. Among my colleagues I have met some of the finest men in the world. For all that, I never allow myself to forget that to play football is my job. I train hard, live a clean life and do everything to make sure I am able to give the cash customers who pass through the turnstiles full value for their money. In return it is my view that football should give me the best possible wage for my services.

"Modesty, I have learnt, is one thing a professional footballer should always retain, for in this game you may be at the top one week, and following a loss of form well and truly in the dumps a little later, so when I say that it is my belief that thousands of folk come specially to see players such as myself, I do not want you to think I have a head which has become too big for my hat.

"This viewpoint of mine was the basis for the disagreement I had with Glasgow Rangers. It was my contention that George Young was the fellow playing a mighty part in helping attract the crowds. The negotiations between Rangers and myself proceeded for several weeks – the number for and against me were about level, and in the end as I did not wish to be shut out of the game I re-signed for the club. There was no bitterness on either side. So far as I was concerned it was like any employee trying to get a rise."

Young used his circumstances as a poweful tool for illustrating his belief that the need of modernisation was crucial to football's development in the post-war years. It was not until 1961, two years after Young's retirement from playing and a full decade after the release of his thought provoking book, that the cap on earnings was finally lifted.

In 1951 Young's mind was full of ideas for taking the game to the next level and for ensuring the welfare of the men who were satisfying the demands of increasingly demanding audiences.

He said: "The first thing I would do is to remember that in all other branches of entertainment the star attractions receive a bigger salary than the supporting cast. Who, for instance, would ever think of offering Danny Kaye the same salary as an act at the foot of the bill? No one in their right senses. Why should football be approached from a different angle? The solution, in my view, is the drawing up of individual contracts with clubs paying their players just what they, and the footballer, consider they are worth to each other.

"The critics of this move, I know, would be quick to point out that soccer is a team game, and that team spirit would be killed. To this my answer is 'nonsense'! The contracts between the club and its players would be secret. There would be no reason for one footballer to know what the other was receiving each week – and I can assure you the average player is concerned only with his own affairs and is not very much interested in the financial side of his colleagues' business, which is as it should be."

Young, after tax, received £365 from his benefit game. He candidly revealed he had been tapped by a leading English club offering £3,000 in cash as a signing incentive. He thanked him and wished him a good evening. His loyalty to the club never wavered, even in the face of his hardline negotiating stance.

Young wanted the maximum wage abolished but he was not motivated by greed. In the same breath he called for the bonus system to be scrapped, claiming offering incentives for wins and draws was an insult to the profession he was proud to call his own. He argued pride and not a few shillings was what drove him to succeed. Bonus or no bonus, nobody could argue that the strapping boy from Grangemouth turned into one of Scottish football's biggest success stories.

**MAGIC MOMENT:** The Wee Blue Devil tormented the Auld Enemy, Slim and his ball juggling act toyed with them. Another Light Blue hero who became a legend in Dark Blue.

# JIM BAXTER
## *'SLIM'* 1960-1965 and 1969-70

**GERS CAREER:** Games 254; Goals 24; Caps 34

I T IS an unusual story that lends itself to starting at the final page. But then Jim Baxter was no ordinary player and no ordinary man. He was, and remains, the ultimate Rangers cult hero and no misdemeanour could force his army of admirers to drop him from their collective heart.

Everyone knows the caricature: the loveable rogue who battled the bottle, the cheeky chap who played keepie-up deep in enemy territory at Wembley, the arrogant Fifer who could mix it with the best ... and knew it.

But it was at the 2001 funeral of the legend that the real story began to unfold. Baxter was not a disposable celebrity, the outpouring of warmth and genuine affection was proof positive that despite his off-field antics his ability with a ball at his feet had conquered all. At times his behaviour was loathsome, his love of

drink and the high life led him to treat his talents with contempt, but that did not matter one bit to his public. From politics and the literary world to his football contemporaries, the praise of the late Jim Curran Baxter was as fulsome as it was sincere.

His passing, having overcome two liver transplants before finally being beaten by cancer, prompted the inevitable question: Just what would a player of Baxter's calibre command in today's transfer market? Former Rangers captain Eric Caldow estimated £20million – and that was just for his left leg, never mind the complete package. Caldow's tongue in cheek quip at a time of national mourning would have earned the approval of Slim Jim, a man not renowned for standing on ceremony. Caldow qualified his valuation of Baxter's lorded left peg by adding: "He loved football – all he could talk about was football, he was just a genius. He was arrogant, but he wanted to win."

The defining, shining example of that arrogance was the centre of attention as a who's who of football turned out at Glasgow Cathedral for Baxter's funeral. By definition it should have been a sombre occasion but the memories of the man in full flight, at his cocky best, raised more than an isolated smile.

Talk Baxter and before long the conversation swings inevitably to Wembley, 1967. The date was April 15, World Cup winners England were humbled 3-2 by the new unofficial champions of the planet and it was the Fifer who twisted the knife with his impromptu keepie-up display on the sacred Wembley turf. He didn't just help beat the Auld Enemy, he toyed with them. And how the Tartan Army loved it.

Speaking at the time of Baxter's death, broadcasting doyen and renowned football historian Bob Crampsey said: "That's a defining moment for almost every football fan in Scotland irrespective of where their club allegiance lies. Baxter going up and down that left wing at no great pace, keeping the ball off the deck with 90,000 people there was phenomenal. England had no idea what to do about it and Baxter was not about to solve that problem for them – it was a wonderful moment. Almost from the word go, he became a cult figure and he achieved almost messianic status. I would seldom use this word about football, but I think Baxter was loved and loved in the totality. Fans weren't blind to what others might have seen as faults. They knew he liked a drink, that he liked to stay out late and they knew he wasn't a dedicated pounder of the track, but they liked the package. I think, more than anything else, that he was the player they would have liked to have been."

Cult hero and messiah. Baxter was as far removed from the Rangers heroes who had gone before him as it is possible to imagine. He could not have lived with the hard line disciplinary approach of Bill Struth, his off-field conduct at times made a mockery of his club's reputation for clean living and straight-laced principles. But all of that was forgiven. Baxter, in the eyes of the Rangers fans and the Scotland supporters he converted in a few flicks of his boot at Wembley one afternoon, could do no wrong.

The outpouring of grief when cancer claimed one of Scotland's most colourful characters was nothing short of breathtaking. Former Scotland team-mate Denis Law said: "He was just a wonderful player, a lovely passer of the ball." Celtic skipper Billy McNeill was a foe on the pitch but an admirer outside the heat of battle, the Hoops legend admitting: "He was a typical cheeky, confident type of character. He had this enormous ability and I think Rangers spotted that more quickly than anyone else." Rangers and Scotland star Sandy Jardine added: "Jim was a wonderful player who had outrageous skill and huge confidence in his own ability. People band about the phrase 'world class', but Jim genuinely was a world class player. Jim could have played at any time and anywhere because of his skill level." Kenny Dalglish added: "My lasting memory of him will be of Wembley in 1967. To keep the ball up just when it looked as though Scotland were going to beat them was beyond belief."

*Don't bother just to be better than your contemporaries or predecessors, try to be better than yourself.*
**William Faulkner**

For a man who, by his own admission, did not live by the highest moral code there is a contradiction in the fact that the bible holds a passage that succinctly got to the root of the life of arguably the nation's most famous football player. Author and broadcaster William McIlvanney delivered the eulogy in which he tackled the well worn line that Baxter was cursed with "feet of clay". It was a reference to a phrase in the good book, taken from the tale of a dream King Nebuchadnezzar had in which the image that appeared to him had a head of gold, breast and arms of silver, belly and thighs of brass and legs of iron. The feet , however, were made of clay – a stone hit the feet and the whole image broke into pieces. Baxter's off-field indulgences were his very own "feet of clay", his downfall at a time when he should have been at his peak. McIlvanney begged to differ, telling his cathedral audience that, if anything, Baxter had feet of pure gold and the left one was probably inlaid with precious stones. It was the rest of him that was made of fallible human clay.

Drink was one of the factors that eroded that human clay. He would regularly miss training on the morning after the night before and he made no secret of the fact, in his post football days, that he had a serious problem with the bottle. But booze was not his only vice, gambling was another and that ultimately ended his marriage to Rangers. When asked if his life would have been different if he had been earning the salary of a modern player, he retorted: "Definitely. I'd have spent £50,000 a week at the bookies instead of £100."

Baxter's antics would today have been tabloid fodder, manna from heaven for the headline writer, yet the complex character of Slim Jim and his many facets gave him broadsheet appeal. Speaking candidly in his final years in an interview with the *Telegraph*, he admitted his talent for squandering cash had forced his hand when it came to his initial departure from Rangers when he joined Sunderland in 1965. It was the beginning of the end for a player who had been at the height of his power, with Baxter saying: "I went downhill because I left Rangers and went to a bad side, simple as that. I would never have wanted to leave Rangers if I hadn't gambled away all my money. I'd bet on anything. Fifty quid the next man to walk in here is wearing black shoes, that kind of thing. The bevvy did my liver in and the gambling did my brain in." There was an intrigue surrounding Baxter that made him a broadsheet writer's dream, indeed it was the *Telegraph* who once claimed Baxter "burned the candle at both ends then torched the bit in the middle". It was true.

He was Scotland's original flawed genius and he played the role to perfection. His quirks were infuriating yet endearing to so many but beneath all of that was the underlying fact that the man who talked the talk could walk the walk.

Baxter was born in Hill O' Beath in 1939 and worked in the local mining industry while starting out in the game with Raith Rovers. He carried props to the coal face for £6 a week and once narrowly escaped serious injury when there was a roof fall at the mine. It was not a glamorous start in life but that would all change.

He was an under-21 international when Rangers paid a club record fee of £17,500 to tempt him to Ibrox in 1960. His debut season brought the first of three championship winner's medals, with further title triumphs in 1963 and 1964. His first Scottish Cup badge came in 1962, the first of three consecutive victories for Baxter and his Rangers colleagues. The League Cup was even more fruitful as he steered the club to success in the finals of 1960, 1961, 1963 and 1964. The cultured schemer was the creative force of the 1963 treble winning side with vision and precision.

European honours were illusive, with Baxter part of the Light Blues side defeated in the 1961 final of the European Cup Winners' Cup against Fiorentina. In his first five year spell with Rangers the Fifer had the Indian sign over Celtic, tasting defeat only twice in an odds-busting string of 18 Old Firm games.

He excelled for his country too. The first of Baxter's first 34 caps came just after his move to Rangers in the summer of 1960. He made his debut in a 5-2 win against Northern Ireland but it was against the men in white that he truly sparkled.

In 1963 he inspired 10-man Scotland to a 2-1 victory over the English, scoring both goals himself after Eric Caldow had broken his leg. Baxter classed that performance as far better than his 1967 exhibition at Wembley. His first goal in 63 was a penalty, the other was a perfectly struck effort after he had cut out a clearance outside of the England box. Spurs legend John White was the first to congratulate Baxter. White revealed at the time: "As I ran up to Jim he was standing perfectly still, arms raised above his head, eyes closed. I heard him say: 'That's the greatest goal in Wembley's history'."

Mixing with some of the best international football had to offer first sowed the seeds of doubt in Baxter's mind as far as his Rangers future was concerned. In 1963 he was selected to play for the Rest of the World against England in a match at Wembley to celebrate the centenary of the FA alongside leading lights such as Ferenc Puskas. The Hungarian star and Baxter struck up a friendship ... and the Scotsman soon discovered what type of wages his new pal's Real Madrid paymasters were prepared to shell out. His head was turned and within two years Baxter was on his way to the promised land of English league football.

The squad for that 100 year celebration was: Lev Yashin (USSR), Djalma Santos (Brazil), Raymond Kopa (France), Eusebio (Portugal), Uwe Seeler (West Germany), Luis Eyzaguirre (Chile), Karl-Heinz Schnellinger (West Germany), Svatopluk Pluskal, Jan Popluhar, Josef

Masopust (Czechoslovakia), Jim Baxter, Denis Law (Scotland), Francisco Gento Lopez (Spain), Ferenc Puskas (Spain), Alfredo Di Stefano, Laulhe (Spain), and Edson Arantes Nascimento Pele (Brazil). Not bad company for a boy who started out with Crossgates Primrose in the hurly burly of junior football.

Baxter was at ease in those surroundings, with his arrogance on the football pitch legendary. In any company he refused to hide and the supporters appreciated that. Former Rangers team-mate Ronnie Mackinnon's anecdote from the 1966 meeting with Brazil at Hampden hits the spot. Mackinnon asked who would be looking after Pele, to which Baxter replied: "Who's Pele? Wait until I get out there." If Pele and the Brazilians didn't know too much about Slim Jim before they soon would. Indeed, the World Cup winner is reported to have claimed he wished Baxter had come from Rio rather than Fife. True or not, it is all part of the myth and mystique surrounding the man.

His arrogance in playing days was replaced with a more humble approach in Baxter's final days. The man himself reflected: "I was a rascal, alright – but you don't know how that makes me feel when people talk about me and the likes of di Stefano and Puskas in the same breath. It was only when I knew I was dying I realised what I meant to people. I got cards from all over the world. Every time the post arrived at the hospital I was in tears."

In his prime the proud Scotsman was in the bracket of di Stefano and Puskas but devoid of the bumper pay packets of that international cast, Baxter had to innovate to even try and keep pace in the financial league. On one Scotland trip in West Germany he secured a boot deal for himself and Rangers team-mate John Greig, the princely sum of £10 handed over by Adidas to secure the services of each of the players. It was cheap at the price – four decades later the German manufacturers are lining David Beckham's pockets with £3million a year as his reward for wearing the three stripes. Changed times? Not half.

At Rangers his basic wage was £45 – at Sunderland, when he moved in 1965, it leapt to £85 and the star had a wage packet at least close to matching his sizeable chunk of confidence. He also earned a significant signing fee, vindicating his decision to exploit the opportunities across the border and feeding his spending requirements. Former Rangers stalwart and one-time Scotland manager Ian McColl was the man who persuaded his country's enigmatic star to break ranks. McColl pulled off what remains arguably the biggest transfer coup in the club's history. Sunderland teamed Baxter up with his cousin, George Kinell, 18 months after his arrival south of the border. Roker Park fans saw the recruitment of the former Aberdeen player, who had already been plying his trade in England with Stoke and Oldham, as a last throw of the dice to try and help the import settle.

Baxter spent two and a half seasons at Roker Park, playing 87 games and scoring 10 goals, before being moved on to Nottingham Forest for £100,000 in 1967. He is still remembered by Sunderland fans who saw him play for flashes of skill – and also for his Beatles-style haircut. It was, after all, the Swinging Sixties and Baxter wanted to look the star on and off the park.

His hard living was as legendary as his talents in Sunderland. In the 2005 book *The Black Catalogue* fans put pen to paper to record their most vivid memories, with one recalling team-mates carrying a "dead drunk" Scotland international out of a local nightclub in the early hours of the morning. That afternoon he watched Baxter go out and destroy Newcastle.

Despite his excesses, he was still a sought-after commodity when he switched to Nottingham Forest it was a headline grabbing move. Forest, who had tracked Baxter since his Rangers days, were overjoyed to finally land the man in December 1967. Manager Johnny Carey said: "This is the best Christmas present I have ever given to any club." When Carey was asked if the six-figure fee was a risk, he replied: "No, I am not a gambler and I don't think this is a gamble." If only his new recruit could say the same.

Slim Jim's time with Forest was short, if not exactly sweet. After 48 appearances and one goal, the Scot was heading back for Rangers with questions about his commitment and physical shape ringing in his ears. The player himself admitted: "I let Nottingham down. I didn't play at all."

The club made him available on a free transfer and when Rangers weighed in with a £10,000 signing on fee the deal was done. Baxter was met by a flurry of attention when he breezed back into Ibrox, with a pack of television and press cameramen camped outside waiting for news on his decision after his intenstive negotiations. He emerged to tell them: "It's great to be a Ranger again." He was back in the full glare of the Old Firm media bubble and loved every minute. Football's first man was back on the stage he loved most.

Baxter was given a golden chance to prove his doubters wrong by Gers manager Davie White but failed to seize it. In his second spell in Govan he got off to an inauspicious start, making his second debut in a 0-0 draw at Dundee United. In the season prior to their talisman's reappearance the club finished five points behind Celtic but that gap widened to 12 points in the 1969/70 campaign when Baxter started in his usual No.6 shirt.

He lasted 14 league games and four in the League Cup, switching to No.8 for his final First Division game and bringing a touch of luck as he signed off with a 3-2 win at Aberdeen.

That came on December 20, 1969. By that time Willie Waddell had replaced White at the helm and a wind of change was blowing through the Ibrox corridors.

When Waddell was appointed he said: "Rangers must have pride in themselves, in their character and in their image. The greatness of a club is not always judged on what the team is doing on the field but how everyone is judged off it as well."

The writing was on the wall for Baxter, whose taste for the high life was as strong as ever.

He and Willie Henderson knew exactly what Waddell stood for. The duo went to the extent of shaving off their moustaches before Waddell's first team meeting, with the manager admitting: "They have both been thanked for their clean-shaven look."

It was to be only a temporary reprieve and, with fitness fanatic and ex-commando Jock Wallace beside him on the training field, Waddell dispensed with Baxter's services.

After 254 games, at the age of 30, the prodigal son retired from the game. Regrets? Not likely. In later life Baxter claimed: "Everything I did on the pitch was off-the-cuff. Sheer instinct. If I'd been a good boy maybe the swashbuckling stuff would have got stifled."

His second spell with the club was entirely unremarkable yet that did not block his copybook as far as the Rangers supporters were concerned. In the process of writing this book I turned to all corners of the country, to all walks of life, in search of people with an affinity to the cult heroes of Rangers. When it came to testifying to Baxter's pavement appeal there was no shortage of volunteers.

Jim Templeton, who has risen to become president of the Rangers Supporters Assembly, was an impressionable schoolboy when he first caught sight of Jim Baxter plying his trade at Ibrox. And what an impression he made.

Templeton's enthusiasm for his subject is obvious as he drifts back down memory lane, recalling: "I went to my first Rangers match in 1961 with my dad. I was nine at the time and Jim Baxter became my hero – I'll always remember the way he used to wear his shirt hanging half out of his shorts. I decided I'd wear mine the same way, I wanted to be just like Slim. It wasn't just the way he looked – I wanted to play like him. Who wouldn't want to?"

That desire to emulate Scotland's star man led to a daily ritual for Templeton, who explained: "I was naturally right footed but spent hours kicking a ball off a wall with my left foot to try and copy Baxter. It worked to an extent because I became two-footed and three senior clubs did look at me when I was at school – but unfortunately I never quite hit the heights Jim did!"

Baxter had the skill, had the killer instinct. But it was his attitude as much as anything that trickled through the supporters to eventually create a torrent of belief that he could lead the Light Blues to greatness.

Templeton said: "Even just looking at Jim Baxter on the park, with his shirt untucked and the swagger he had, you knew he was gallous and cocky. That appealed to supporters because if he was confident then it meant you could be. With somebody like that in your team there's always hope that something special can happen, that no game is ever beyond you."

Templeton has lived through some of the most momentous occasions in the history of Rangers and watched legend after legend grace Ibrox yet he is unequivocal about Baxter's place in the pecking order.

He said: "People talk about George Best but, for me, Jim Baxter was the first real idol in football. At Rangers many, many fantastic players went before and were loved by the supporters for the job they did – but Baxter was different. He was more than just a great player, he was a hero.

"I watched a short video of him just the other day and his skills were unbelievable. He could destroy a team on his own and not many half-backs, or midfielders as we'd class them now, could do that. The forwards had traditionally been the dangermen but Baxter changed all of that.

"I remember being on the terraces at Ibrox when he started playing keepie-up inside his own six-yard box. The stands were going mad, with people yelling for him to get rid of the ball. He didn't, because he knew nobody would take it off of him. He had that arrogance but with the talent to back it up.

"I know many Celtic fans who would tell you that the day he walked away from Ibrox was a happy one for them. They were glad to see the back of Baxter more than any other player. In my opinion he is the greatest player we have ever had and I'm not alone in thinking that.

"He was a bit of a rebel and fans related to that. The country was coming out of some dark days, the end of the war wasn't too far back, and here was an ordinary guy, a miner, out there doing the things every supporter wished they could do.

"He knew he had ability and he used it on his terms. If that wasn't suitable then tough. Jim Baxter had his flaws and everyone knew that but there was nothing he could do that would tarnish him in the eyes of the fans. I was listening to a radio phone in not so long ago and Paul Le Guen's views on the drinking culture in Scottish football were being discussed. A Rangers fan phoned in to say what about Jim Baxter, that 'drinking never did him any harm'. He must have forgotten about the two liver transplants and the years of illness! Supporters don't dwell on those parts of his life, they remember the good times and the hours of entertainment he provided. When he came back to the club for his second spell at Ibrox he was no longer 'Slim' Jim. But he still had it – I remember his first game against Celtic when he controlled the match. The problem was, because of his physical condition, he couldn't sustain that level of performance. That was accepted, he wasn't criticized because he was above that.

"The interesting thing is that his time with Rangers was actually pretty short in comparison to so many of the greats. Yet I doubt if there is a single Rangers supporter anywhere in the world who wouldn't know Jim Baxter, whereas there are some wonderful players from the past who a lot of fans might not have too much knowledge of. Baxter was a phenomenon.

"He played in what is arguably the greatest team Rangers have ever had and there was an embarrassment of riches – he came into the team at the expense of Billy Stevenson, another player I remember watching when he went on to star with Liverpool and was a tremendous player. At that time there were almost two star players for every position.

"Even in great teams there is room for individuals. Brian Laudrup and Paul Gascoigne played in dominant sides but they had a special bond with the supporters because they brought something different to the table, they weren't just good team players. Baxter was the same, he was somebody the fans could see a bit of themselves in. Or at least a bit of what they would like to be if they ever got the chance to play for Rangers. I wish we had another one like him now."

But would another Jim Baxter thrive in today's game? For one thing his off-field habits wouldn't be tolerated and his on-field style would have to fit the masterplan.

Being stifled in that way was a huge fear for the free flowing playmaker and he was well aware that he was fortunate to play in an era that enabled him to thrive, free from the shackles of tactical minutiae. Would a team with Baxter in it have been happy to have gone into an away game to carry out the tried and tested modern ploy of sitting back and playing on the counter?

In his 1984 autobiography *The Party's Over,* Baxter said: "As far as I am concerned a football park is a football park, wherever it may be. If you can play at all, what does it matter whether you're in Glasgow or Moscow. Too many players away from home are looking for excuses in advance. It's time managers – who are responsible for much of the brainwashing – recognized this. The problem is managers are also seeking excuses."

Baxter and fellow errant star George Best later teamed up to host, meet and greet sports nights with fans across the country in the early 1990s, their outspoken views currying favour with fans across Britain. At one event in Aberdeen in 1993 Baxter made his views on the transition his beloved game was going through crystal clear when he told the audience: "I don't go to football often because there is a lack of personalities. Rangers let Davie Cooper go too early, he's still the best player in Scottish football. He still keeps fit and I'd rather see 20 minutes of him than 90 minutes of someone else."

By that stage Baxter had been retired from frontline duty for more than two decades but his opinions still carried weight, even if he had chosen to turn his back on football following his second departure from Ibrox.

Within six months of the announcement by Rangers that Baxter was being released in 1970, he was granted a licence to begin life as a publican. Baxters on Paisley Road West, in the heart of Light Blues territory, became a popular venue and he carved out a lengthy career in a trade that was not best suited to a man not equipped to resist the obvious temptations awaiting him at the office. He had two life-saving liver transplants in the mid-90s. When Baxter had his first operation in 1994 he became Scotland's 50th liver transplant patient. When it failed he underwent a second transplant immediately and battled back to health at the age of 55, having vowed never to drink again. He said prior to the operation: "I know my whole lifestyle will have to change but there is no alternative."

He managed to make the best of what life had thrown at him. Former Rangers team-mate John Greig's son attended the same school as Baxter's two boys and the Ibrox greats saw plenty of each other in later life. Greig witnessed at first hand Baxter's struggles but insists the man's spirits never dropped. In his 2005 biography *My Story*, Greig said: "Jim died at the age of just 61 but he had few regrets, publicly at least. He used to say that he had lived three lifetimes in one and I suppose there was a lot of truth in that statement. He certainly knew how to enjoy himself. I saw quite a lot of Jim in later years and he never lost his talent for raising a smile, often in a manner that made others cringe. But no matter what anyone says about Jim Baxter, he stands alongside any of the greats of the game. He was blessed with a remarkable football brain, great vision and an abundance of skill. I could never praise Jim highly enough as a football player and you rarely see his likes in the modern game – more is the pity. I was given the accolade of Greatest Ever Ranger, but Jim Baxter would have been my personal choice. Jim was one of the true greats of the game: a player who would have left his mark on any generation, because he would have been able to adapt to suit the demands of the modern game. He was blessed with magnificent talent and the ability to win a game almost single-handed – and he knew it. That was what made Jim the player he was. He had the utmost confidence in himself. Jim gave the appearance of being the coolest man around and he probably was. He refused to show nerves and the bigger the stage the better he played."

Even after his transplants Baxter did not take his foot off the pedal and his cult status continued to open doors. Just a couple of years prior to his death, he had an unexpected shot at film stardom. He and former Celtic rival Jimmy Johnstone were offered cameo roles in Hollywood director Robert Duvall's film *The Cup*. Duvall had pencilled in the pair for a number of scenes, in each one he wanted them to appear pouring a pint of beer in a reference to their hard drinking past. Both politely declined the invitation, preferring fans to remember them for their magic on the pitch rather than opting to poke fun at their own reputations.

As it happened Baxter's reputation as a player, for all of his dalliances with the darker sides of life, has outlived him. He became a hero at club and international level and, almost uniquely, maintains that status years after his death. Radio bosses at Five Live famously fell victim to Baxter's cult status. Even after his death, Slim Jim still had a hold on the Auld Enemy. When the station opened a poll in 2005 to name the footbridge leading to the new Wembley Stadium they hadn't bargained for the Tartan Army's input. Scotland fans flooded the lines to nominate Jim Baxter as the man the structure should be named after. He had, after all, been a star performer at Wembley. An incredible 90% of the 80,000 votes cast were in Baxter's favour and, as the campaign gathered pace, there was even support in the Commons from SNP Member of Parliament Peter Wishart. In his representation to the House, Wishart said the move would be recognition of the day England were "humbled by an impudent genius". In the end Baxter was beaten by a horse, Billy the White Horse to be exact, as England fans paid homage to the equestrian police hero who cleared the pitch following a mass pitch invasion during the 1923 FA Cup final.

Baxter's personal monument actually lies closer to home by virtue of the fact his talents, just like Alan Morton before him, had the power to unite football fans. He didn't belong solely to the Rangers fans, more of a national treasure. In 2003 a lasting memorial was unveiled in Hill o' Beath by Gordon Brown, then serving as Chancellor. Brown, a devoted Raith Rovers fan, had marvelled at Baxter's skills from the terraces of Stark's Park as a boy. Brown has been lambasted in recent years for his Britishness, sitting decidely on the fence when it comes to Scotland's rivalry with the Auld Enemy he finds himself on the brink of governing. On one particular player from his home patch his views are unequivocal. According to Brown, Baxter is the greatest talent his home country has ever produced. The £80,000 bronze statue which now stands in the Baxter's birthplace is testament to his appeal. Even from beyond the grave Slim could pull in the crowds and a series of fundraising events soon found the necessary cash to fund the project.

The famous name still carries considerable financial clout and the clamour for memorabilia is still strong. In a recent auction two of his international shirts, from his Sunderland days, sold for close to

£3,000 – while a Michael Owen cup final jersey fetched £300. Fans will still pay top dollar for a small slice of the Baxter magic. Another of the kits to have been auctioned was the one Baxter wore on his international debut, the No.6 top swapped with Northern Ireland player Bill McAdams. When his opponent suggested Baxter might want to keep hold of his first international jersey, he replied: "Dinnae worry, Bill. It'll be the first of many." Not for the last time, his confidence had solid foundations and he went on to captain Scotland just as he had skippered Rangers.

When Baxter was diagnosed with cancer of the pancreas at the beginning of February in 2001, and died at home in Glasgow just two months later, Scottish football lost one of its favourite sons but his presence in the game lives on.

Baxter's son Alex once recalled a moment on holiday in Rothesay when, side by side with his long since retired dad, a stranger approached to ask: "What's it like to be the son of God then, eh?"

In that one sentence, the lone football philosopher spoke for the legions of Rangers of fans who class the late great as an immortal.

**MAGIC MOMENT:** Wonderful Willie's wing play undid
Dundee to earn Rangers the 1964 treble in style.

# WILLIE HENDERSON
## 'WEE WILLIE' 1960-1972

### GERS CAREER: Games 426; Goals 62; Caps 29

T HE BIGGER they are the harder they fall, that's what every
football coach up and down the land will try and tell his
charges. What they conveniently forget to
add is that the smaller they are the faster they
tend to run past you. Many, many full-backs in
the 1960s and 1970s found that out to their cost.
Here was a player who looked like an underdog
until he had the ball at his feet, then he was very
much top dog. A cross between a greyhound
with pace to burn and a Rotweiler who wouldn't
let go once he had the ball in his possession –
but a true pedigree performer, a breed apart.

Wee Willie Henderson stands 5ft 4inches tall.
A connoisseur of Cuba's most famous export,
the Rangers legend has the odd honour of once smoking a cigar that
stood every inch as tall as he did. He wouldn't get away with that
now of course, the club dietician would have it snuffed out and
replaced it with an energy bar.

A lack of height was not the only physical disadvantage he had to
conquer, Henderson also suffered from acute eyesight problems.
Famously he once ran to the dugout during the closing stages of a
pulsating Old Firm game to ask: "How long to go, how long to go?"
It was left to Celtic manager Jock Stein to boom back: "Go and ask

the other dugout you bloody fool, this is the Celtic bench." Fact or fiction? That is at least the most popular recollection of the moment, although Henderson likes to remember it differently. He claims Stein actually shouted back that there were 10 minutes to go ... knowing full well there were only two. The Hoops manager was always looking to gain an advantage for his side.

Henderson was small, but was as tenacious as he was skilful. This was a player well versed in the dark arts of wing sorcery. Henderson, as anyone lucky enough to have cheered him on during his rapid raids down the flanks will testify to, was a treasure to behold. Speed, trickery and the ability to sell the type of dummy that left defenders paying at the gate to get back in the ground were the key features to his game.

*It's not the size of the dog in the fight, it's the size of the fight in the dog.*

**Mark Twain**

He used his stature to his advantage, darting past opponents with consummate ease time after time. He was also not a man to be bullied on or off the field. The Rangers fans responded and afforded him the freedom of Ibrox. The supporters were elevated to the highest highs by the smallest man in their team.

Tommy Malcolm, a football historian based at the Scottish Football Museum at Hampden Park, is in no doubt about Henderson's standing in the grand scheme of Scottish wingers. Malcolm has the distinction of witnessing the moment Wee Willie took his first step on the path to stardom and from that day on he was a huge fan of the little man.

He said: "The first time I saw Willie Henderson was in a Rangers trial match in 1959. The club would stage matches between the first team and the second team but in that particular year a third side had been introduced and Willie played for them on that occasion. He was up against Eric Caldow, an absolutely top notch full-back, and he gave Eric and an absolute roasting. Those games attracted up to 30,000 fans and the supporters took to him straight away. He had a bit of magic about him.

"Wee Willie Henderson was a tremendous player. People compared him and Jimmy Johnstone – maybe I'm biased, but I always felt Willie was a far more productive player than Jinky. Johnstone was very, very tricky but sometimes he would tie himself up in knots, Willie was more direct and would beat his man and fire in an accurate cross nine times out of 10. The other big difference between the two was Willie would just pick himself up and get on with it if he was hit by a heavy challenge. Jimmy Johnstone was more likely to get up and try and kick the defender back. Willie was like India rubber, he just bounced back and the supporters loved that attitude.

"I would always have had Willie in my team ahead of Jimmy Johnstone and I think their respective records in international football supports that, Willie was more effective for Scotland. Mind you, so many great wingers of that era didn't get anywhere near a cap because there were so many outstanding performers. Alex Edwards, a fantastic player for Hibs and Dunfermline, could only get as close as an under-23 cap."

Johnstone of Celtic and Henderson of Rangers were the two highest profile flankers in the Scottish game in that era but they were not alone. A plethora of hugely talented men graced grounds the length and breadth of the country and Malcolm, who first watched Rangers as a schoolboy in 1954, dreams of a return to those heady days.

He added: "People raved about Brian Laudrup when he came to Rangers in the 1990s because he was different, because he could excite the crowd. In the 1950s and 1960s he would have been just another winger because that type of ability was commonplace, every team from the top to the very bottom played with two wingers who could beat their man. It's such a shame we no longer produce them, there seems to be a dearth of that type of player. I watched Scotland play the Faroe Islands recently and the game was crying out for somebody who could take the ball past them, we simply don't have it.

"When Willie Henderson was at his peak it was a golden era for wingers, with Davie Wilson on the opposite side of the park and later Willie Johnston. Willie Henderson was a provider of goals while Davie was a goalscorer despite playing on the wing, he would pop up at the back post time and time again and scored a phenomenal amount for a winger."

While Malcolm followed Henderson's Rangers career from his first kick of the ball, he had to wait just a little longer to catch his first sight of the winger in the dark blue of Scotland.

He recalled: "Nowadays players don't get into the Scotland team until they are into their 20s. Willie was only 18 when he scored on his debut in a 3-2 win against Wales – I didn't see that game in Cardiff but I did see his first appearance at Hampden in the next match, when he scored again with a wonderful solo goal in a 5-1 win against Northern Ireland. He outshone George Best that day."

All good things come to an end and when that time came for Henderson there were no demonstrations on Edmiston Drive, no sit-in protests at Ibrox. The manager made his decision, the player left and the fans got on with it.

Malcolm said: "I don't think Willie was too impressed but there was no outcry. Supporters accepted his time had come and gone, although I think Tommy McLean struggled a bit to win over the fans after taking Willie's place. It is always difficult to come in and replace a legend, which is what Willie was. He had done something similar himself when he took over from Alex Scott. The fans perhaps felt a bit sorry for Alex when he left for Everton but they were happy to have Willie in the side, they were different players with Alex relying on pace to get past defenders while Willie had tricks that could make opponents look stupid at times.

"It was like an electric shock when he got the ball, the fans were jolted because they knew something was about to happen. Willie was always an emotional type of fellow. He cried he won his first medal, in the Scottish Cup in 1962, and it was the same when Rangers won the treble two years later. Even now he is the same, when he came to Hampden to accept his place in our hall of fame you could hear the emotion in his voice. He has always appreciated the position his talents put him in and I think in return the fans appreciate him because of that.

"Mind you, he can be cutting when he wants to. Willie tells the story when he was playing at Sheffield Wednesday and a player from the opposition team directed a comment towards him going up the tunnel at half-time. He shouted 'hey Henderson, you're crap'. Willie took one look at him and just said 'Well, you know my name. Who are you?'. He had a point, everyone in football was aware of Willie Henderson in that era, he was a big name player and not just in Scotland."

Wee Willie was not the only name the winger was known by. The tag 'Scotland's Garrincha' was bestowed upon Henderson by sections of the Light Blues faithful, high praise indeed but even comparisons with the Brazilian star, the 1962 World Cup's player of the tournament, would not faze the assured young protégé.

In any case, at an even younger age he had already had a more onerous comparison drawn. In the 1950s an excited Airdrie director,

Peter Bennie, called a contact on the *Sunday Post* with a simple message: "If you want to see another Alan Morton in the making, come out to Broomfield tonight." That night a 12 year-old Willie Henderson starred for Caldercruix in the Airdrie schools tournament. The *Sunday Post* reporter was among the interested spectators, as was an old timer by the name of Alan Morton. No doubt he approved of the boy being tipped as his heir to the throne of Ibrox wing king.

He became a child star, a schoolboy international who was tipped for big things from his teenage years. The Ballieston-born winger was courted by a string of clubs during his school days as Everton, Arsenal, Manchester United, Manchester City, Newcastle United, West Brom, Chelsea, Hearts, Hibs and Aberdeen all jostled for his attention. In the end it was Rangers who pushed to the front of the queue and Scottish youth football's hottest property was on his way to start a new life at the Glasgow club straight from school in 1960.

Henderson, who had grown up idolising the wing play of Sir Stanley Matthews, was only 17 when Scot Symon handed him his debut after serving a brief apprenticeship in the Gers reserve side.

He took his bow in the latter stages of the 1960/61 season, with three cameo appearances as his new side clinched the championship. The following term it was Dundee who claimed the league honours but the consolation for Rangers was a knock-out double and the Scottish Cup final of 1962 provided Henderson with his first winner's medal, the emerging talent earning the No.7 shirt for the 2-0 victory against Morton.

It was not all plain sailing in the early days. In the first week of 1962 Henderson's impatience to hit the big time threatened to take over and he demanded a transfer. At just 17 he was already itching to play week in and week out but thought opportunities would be hindered by established Ibrox hero Alex Scott, who himself was only 24 and a favourite with the fans. Scott was an international but Henderson was pushing him hard, earning a Scotland under-23 call after just a handful of first team appearances before submitting his request for a move. The Rangers management declined and Scott was soon sold to Everton to make way for the new kid on the block.

When you consider just how influential Scott had been, it rams home the esteem in which his successor was held by the coaching team. The men from Merseyside paid £39,000 early in 1963 to take

Scott south, a player who had scored 117 goals in 347 games and created many, many more. Yet he found his opportunities blocked by a fresh faced, confident colleague. The rivalry between the two men was intense, both determined to fight their corner and win the jersey, and it was Henderson who came out on top.

By the time the league and cup double of 1963 and the treble of 1964 was won he was a key man, not least in the 1964 Scottish Cup final against Dundee. It was Henderson's final, with the Sunday Mail headlines screaming 'Wonderful Willie' in the hours after his superlative display at Hampden. He enthralled a crowd of 120,000 at the national stadium, provider of an inch perfect corner for Jimmy Millar to open the scoring in the 71$^{st}$ minute against a resolute team from Tayside. The Dens side equalised but Jim Baxter and Henderson combined, this time the winger crossing from open play, for Millar to make it 2-1. With the final whistle set to ring around the ground Henderson produced his third telling pass, this time a perfectly executed lob for Davie Wilson to fire in a shot that allowed Ralph Brand to score from the rebound. The treble had been completed and there was no doubt who the architect supreme had been, the initials WH were stamped all over it.

Surprisingly the league celebrations of '64 marked Henderson's last taste of championship champagne as Celtic embarked on their nine in a row run. Henderson's appetite for success was at least tickled by the Scottish Cup triumph in 1966 and League Cup win in 1970. Under Scot Symon and Davie White the star wide man was indispensable but Willie Waddell needed more convincing. Two strong personalities, the men appeared set on a collision course and the impact occurred during what should have been a momentous period for Henderson and his bag of tricks.

Waddell was a man who knew a thing or two about wide men, having himself etched himself into Rangers history as one of the finest to grace the Ibrox flanks, but for all of Henderson's undoubted plus points he could not see past the personality clashes that occurred. Tommy McLean, a more industrious winger who had proven his worth as a championship winner with Kilmarnock, was the manager's choice as patience wore thin.

Henderson had played in all nine of the 1966/67 European Cup Winners' Cup ties, scoring the winner in the semi-final second leg against Slavia Sofia, which had ended in the bitter pain of defeat against Bayern Munich. Played in Nuremburg, Henderson always maintained that home advantage had been crucial to the Germans as they ran out 1-0 winners to shatter his dream.

He set out to right those wrongs in the 1971/72 competition. Having played against Rennes in the opening round, Henderson took control in the second round when Sporting Lisbon provided the opposition, scoring both at Ibrox and in Portugal against Lisbon as the sides played out a 6-6 aggregate draw. It was the famous game settled by the away goal rule well after the last ball had been kicked while Rangers thought they were out of the competition.

That double was crucial to the run but were to be his final contribution. By the time his former team-mates collected the European silverware in Barcelona, Henderson was out of the first team picture after one fallout too many with his Ibrox boss. In 1970 he had been suspended for a fortnight by Willie Waddell after he and partner in crime Jim Baxter had slept in and missed training. Baxter and Henderson had been team-mates in the early 1960s, two stars who enjoyed their status and who lived life to the full away from football. Glance at a celebration picture from the glory days and more likely than not Slim Jim and Wee Willie will be side by side, a pair of cheeky grins smiling back at the lens from two of the era's entertainers. You don't have to have seen him in the flesh to realise Henderson played the game with a smile on his face, the trail of images tells the story. As Rangers themselves claim in their hall of fame profile of Henderson, he was football's equivalent to the Rolling Stones and Beatles combined in the Swinging Sixties.

On occasion the Henderson and Baxter good time approach spilled into the day job, just as it had when one too many had kept them off the training field in 1970. Waddell sent out an early signal that he would not stand for it with his suspension – a warning was one thing, getting a stubborn star to change his approach was another.

Henderson, nudged out of the team by McLean, walked out on Rangers early in 1972 after failing to report for reserve duty in a second string game against Aberdeen, staying away from the club for eight weeks. When he returned he was immediately hit with a one month suspension by furious club bosses. It was one of the final nails in the coffin, his 13 year stay was drawing to an end even though he was just 28.

He did not part on the best of terms but his relationship with the Ibrox fans survived, his skills going down in folklore and memories of his dazzling displays passed from generation to generation with the type of care bestowed upon the most treasured of family heirlooms. Today you can still buy yourself a Willie Henderson T-shirt to wear while you watch your Willie Henderson DVD under the shadow of your Willie Henderson caricature – paying homage to the legend has become a cottage industry. If you look hard enough you might even be able to get your hands on footage of Henderson representing Rangers on Stuart Hall's game show *Quiz Ball*. Surely you know you've hit the giddy heights of fame and fortune when you've appeared alongside Stuart Hall.

In 2006 Henderson was inducted to Scottish football's hall of fame during a glitzy evening at Hampden. Joining him on the night in adding his name to the elite list was Henrik Larsson, a modern day Celtic cult hero alongside a vintage Rangers icon. Larsson left Old Firm life behind to move to the sun and sea of Barcelona, the megastars of the Nou Camp. My, how times have changed.

When it was time for Henderson to depart in 1972, a string of admirers in Scotland circled but a player of Henderson's standing was out of their financial league and it was Sheffield Wednesday who weighed in with the signing-on fee that trumped the rest of the offers after the winger had spent the summer guesting with Durban in South Africa.

When Rangers collected the European Cup Winners' Cup at the Nou Camp, their one-time talisman was sunning himself on a South African beach. He would far preferred to have been in amongst the action but instead was preparing for an altogether different and far less glamorous assignment.

He went on to stay for two seasons at Hillsborough, claiming the period marked some of the best form of his career even if it went largely unnoticed, before sampling life  with Hong Kong Rangers as player-coach in 1974. Wednesday fans of a certain vintage still recall with fondness the mesmeric skills Henderson took to the Owls but those forays down the right side were flickering embers in a dark and cold period for a proud club in a desperate lull.

The  Yorkshire club were managed by Derek Dooley, a man who knew a thing or two about attacking play and cult status. Dooley's 46 goals in a single campaign in the early 1950s is a record which still stands. Dooley took over a year prior to Henderson's arrival and was entrusted with restoring the club to the English top flight. A 60,000 capacity ground and a fanatical support made the Owls a sleeping giant but Dooley failed to stir them.

Henderson went straight into the Yorkshire team at the start of the 1972/73 campaign and missed only a handful of games but his magic did not rub off on those around them. Wednesday briefly led the Second Division in the opening months of the campaign but fell back to 10th at the end of the term.

It was a similar story the following season, when Dooley was replaced by Steve Burtenshaw. New man at the helm but the same old story for the slumbering club, who this time just scraped clear of the ignominy of relegation to the Third Division with a last gasp win in which their star Scot played his part.

To rub salt into the wounds, across the city Sheffield United were holding their own in the First Division and pushing for a place in the top half of the table. Without Henderson, Wednesday slumped to new lows and endured their worst ever campaign immediately after his departure.

The next stop was the Far East. It was an exciting time to be joining Hong Kong's version of Henderson's beloved Rangers. The club, founded in 1958, was still basking in the reflective glory of its one and only championship victory.

That came in 1971, three years before Henderson joined the trail of Scottish players who had turned out for the flourishing club. Former Rangers player Billy Semple was one who made the move in the 1970s along with Jimmy Bone.

During Henderson's time with the Hong Kong Rangers they won the country's Senior Shield and FA Cup, justifying their policy of mixing the best the Asian game had to offer with high profile imports. George Best, briefly, was the biggest name of them all to pull on the jersey.

Henderson's switch to Asia promised the first step on the coaching ladder but the talents he possessed were not those you can teach. A rugged centre half may be able to teach a budding football Rotweiler how to thwart a forward but tutoring the finer arts of wing wizardry is a different ball game. Henderson's abilities were natural, not man made, and maybe that is why there are so few players who have even come close to imitating him in modern times. With the emphasis on coaching, on pass and move, the flair is being drummed out at an early age. If it was possible to teach the type of moves and improvisation Henderson used to such great effect it would be football's most prized instruction manual and a bestseller on every continent.

After life in Asia he returned briefly to Scottish league football with Ross County and Airdrie in the 1978/79 season but played only a handful of games before retiring.

He now appears on the after dinner speaking circuit, where rapturous applause greets him at every turn as Rangers' supporters seek to reinforce the message that once you earn cult status you never lose it. There is still a twinkle in Henderson's eye as he reels off his repertoire of anecdotes from a career not lacking in incident, humour or highlights.

He thrilled tens of thousands of supporters every time he graced the Ibrox turf and collected a pocketful of medals but is not a man devoid of regrets. At club level one is that Rangers could not get the better of Bayern in his European Cup Winners' Cup final appearance and the other is that he did not get the opportunity to play in Barcelona in 1972.

On the international stage his major disappointment was never getting the chance to play against Garrincha and company in the World Cup finals, part of the Scotland squad who narrowly missed out on a place in both 1966 and four years later when they appeared destined to do it.

The decade when Henderson was at his peak was, with the benefit of glorious hindsight, Scotland's best opportunity to make an impact on the global game. The star names from that golden era trip off the tongue yet the unit could not make it past the qualification hurdle. There was no questioning the individual talent but as a unit, at least when it mattered most, it did not click. Reminiscent in many ways of England's struggles in the current superstar-laden period.

Despite beating Italy's glamorous national side in qualifying for the 1966 tournament across the border in England it was not enough. The team that got the better of the Azzurri included Henderson, Jim Baxter, John Greig, Billy Bremner, Alan Gilzean, Bobby Murdoch among an all star cast but they could not earn a spot in the finals. Celtic heroes Jimmy Johnstone and Billy McNeill were also in full flow but it was not enough to blaze a trail to the World Cup finals.

Johnstone and Henderson won recognition as two of the finest players ever to emerge from Scottish shores yet they shared an era and competed for the same shirt in the national side. It was an embarrassment of riches to say the least and it has often been argued the pair split the 1960s in half, with Henderson taking his turn in the first half of the decade and Johnstone, in line with his club's parallel superiority, bossing the second half.

The merits of the two players could be debated endlessly and even Jock Stein, who was the man who masterminded the famous 1-0 victory against the Italians, found it difficult to choose between his Celtic charge and their Rangers adversary. Against the defensive giants of Italy, Henderson was a key pawn in Stein's game of chess. Despite his lack of inches, Stein wanted Henderson to run legendary full-back Franchetti inside and it proved to be a killer move. When Henderson dragged the opposition across the pitch, the path opened up for club-mate John Greig to crack home a spectacular winner in front of 100,000 at Hampden. Henderson, despite the fierce Old Firm rivalry, struck up a fond relationship with Stein. He classed him as a friend as well as a mentor.

The same could be said for Hoops wing rival Johnstone. Both were worshipped by their own fans yet both had the rare ability to draw appreciation from the opposite side of the divide. There was an empathy between Johnstone and Henderson and right up to Jinky's death in 2006 the pair remained in close contact.

The fact the two thrilled the masses at the same time demonstrated the seemingly bottomless pit of genuine talent Scotland could call on during the two failed World Cup qualifying attempts of that period.

In 1970 there was arguably an even finer crop of internationals than there had been four years earlier but again qualification proved a dream impossible to realise. By then Henderson was joined in the Scotland ranks by the likes of Pat Stanton and Chelsea hero Charlie Cooke but again it was a fruitless campaign. In the face of opposition from Austria and West Germany, Scotland were edged out at a time when many felt the national team's squad could rival the best in the business. Not before and not since has there been such a renowned clutch of stars on call and it's difficult to imagine a day when that will change.

The adventures in Dark Blue began in 1962 when he was still just a boy, aged 18 to be precise and only beaten in terms of age by international colleague Denis Law. The rookie did not let nerves get the better of him and scored on his debut to help his country to a 3-2 win over Wales in Cardiff. Former Rangers player Ian McColl gave him his big break with Scotland, throwing him in at the expense of

Alex Scott as he continued to be haunted by the rookie. He was in good company, alongside clubmates Eric Caldow, Bobby Shearer and Jimmy Millar, and Henderson went on to be capped 29 times over an eight and a half year period, scoring five goals for his country, but never making it to the World Cup carnival he craved. The closest he got to mixing it in that type of cosmopolitan company, outside of European ties with his club, was when he was selected to play for a European select side against Benfica in Mario Coluna's 1970 testimonial. It was Coluna, the Portuguese side's captain, who declared Henderson to be the best winger in Europe while contemporary George Best described him as a "genius" and Sir Matt Busby hailed his fellow Scot as "world class".

Talents deserving of a global audience never got that exposure but plenty of archive material from Henderson's club days remain and continue to be constantly in demand.

Despite the exalted companions for his first international start, at Ninian Park in Cardiff, Henderson was totally undaunted. Denis Law and Caldow sat alongside Henderson's name on the scoresheet.

McColl was in charge when the Rangers prospect was introduced to international football but it was Bobby Brown who was at the helm when Wee Willie's final appearance in Dark Blue came in 1971. The swansong was in a 2-0 defeat at the hands of Portugal in Lisbon and came as his Rangers career was drawing to an inevitable end under the new management regime. From the outpost of England's second league tier he was never likely to gain another shot at Scotland glory.

Henderson loved to put on a show and came to the fore in some of Scotland's most remarkable results of that period. His five international goals came in an 8-0 rout against Cyprus, 4-1 and 3-2 wins against Wales, a 5-1 hammering of Northern Ireland and the epic 6-2 win against Spain at the Bernabeu in Madrid in 1963. There was never a dull moment when Henderson was in the mood for scoring goals it would appear.

In fact, there was never a dull moment when Henderson was around and that was what the Rangers fans grew to appreciate and grew to love. They turned up at Ibrox not knowing exactly what to expect but anticipating an individual performance worthy of the admission price. He had the ability to draw gasps from the terraces, to have thousands on their tip toes. Not big in inches but huge in entertainment, Wee Willie will forever be a jewel in the Ibrox crown.

**MAGIC MOMENT:** The commentator cried
'It's a goal, Willie Johnston' in 1972 as Bud's double
helped claim European silverware at last.

# WILLIE JOHNSTON
## *'BUD'* 1964-1972 and 1980-1982

### GERS CAREER: Games 393; Goals 125; Caps 22

IN A cauldron of passion and bitter rivalry, amid a cacophony of noise and riotous exuberance, a man in a light blue shirt sat perched on a size five in the middle of the Hampden pitch. He wasn't taking advantage of a lull in proceedings, he was in fact taking the sting out of a major cup final and at the same time taking the rise out of 50,000 Celtic fans.

The 1970 League Cup was Derek Johnstone's day, the teenager who scored the dramatic winner against the Hoops. But it was not Derek Johnstone who had the audacity to plant himself on the ball, it was Willie Johnston.

Johnston had a major hand in the game, laying on the cross for his rookie near-namesake to score the decisive goal and taking the opportunity for a spot of Celt-baiting. He knew how to push the buttons of the Rangers' fans but he backed up his cheek with raw talent, the cold hard currency that buys more favour than any other in football.

The episode was perfect fodder for the bar-room philosophers of Glasgow and even now it remains a topic for debate, the lounges replaced by the modern equivalent of internet forums. More than three decades on, if you ask the man about it he responds with a knowing laugh. He enjoyed the tricks and the bare faced cheek at the time and the enjoyment has faded with age.

The ball-sitting was not isolated to the Hampden tussle, it was a regular feature of Johnston's repertoire in an act that travelled the world. Nutmegs, flicking the ball over stricken defenders, mooning at the opposition bench and swigging beer from a supporter's carry out were some of the other party pieces. Oh, and kicking a referee was thrown in for good measure.

That little touch of comedy came in his West Brom days, Derek Lloyd was the official on the receiving end of the playful boot up the backside during a League Cup tie against Brighton. His response was instant and decisive, Johnston was shown the red card and ended up banned for five games after being found guilty of bringing the game into disrepute. Johnston's tongue in cheek explanation that the referee kept blocking his runs didn't wash with the FA's disciplinary chiefs, maybe it got lost in translation somewhere along the way.

*To win without risk is to triumph without glory.*

**Pierre Corneille**

Lloyd-gate was far from Johnston's first brush with the game's internal police and nor was it his last. Trouble, it seemed, followed him wherever he went. From Rangers to West Brom and all the way to Hearts, he suffered from a series of lengthy suspensions through his playing days.

The greatest scripts of all time feature a prominent role for a loveable rogue and if anyone were to be brave enough to take on a screenplay of the many twists and turns in the history of Glasgow Rangers there would surely be no better candidate to fill that berth.

The tangles with the authorities began to take a familiar pattern relatively early in his career. In the late 1960s he was twice suspended for clocking up too many disciplinary points, not aided by red cards against Falkirk, Bilbao in the Fairs Cup and during a friendly on a tour of Canada.

By the time he was sent off against Clyde in December, 1969, he was on the brink of his fourth ban in five years as a professional in an era when suspensions were still big headline making news and a relative rarity. When men were men the cards tended to stay in the pocket but the long walk against the Bully Wee sidelined him for three games – a walk in the park compared to some of the punishments meted out to him.

By the time he was 23 he had spent 12 weeks suspended but that record shot up in December 1970 when a red card against Hibs in a stormy encounter at Easter Road saw him hit with a whopping six week ban covering nine games as the result of his fifth red card in the space of just 22 months.

In 1972, in the wake of the European Cup Winners' Cup final, he was hammered with a 10 week suspension following another early bath, this time against Partick Thistle. That, and being fined by the club for gesturing to the crowd after a match against Ayr United, proved to be the straw that broke the winger's patience. Johnston packed his boots and headed for England.

When he returned to Scotland for his second spell with Rangers the controversy followed, caught up in a storm in 1980 when he was accused of stamping on Aberdeen's John McMaster. He was red carded, again.

By the time he was with Hearts in 1983, aged 36, the red card tally reached an incredible 19 when he was sent off by Brian McGinlay during a 4-1 defeat by old victims Celtic in the semi-final of the Scottish Cup. An off the ball collision with Davie Provan was McGinlay's explanation.

Hearts were furious, threatening court action to defend their veteran in the face of what they considered to be victimisation on the back of his previous convictions. The late Wallace Mercer was a chairman who demanded discipline from his stars but at the time he said: "If Willie Johnston had been clearly guilty of a serious offence he would not kick another ball for the club. However, there is an element of doubt and absence of hard evidence that he committed the offence for which he was ordered off. I've not spoken to a single person who witnessed anything. Johnston admits he gave Provan a playful slap as he ran past, but there is a line of thinking that the Celtic player feigned. He just crumpled like a pack of cards. Sadly Johnston's reputation tends to go before him and he now believes he is being victimised."

Manager Alex MacDonald, a former Rangers team-mate who knew all about Johnston's temper and steely streak, backed him to the hilt despite watching his man receive his marching orders in his first game back from a four game ban after being sent off earlier in the cup campaign.

The cup tie that brought Johnston's 19th red card was watched by SFA president Willie Harkness and secretary Ernie Walker but the player could expect no favours from the observers in the stand as he sought to protest his innocence. It was the SFA who, according to Johnston, were guilty of the biggest miscarriage of justice in his tempestuous professional career.

The association's treatment of Johnston following his positive drugs test at the 1978 World Cup in Argentina hurt him far more than any of the lunging tackles that so often led to the retaliation that led, in turn, to many of his red cards.

Johnston admitted to taking Reactivan, a hayfever treatment, without knowing it contained a substance banned by FIFA. Despite holding his hands up, he was hung out to dry by the SFA and never kicked a ball again for Scotland.

Reactivan, it transpired, contained fencamfamin which was one of 400 on the prohibited list. The SFA were unsympathetic and bundled him into the cheapest plane seats they could find before abandoning him back on home soil.

As West Brom team-mate John Osborne observed at the time: "Even the French Foreign Legion allowed their convicted criminals the comfort of a last cigarette before the firing squad blasted them to eternity. The SFA does not even let Willie have a quick drag. I'm disgusted and outraged over the diabolical way Willie's character has been assassinated. In this case, it seems the SFA panicked in keeping their 'holier than thou' image."

It has since be claimed by journalists who were on the ill-fated trip that Johnston was one of a string of Scotland players who had used Reactivan but he has never pointed the finger at any of his team-mates, even if that loyalty has not always been reciprocated by squad members who used tales of the incident to publicise their own biographies.

To this day he remains hurt by the SFA's treatment of him in his hour of need, maintaining the over the counter decongestant was not performance enhancing. Those pleas fell on deaf ears and the Scotland star became a 'former international' when he was left high and dry, never picked again to play in the dark blue of his country.

Up to that point he had won 22 caps between 1965 and 1978, losing just seven of those games. Johnston was in the side which beat England 2-1 at Wembley in 1977, not guessing his days on the world stage were drawing to an abrupt conclusion.

His name goes hand in hand with the Argentina furore. He became the country's most talked about sportsman but it was not a situation he felt comfortable in. Johnston was undoubtedly a rough diamond but he does not play on that image, he does not court publicity and he does not attempt to cash in. The riches of the after dinner circuit patrolled by so many of his contemporaries hold no appeal.

For him the impish element to his game was not about cultivating a persona, it was simply part and parcel of what made him one of Scotland's greats. It transpired those elements also made him a hero to tens of thousands, the unpredictability as much of a vote winner as the talents that propelled him into the company of the country's greatest wingers.

Commentator Archie MacPherson has had the good fortune to watch the greats of the Scottish game at home and abroad. He classes Johnston, even with his red card tendencies among those legends, and believes the fine line between indiscipline and commitment was blurred by contributing factors.

MacPherson told me: "I remember a League Cup final against Celtic when Willie Johnston was fouled inside the first minute with a tackle that almost put him out of the game. Jock Stein felt Celtic had been pushed around far too much by Rangers and wanted to muscle them out, although it wasn't a direct instruction to put Johnston out of the game it was certainly clear that Stein had identified where the threat would come from.

"He wasn't a pansy, that is for sure, but he had to look after himself in the face of some pretty harsh treatment from the opposition week in and week out. That in a way is as big a back-handed compliment a player can get, if they are being singled out in that way. There are times when Old Firm players, on both sides, can play up to the role but I don't think that was primarily the reason for his brushes with the officials, he had a fierce competitive streak and that coupled with the treatment he was prone to receiving led to flashpoints."

It is not one of the many confrontations that defines Johnston in MacPherson's eyes. The seasoned broadcaster let his mind wander back to a bracing October day in Glasgow to come up with the moment Johnston turned from player to national treasure and household name.

He said: "He was a young fresh faced player when he first made the impact that caused him to move from the ordinary to the extraordinary, with his performance against Poland in 1965. He was wonderful in that game, people were describing him as the new Alan Morton and it took him above and beyond adulation purely from

Rangers supporters. He won the attention of the general public in Scotland with that display. I remember being on the terracing at Hampden for that game, at the back of the King's Park end, and Johnston shone. Scotland actually lost that day, with Poland scoring two late goals, but that did not detract from his personal performance – I can still picture him bearing down on the defence."

MacPherson's bread and butter as a broadcaster was following Scotland's club sides and Johnston's exploits provided plenty of commentary highlights, not least the European Cup Winners' Cup final at the Nou Camp.

The familiar tones of MacPherson accompany the well worn highlights of that famous night, when Johnston's double and Colin Stein's strike gave Rangers the 3-2 win that earned the coveted continental prize.

When I caught up with MacPherson it was days after a gala testimonial dinner in Glasgow to honour the 1972 team and mark the 35th anniversary of that victory. MacPherson addressed the audience to mark the occasion, one he never imagined would take on such significance.

He said: "I did the commentary in Barcelona that night and did not for a moment expect it would not be repeated for the length of time that has passed since then. Again it was Johnston's pace and tenacity that was so important and his legend grows with every year that passes because of his part in that occasion.

"There was much more to his game than scoring goals. His speed was what caught the eye, he was enormously fast physically and mentally. He also had that attitutude that said 'I am a Rangers player'. That is easy to identify but so difficult to define, something the heroes and idols all had.

"I well remember standing in the tunnel before a Hibs versus Hearts game at Tynecastle, when Eddie Turnbull was talking about what his Hibernian team needed. As far as he was concerned Willie Johnston was the perfect player because he had pace, control, could play the ball with either foot and could score goals. Turnbull was a great technician and coach, so his opinions always carried a great deal of weight."

MacPherson was also part of the television contingent in Argentina for the ill-fated 1978 World Cup campaign, his memories of the Johnston drugs scandal featuring prominently in his 2005 book *Flower of Scotland?*.

MacPherson said: "Those players were taking uppers like sweeties at that time, they were all over the place. I'm not saying that makes it right, but it was certainly part of life in the game in that era. He was the one who was caught but I know for a fact the Scotland doctors were going through the rooms of players flushing tablets down toilet pans. He was unlucky in that he got caught, it doesn't vindicate it but it was wrong for one player to be singled out the way he was."

Bud is a player who left a lasting impression on all who watched him in full flight, and some who didn't. In 2005 I had the pleasure of conducting one of the most illuminating interviews of my career as a journalist and author. It was part of a quest to track down the 11 men who made Rangers winners in the European Cup Winners' Cup in 1972 and coming in at No.11 was Johnston. That was the number he wore on that famous night in Barcelona, the number that was on his back as he grabbed two goals in the 3-2 win against the men from Moscow and that was the chapter he filled in 'To Barcelona and Beyond'.

That evening, in a matter of minutes Johnston, from the comfort of his Fife home, righted the wrongs of football. There is no trace of arrogance when Johnston speaks, quite the opposite, but behind the words are the recollections of the actions which give him more credence than the majority of commentators on a beautiful game which somewhere along the way has lost some of its attractiveness.

I never had the good fortune to watch him play but, perhaps more than any other player, I wish I had having been initiated in his football philosophy. Laying down the Johnston mantra, he told me: "Football's the easiest game in the world, good players make it look that way but some players, and managers, make it difficult." That isn't some well rehearsed soundbite, it's a deep-seated belief.

He despairs at the oppressive majority but can still find tiny ripples of joy in the sea of mediocrity. When I interviewed Johnston it was just days after Robert Pires had failed to convert from a short penalty routine, drawing howls of derision throughout football. The Frenchman did not know it, but in a corner of Scotland a past master was nodding his approval. Better to have tried and failed than never to have tried at all.

Johnston said: "The entertainment has gone out of the game because people are told not to do it, it's coached out of them. I'd do things like trapping the ball by sitting on it, flicking it over people, putting it through their legs – it was what the people who paid their money enjoyed seeing. Now all that is gone."

In a nutshell, sack the coaches and let the entertainers entertain. Difficult to argue with that, especially if you are one of those parting with cash on a Saturday afternoon. Instead we have the game being squeezed to within an inch of its life by a weight of tactical complication and suffocating technicalities in every area of the pitch.

He added: "We didn't have anyone telling us what to do or helping us learn from our mistakes, you were left to go over it yourself in your own mind after every game. Maybe better coaching would have made us better players but on the other hand we were able to go out and express ourselves – once you cross the white line you're on your own anyway."

Supporters were happy to pay their money to see Johnston express himself, with his left wing artistry a feature on both sides of the border in the 1960s and 70s at a time when flair was to be encouraged rather than frowned upon.

A player who had an array of subtle feints and ballet like turns came from a more workmanlike backdrop than those moves suggested. Despite being a Glaswegian by birth, Johnston came from the earthy backdrop of Fife's mining community and was an apprentice at the pits, fortunate enough to work above the surface but not spared from the hard graft associated with the notoriously tough environment. It was the same profession that gave Jim Baxter his grounding in life, football was the great escape.

Manchester United were confident of landing the emerging talent but Johnston was a homebody and did not fancy straying far from what he knew best. His preferred option was to stay on Scottish soil, switching from his home territory on the east coast to his home city on the west when he joined Rangers under Scot Symon in 1964. Glasgow, on visits to his grandparents, had been his furthest excursion to that point and he hadn't yet been struck by the wanderlust. That would come later in life.

His first start came in the 1964/65 campaign as a left winger. He fancied himself as a striker, the position he had played when the Light Blues recruited him, but the ability to run with the ball at pace and deadly distribution led to a change in direction. At times he grudged being edged out of the thick of the action, as a Hearts player he once got down on his knees to beg for the ball during one particularly frustrating cup tie. The crowd loved it, even his team-mates could afford to smile.

Even on his lonely beat on the wing, Johnston could still find the way to goal given the slightest sniff. Whether from open play or dead balls, he was a potent weapon for every club he was employed by. In 1971 against St Johnstone he came on from the bench for Rangers with 18 minutes to play and trooped off with the match ball tucked under his arm after a rapid fire hat-trick of penalties against the luckless Perth Saints.

Goals win prizes and he was not short of honours during his two stops with Rangers. Johnston collected a League Cup winner's medal in his rookie season and added a Scottish Cup gong in 1966 when he was still only 19 years-old.

As a teenager he gained early international experience, blooded by Jock Stein for Scotland as an 18 year-old against Poland in 1965. The Glaswegian had already won youth and under-23 honours and was being lauded as a youngster bursting with talent and potential.

With his club he was also amassing a strong continental CV, playing in two thirds of the ties on the way to the 1967 European Cup Winners' Cup final against Bayern Munich. There was no winner's medal on that occasion but 1972 sorted that discrepancy, having added another League Cup winner's medal in 1970 in between.

Johnston missed only the first leg of the second round clash with Sporting Lisbon in the 1972 European campaign. He scored against Rennes and Torino as well as creating a string of other goals, leading continental journalists to vote him among the top three attackers in European football that year.

His performance in the famous final at the Nou Camp cemented his growing reputation with the professional observers and the punters who kicked every ball with him from their vantage point on the sprawling Spanish terraces. The first goal was a first half header from a Dave Smith cross, his second was a cool finish from Peter McCloy's long clearance early in the second half. Film of those key moments preserves the occasion for the generations who missed the chance to be there, although Johnston himself insists he has never watched them back. That was then, this is now and he isn't interested in living in the past.

The fans, however, are free to watch the goals which helped land the European silverware which before, and since, bore all the hallmarks of a holy grail. If he had done nothing else in a blue shirt, those two goals would have made Johnston a legend and a hero for all-time. As it happened, he did much, much more but by his own admission hit his Rangers peak when he and his team-mates conquered the cross-channel mountain which has proved too steep for every other Ibrox side.

In the final his two goal contribution, to add to Colin Stein's goal in the 3-2 win, led to a post-match assessment that he could not possibly follow what he had just achieved. He had predicted what was to follow, with a 10 week suspension from the SFA after the latest in a string of brushes with the disciplinary chiefs proving to be the straw that broke the camel's back. By the time he retired, Johnston had been red carded 21 times according to those who managed to keep track. They were too frequent to be considered collectors' items, more a matter of course.

Unlike Willie Henderson and Jim Baxter, both shown the door by the iron hand of manager Willie Waddell, the winger's relationship with the renowned disciplinarian was strong if not always smooth. Johnston recalls: "I must have been up the marble stairs to his office more than any other player. He always had the last word but never held a grudge."

After all Johnston did respect the traditions, even when he had moved on to Hearts he caused more than a little consternation among his Tynecastle team-mates by continuing the Ibrox tradition of turning up to work sporting a collar and tie. He had grown up at the Struth-inspired Ibrox, with the traditions upheld by Waddell, and knew what playing for the club was about. Above all else, the supporters responded to players who had a passion for the cause and with Johnston involved that was a quality never lacking. Just ask the opposition defenders who tried to keep a lid on him.

It was not Waddell, who had handed over the tiller to Jock Wallace by the time Johnston left, who forced the star's departure. Instead it was his growing problems with Scotland's referees which proved to be a telling factor. He picked up his boots and headed south in 1972 to join West Brom.

It was the dour Don Howe who made the signing, although Johnston had his suspicions that a slightly more flamboyant chairman may have been his secret admirer at the English club and quipped: "If you played football on a blackboard, Don Howe would easily win the World Cup."

In spite of the initial stewardship in England, with the Baggies he repeated the formula that won the affections of the Rangers' supporters and remains one of the most admired flair players ever to turn out at the Hawthorns. West Brom had to shatter the cross border transfer record to clinch the £138,000 transfer and the fans felt they got value for money, even if the star's spell included the frustration of relegation from the top flight.

He played under a succession of managers at the English club, most notably Ron Atkinson and his sheepskin jacket. Big Ron met Wee Bud and not surprisingly two of the game's raw characters hit it off. Despite his reluctant approach to the merits of coaching, Johnston appreciated the role of a good manager. He classed Jock Stein as Celtic's greatest "conductor", not employed to play the instruments but simply to set the pace and he carried that approach throughout his career.

Johnston helped West Brom bounce back to the First Division in 1976 and this time they were a force in the top half of the table. In 1979 Johnston signed off, joining Vancouver in a £100,000 transfer after 261 appearances for the Baggies and 18 goals.

He won the Soccer Bowl, America's main prize, with the Canadians and became a firm fans favourite. Spot the trend yet? Even now he receives regular invites to return to Vancouver to relive the glory days. It was in the land of the free that some of Johnston's more liberal moments occurred, the American fans bemused when their imported athlete stopped mid-game to swig from a fan's beer bottle before swinging in a corner to create another Vancouver goal and stunned when he celebrated another by dropping his shorts to the opposition bench. His down to earth charm warmed the hearts of the Canadians just as it had done in the English Midlands, where the West Brom supporters took to him instantly and installed him as one of their own cult heroes. The North American Soccer League was an entertainment business played out in front of supporters who, in many cases, were still struggling to grasp the finer points of a game of football in which the players couldn't use their hands. The players who thrived were those who stood out from the crowd, who made the trainee soccer followers sit up and take notice. Johnston was one of those.

He had the ability to draw supporters to the edge of their seats in America's sparkling new arenas as a trail of Brits abroad came, played, picked up wages and left again without making any real lasting impression. Whether for his antics around the fringes of games or for the way he left defenders in a spin, a small corner of North America will forever belong to Bud and he was never classed as one of the game's mercenaries in that part of the world because of the bond he struck up, just as he had done in Scotland and England.

Let's face it, everyone loves a bad boy. Maybe the fans love them because they do the things everyone else would love to if they had the guts. Managers love them because they give their team the edge, the attitude that separates the good from the great and the edge that divides winners from losers. Former Aberdeen manager Jimmy Calderwood, a Govan boy brought up in a Rangers family, frequently waxes lyrical about his desire to seek out recruits with the "nastiness" to unsettle rivals and get under the skin of defenders. From time to time he can also be found letting his mind wander back to the days when Johnston, one of his playing heroes, was in full flow. He played against him and alongside him too as a Birmingham defender, so the Dons gaffer is well placed to judge. For all the flaws and hot-headed incidents any manager would take the risk for a player who had it all.

In Johnston's own era there were certainly no shortages of admirers within the coaching fraternity, even in the face of the down time caused by the inevitable suspensions each season.

Johnston returned to Britain from his stint in the NASL for a loan spell with Birmingham City in the 1979-80 season. He was 32 but still more than capable of bamboozling defences, something not lost on former team-mate John Greig.

Greig, by that time in charge of Rangers, tempted Johnston back to Ibrox in the summer of 1980 and won the Scottish Cup that season before joining Hearts in 1982 as he wound down his playing days, briefly turning out for East Fife and dabbling in coaching before finally retiring in 1985 at the age of 38 to concentrate on what proved to be a long and successful career in the licensed trade at the Port Brae Bar in Kirkcaldy. Still run by the Johnston family, Bud can still be found up to mischief with the regulars who have stuck with him in business just as the Rangers' fans did in football. A little bit longer in the tooth and slower over 10-yards, but the loveable rogue is alive and well, keeping Fife on its toes.

**MAGIC MOMENT:** It was Stein's goal that ended Celtic's 10 in a row hopes and launched a new era of success for Rangers in 1976.

# COLIN STEIN
## *'THE HOT SHOT'* 1968-1973 and 1975-1977

### GERS CAREER: Games 206; Goals 97; Caps 21

WHERE WERE you when man walked on the moon? Where were you when the Berlin wall toppled? Where were you when Colin Stein made his Rangers debut? It is one of *those* moments for Bears, an occasion never to forget and for memories to be passed down through the generations like treasured heirlooms.

The magic date was November 2, the year was 1968 and the venue was the far from glamorous Gayfield Park in Arbroath on a dank and uninviting Angus afternoon. The surroundings did not matter one bit to the Rangers fans who made up the bulk of the crowd crammed into the tiny coastal ground. What counted was the birth of a new hero.

Four years earlier Stein had been a junior striker given his crack at the big time by Hibs. Within three years he was a major player in the Scottish game, in the 1967/68 campaign Hibs climbed to third in Scotland's top flight and Stein's 29 goals in all competitions were a major contributing factor.

He topped the Hibees scoring chart and was attracting attention from all quarters. Everton moved in for the kill in the closing months of 1968 but their target was a Blue Nose of a different persuasion, a Rangers fan from his schooldays and desperate to earn a crack at Ibrox life. A cheque for £100,000 from Gers manager Davie White finally tempted Hibs to allow their main man to join a rival Scottish club. It ended an 11-month chase for White and broke the resistance from the Edinburgh club's chairman, who had claimed his player would never sign for Rangers.

Until then the recruitment of Alex Ferguson for £65,000 the previous year had been the bank-busting deal for Rangers but the momentous six-figure deal to secure the services of a 21 year-old with goals in his boots blew that to pieces. It took nine years, and the arrival of Davie Cooper, for the new record to even be equalled. Rangers' fan could quite justifiably be concerned about the apparent extravagance. After all they could have had two Alex MacDonald's for the price of one Colin Stein. The nagging doubts passed quickly, in the space of an hour and a half at Gayfield with a debut that dreams are made of.

Were you there? Colin Glass, an Ibrox season ticket holder from Bearsden, was as a wide eyed 11 year-old and almost four decades on the recollections are as vivid as he watched a future Rangers favourite announce his arrival in Light Blue.

Glass recalls: "I was in primary seven at school in Dundee, so I only got to watch Rangers a couple of times a season when they were in the city. When Arbroath won promotion to the First Division it was great news because it was another chance to watch my team close to home. As soon as they stepped up, we wrote to Arbroath to get tickets for the Rangers game. In those days clubs weren't as hostile towards away supporters and were happy to let you in. I grew up on Arbroath Road in Dundee and there was no way I was going to sit at home watching the Rangers buses pass my door on the way to Gayfield without going along myself.

"It was a typical traditional Scottish ground, with the old stand on one side and covered enclosures on the other three. It was a windy day and I'll always remember taking my ticket out to have a look – it blew away. I got a real fright, but managed to get it back. I went with my friends Craig Millar and Brian Foster. A friend of Craig's grandfather came and collected us in his big blue Rover to take us through to the game.

"Rangers had beaten Dundalk 6-1 in the Fairs Cup just before Colin Stein signed. Everyone was excited about the prospect of seeing him in a Rangers shirt – we all knew about the great English centre forwards, with Bobby Charlton at Manchester United and Jeff Astle at West Brom regarded as the best in their league and among the best in the game. We now had the best Scottish centre forward and in my opinion Colin Stein went on to become the best in Britain with his performances for Rangers.

"The previous experience we had of him was a punch up with Alex Ferguson, when Stein was with Hibs and Fergie was with Rangers. That didn't cloud my judgement of Stein because I always felt Alex Ferguson could be sneaky and furtive in his clashes with opponents, he liked to use his elbows.

"The Arbroath game was in the run-up to Guy Fawkes night and the Rangers fans were letting off bangers before and even during the game. Some were stuffing fireworks inside the hollow crush barriers and the bangs were echoing around the ground like gun shots, with 13,000 packed into such a confined ground it was quite an atmosphere.

*In every phenomenon the beginning remains always the most notable moment*

**Thomas Carlyle**

"I actually missed the opening goal, when Willie Johnston scored, because somebody was lighting a banger near to where we were standing. When Arbroath pulled it back to 2-1 in the second half, with a Dave Smith own goal, there were real fears that they would come back and equalise. Then it happened … bang, bang, bang. Colin Stein scored his hat-trick inside four minutes and a hero was born.

"There are several reasons Colin Stein will always be a cult hero. Some players had that status at the time but are less popular now, with Terry Butcher and Derek Johnstone falling into that category, but Colin is as popular now as he was back then.

"One of the main reasons was his workrate, which was phenomenal. He would run his heart out for Rangers chasing lost causes and the Bears could relate to that – we still supported the team in games that felt like lost causes and here was a player with the same attitude. There was also a visual element to it. It was in the era when clubs didn't change their strip every year, it was a rarity for a new look. Colin Stein's arrival coincided with the introduction of the smart blue top, white shorts and the red socks with white tops. He looked every inch a football star. The other big thing was that we all knew Everton, who were a major team in England at that stage, had agreed a £90,000 fee with Hibs. It was well before freedom of contract so the selling club held all the cards but Colin Stein dug his heels in because he had heard Rangers were interested. He wanted to move to Ibrox, he wanted to be part of Rangers. That meant a lot to supporters, they could identify with his love of the club."

Supporters crave above all else players who would run through a brick wall for their beloved team. Stein may not have bulldozed that metaphorical barricade but he did get through his fair share of defenders and goalkeepers.

Alan Morton, Willie Henderson and Willie Johnston had the trickery and finesse to win affections but that would have counted for nothing without the spirit and willingness to fight for the cause. Those were the qualities that Stein had in spades and the supporters responded to that.

He was the type of striker Rangers have spent decades trying to rediscover, an all action performer with the strength of a bull and the precision of a sniper. He also had the same streak of devilment as his team-mate Willie Johnston and was no stranger to the SFA's disciplinary committee.

Perhaps the closest the club came to finding a modern day Stein was when Mark Hateley charged into Glasgow to strike fear into Scotland's defences once again but, as the fans would testify, there really only ever could be one Colin Stein.

His power and determination won admirers in England following his switch to Coventry. Recounting their fondest memories from Highfield Road before the old ground's demolition, one Sky Blues aficionado recalled the joy Stein brought to Coventry by "running through defenders rather than round them".

His rugged and no nonsense approach was not a substitute for ability with the ball at his feet. He was not just a target man or an easy outlet, in front of goal Stein was clinical with his head and boots. A threat in every game he played during his peak years, his ability to find space and lose his markers set him apart and the fact he had the physical presence to win personal battles when necessary gave him the all important element of surprise.

Once he got into his stride there was little that could nudge him off course and his goals tended to come in groups, hat-trick after hat-trick racked up in the colours of Hibs and Rangers just as he had done as a player starting out in the rough and tumble world of junior football. His willingness to throw himself in where it hurt and get in amongst the action when studs were flying and defenders were looking for blood made him an obvious fans favourite but the die hard attitude was simply the icing on the cake. Goals, goals and more goals provided the substance to the base.

In his two spells at Ibrox he scored 97 goals in 199 starts and in game after game he was an unstoppable force, particularly in the first stint. By his own admission there was no secret to his knack for hitting the net. Stein said: "There were a lot of good players round about me and when you are playing in a good team you will always get chances. You still have to take those chances, and confidence is a big factor for any centre forward – if you don't have confidence, one touch can turn into two touches and the chance is gone. It's difficult to coach a striker because so much of it is about instinct, you can try and teach somebody to make the right runs, to be in the right place at the right time, but you can't turn them into a finisher."

Certainly nobody turned Stein into a goalscorer. It was a natural process, purely accidental and one of the quirks of fate that makes football so unpredictable. A teenager who was a decent defender outwith the senior game became a forward capable of putting Europe's, and the world's, finest to the sword.

Nobody turned him into a cult hero either, he did that all by himself with actions on the pitch that spoke louder than any words off it. Stein is the polar opposite to his one-time team-mate Willie Henderson, a man who commands handsome fees for standing up and delivering wisecracks and anecdotes lapped up by Rangers fans and non-blues up and down the land. Stein is happier out of the public spotlight in contrast, in the same vein as Willie Johnston, yet in his prime he went to work each week in front of tens of thousands and ruled the roost. It shatters the illusion that off-field profile earns hero status, it can help undoubtedly and cement that special place in the hearts of the fans but delivering the goods on the green stuff is what it all boils down to.

The fact he appeared to be persecuted at times by the game's governors helped galvanise the support for a man taking his first steps towards becoming a Rangers striking legend. The six week suspension he received at the business end of the 1968/69 season caused uproar among the Ibrox faithful, not least because Celtic chairman Robert Kelly chaired the referees' committee which dished out the ban. The grievance was the loss of the hit man for the title run in and for the Scottish Cup final against Kelly's own club.

Rangers lost two and drew two of the games that Stein watched from the sidelines, dropping six points, and Celtic won the league by five points. They also lost 4-0 in the final and while one man cannot make a team the consensus was that one Colin Stein could have made a significant difference to those two outcomes. He could also have had a say in Scotland's own World Cup aspirations, with one of the games he missed happening to be the 1-1 qualifying draw against West Germany which proved so costly to the country's hopes of making the finals.

For supporters, even as young as Colin Glass, it was a painful experience. Glass added: "To put into context, Colin Stein was as big a factor to Rangers as Henrik Larsson was to Celtic. People say one man cannot make a team but he was the exception to that in his first season, both for Rangers and Scotland. He scored in every one of the home internationals and hit four against Cyprus – the suspension cut him down in full flight. If it wasn't for the ban I still maintain Scotland would have qualified for the 1970 World Cup and Rangers would have won the league and Scottish Cup. Colin had great ability – he was good in the air and an instinctive finisher, just like Ally McCoist, with either foot. He didn't have the same pace as Willie Johnston but he was fast enough, especially inside the box."

It was not the last time he would suffer a suspension, the danger for any player who walked the fine line between enthusiasm and over-enthusiasm. Playing at anything less than one-hundred percent would have taken the edge from Stein's game and there was no danger he would let that happen. He had the pace to speed away from defenders and the first couple of yards were gained by speed of thought, any hesitation or inclination to hold back would have crippled that advantage.

Stein had barriers to break down before he had even kicked the ball. He came from the green half of Edinburgh, the links between Hibs and Celtic were inextricable and it made his initial task of winning over the Rangers fans all the more difficult. Stein was not just a Hibs player though, he was a Hibee who had rubbed up the Ibrox fans the wrong way more than once.

Firstly he had scored numerous times against his future employers but secondly, and more pertinently at the time of his arrival in Glasgow, he had incurred the wrath of the Govan masses when he was sent off for his part in a clash with Rangers striker Alex Ferguson. That led to a barrage of verbal abuse from the baying home crowd.

Stein was the enemy and went into the second phase of his career with his eyes wide open, desperate to convert the Rangers support he himself had been part of as a boy. He told me: "When I was with Hibs I had the entire Rangers support calling me all of the names under the sun ... a few weeks later I was being treated like a god by them. A lot of players have found it difficult to get the Rangers supporters on their side, even Ally McCoist and Mark Hateley struggled, but the best way for a striker to do that is to score goals. Once you do that, and have them on your side, it is a fantastic feeling."

Having been a target from the terraces while in Hibs colours, Stein was prepared for what would follow as he embarked on life as a blue. His price tag made him a sitting duck but the verbal cascade which flowed in his direction fell like water off his back. He has always maintained that opposition fans, and defenders for that matter, were far more concerned by his big money billing than he ever was and adopted the approach that the time to worry would be when he wasn't provoking a negative reaction from the followers of the teams he was up against.

In the blue corner, however, he soon had the fans on his side. The chants of 'We don't need Eusebio because we've got Colin Stein' paid tribute to his prowess in front of goal, one of the many songs created in his honour by a crowd who quickly grew to appreciate the threat Stein had brought to their side. The fact his name rhymed with the Queen lent itself to a few more for the royalists while the simple but effective 'Colin, Colin, Colin Stein' remains a favourite to this day and still greets him when it is least expected. In the street, in the supermarket, in restaurants ... there's no escape for a cult hero.

Despite the recollections of his muscle, Stein was athletic rather than tank-like. He stood at just under 5ft 11inches tall but had a powerful physique which made him stand out from the crowd. He hit the scales at 12stone 8lbs, making him one of the most imposing strikers of his generation. Few defences had anyone capable of overpowering him, even after his switch to the supposedly superior English top flight. Liverpool's legendary defender Tommy Smith was a stone lighter, Norman Hunter at Leeds was another who couldn't touch him and Manchester United captain Martin Buchan was another who was at almost a stone's disadvantage when he went toe to toe. He looked the part on the pitch, he could have slotted in beside Roy of the Rovers in the Melchester United team without appearing out of place with his fair hair and purposeful gait.

He was a stand out in his era because the physicality was married to ability in front of goal and to link the play and Stein, like so many heroes, is a player who would surely have hurdled the generational barriers. Mind you, in today's game he'd be far from a giant, with Kris Boyd taller and heavier than the No.9 of the 1960s and 70s. When people talk about the changes in the game over the decades pace is so often the factor that springs to the head of the queue but the cold hard statistics suggest power is above all the measure which continues to grow with every year. Stein, at his peak, would have been able to live in present company without exception while others would have had to bulk up or ship out. The recurring theme here is that the players the supporters took to have an ageless quality, both in personality and their play. Every team has performers most certainly of their own time but the stars are the ones who are timeless. They either had physique ahead of their time or the speed of thought to make the apparent disparity irrelevant and Stein ticked both boxes. Perhaps the supporters are more perceptive and knowledgeable than managers tend to give them credit for.

When Stein's physical prowess began to slip he had the good sense to walk away. He said: "When I came back from Coventry, I wasn't the same player. I'd had a couple of hamstring injuries while I was at City and my pace suffered. That had been a big part of my game. I eventually stopped playing when I was 30. I could have kept going, but it is a downward spiral when you leave Rangers and you end up becoming a target for madmen. I've lost count of the number of people who told me they were going to break my legs. I just thought I didn't need that week in and week out. Fine, if that's what they enjoy, but I didn't have to stand there and take it. It might have been different outside of Scotland and I could have gone to play in Australia, but it didn't appeal to me."

Cult hero to Rangers supporters but a villain in the eyes of the opponents he shattered so often. Today Stein is still worshipped whenever he is in Rangers company, I've seen the adulation with my own eyes and for somebody who never watched him play it speaks volumes for the lasting impression he made on the paying public at club level.

Unlike Alan Morton, George Young or Jim Baxter the international experience was more subdued for the Rangers marksman but no less remarkable. He was prolific in dark blue yet he never became a Scotland legend in the mould of the Ibrox heroes who trod the Hampden turf before him.

Stein does not rate alongside Kenny Dalglish or even Joe Jordan in the Tartan Army heirarchy yet he remains a record holder, setting a target that looks unlikely to be beaten any time soon in more cautious times. Typically, he was always courageous in the colours of his country having been fast tracked to the top team after just a single under-23 appearance. That was all it took to prove he could handle the step up a level from the club game.

He is the last player to have hit the net three or more times for Scotland after grabbing four against luckless Cyprus in 1969, all in the space of 39 minutes. Had it not been for the fact Celtic adversary Tommy Gemmell was on penalty duty in the 8-0 win, he could have made it five from the spot. That would have equalled Hughie Gallacher's record haul for a single Scotland game.

The rout against the Cypriots was the the soaraway highlight of the proud Scot's career on the world stage, having made his debut the previous year in a single goal victory against Denmark in Copenhagen. He was 21 when he ran out against the Danes, scoring his first goal just months later in the 5-0 away tie against Cyprus before hitting them for four back on home soil.

The second record against the Stein name is that he is the only Scotland player to have scored in five successive games, punishing England, Northern Ireland, Wales, Cyprus and the Republic or Ireland during a burst of international sharp shooting in 1969.

The Scotland adventure lasted four years, culminating in a 1-0 defeat against England at Wemley in 1973, as Jordan and Dalglish waited in the wings to take centre stage. He played 21 times for the national side, scoring nine times, but was a victim of circumstance, playing at a time when striking talent was plentiful, competition for places was fierce yet success was limited.

Yet there was still the chance to sample the highest highs. In addition to a very respectable haul of caps and healthy return of goals, Stein did play his part in a title win for his country, even if it was a shared one. In the 1970 home nations championship Scotland sat proudly at the top of the table alongside England and Wales on four points, under Bobby Brown they were unbeaten in three games after draws against the Auld Enemy and the Welsh and a win against Northern Ireland.

Stein, the brother of Raith Rovers player Bobby and Montrose's youth international Eric, also won a call-up to the Scottish Football League select four times at his peak. Manager after manager saw the merits of his gutsy style and as long as he was playing for their team rather than against it, scores of fans agreed.

It was amazing how quickly the appreciation switched when he turned from friend to foe. Despite an incredible 10,000 time return on their initial £10 investment in Stein, the Hibs supporters showed no mercy to the departed. He played in an impressive team at Easter Road, starring in the one of the most dramatic European ties the Hibees have ever been involved in. On target in the first leg when the Scots lost 4-1 in Italy to Napoli, Stein also found the target in the 5-0 home leg victory to send his side through in a heart-stopping encounter. For all the goals, the obscene profit and happy memories Stein was never held in the same regard at Hibs as he was at Ibrox. In Govan he found his true place and was welcomed with open arms. Certain players fit certain clubs and Stein to Rangers was like a hand in glove. Maybe blue suited him because the Sky Blues of Coventry took to him in a way their green and white counterparts on the east coast of Scotland never really did. Call it small club insecurity or Old Firm jealousy. David Robertson received death threats when he left Aberdeen to sign for Rangers, so a case of mild indifference from the fans he left behind was getting off lightly.

He was willing to put up with that, it was part and parcel of living the dream which had seemed a long way off when he first dabbled in the game. Stein started life as a stopper in junior football, turning out for Armadale in his native West Lothian, before an injury crisis forced him to appear as an emergency striker. He responded by banging in a hat-trick, the first but far from the last. He was just 18 when the senior clubs began to circle and it was Partick Thistle who thought they had snapped up the bustling young striker. In fact it was Hibs who won the day, legendary manager Bob Shankly stepping in with an offer after watching another Stein treble in a junior cup final at Easter Road. He went on to become one of Scotland's most feared marksmen wearing the green and white of the Edinburgh club but it was in blue that he became a real hero.

His debut hat-trick was just the first part of an extended introduction to his new supporters. The next game was at Ibrox against Hibs and the outcome was familiar, three goals from the No.9

came this time in a 6-1 win against his old side. In his third game Stein was an inch away from a third consecutive hat-trick, the woodwork restricting him to a double in the Fairs Cup against Dundalk.

The six week suspension at the end of his first term at the club which forced him out of the 1969 Scottish Cup final delayed his first medal until the following season, when Celtic were defeated 1-0 in the League Cup final.

The next triumph came in the European Cup Winners' Cup final of 1972 and he proved to be a star turn, playing in each of the nine games. Stein scored four goals over two legs against Sporting Lisbon and added his fifth of the run in the final against Dynamo Moscow, firing home a superb shot from Dave Smith's pass in the historic 3-2 victory to earn a place in Ibrox folklore.

It was one of the final acts of his initial spell in Light Blue. A deal involving £90,000 in cash and the £50,000 rated winger Quinton Young heading in the opposite direction took Stein to Coventry City, deemed surplus to requirements by new manager Jock Wallace.

He fulfilled his role as the Midlands club's record buy, leading by example as a whole hearted captain and scoring valuable goals to help the Sky Blues keep their cherished place in the English First Division.

In March 1975 the call to return home to Ibrox came and Stein didn't hesitate. His aim back in Scotland was very different – from consolidation south of the border he was now tasked with halting the Celtic juggernaut on the back of the Parkhead side's nine in a row league run. It was when Rangers travelled to face Hibs that the dominance ended, Stein scoring the equaliser in the 1-1 win his side needed to secure the 1974/75 title.

The homecoming was eventful for the Philipstoun-born star. More than 42,500 were at Ibrox to welcome him for his second debut. It was a 1-0 victory against St Johnstone, the corresponding home fixture against the men from Perth in 1974 drew a crowd of 8,200. On face value the Stein factor was equal to an incredible 34,000 of bodies through the turnstiles for the Light Blues money men. His emotional first game back was, outside of Old Firm encounters and the all singing and all dancing trophy presentation game, a home record in the title winning season – a phenomenal statistic. Stein was a crowd puller but not a show pony and nobody has been able to combine the two in quite the same way.

His second game back was memorable for a different reason. Instead of scarves being waved it was a red card as he became reacquainted with Scotland's referees, given his marching orders against Dundee at Dens Park.

In addition to his title clincher against Hibs, Stein scored in the 3-2 win against the Dons of Aberdeen and the 2-1 win against Arbroath as Rangers coasted towards the trophy presentation. Three goals, eight games and a thousand cheers were not enough to gain the reward he really wanted – a league winner's medal. Manager Jock Wallace deemed he had not made a significant enough contribution and even refused his striker's offer to have his own memento struck. A screaming injustice if ever there was one for a player who served his club with such distinction during Celtic's domination and returned in time to break the Hoops' grip.

Another League Cup winner's medal, from the 1975/76 season, was added to the collection but in 1977 the ties to Rangers began to fray when Stein was allowed to head for Kilmarnock on loan. He never returned to Ibrox, retiring from the game at the age of 30.

Injuries at Coventry and the general wear and tear of life in the game had hindered the pace which had allowed him to escape defenders in his early days and Stein, by his own admission, felt he could no longer recreate the deadly form which had made him the country's most feared striker. The other factor in his decision to call time on his playing career was the prospect of battling week in and week out against defenders keen to make their mark on a player who had never sought to make friends with his opponents. Stein gave as good as he got and a bit more. He had the scars to prove it but after 12 years at the highest level the threats and confrontations on the park began to grow tiring and he walked away with his head held high and, most importantly, his legs intact.

Stein had opportunities to move abroad and carry on playing, or drop down the leagues in Scotland, but chose to concentrate on life outside of football. He remains in Linlithgow, kept busy with work as a joiner but finding time to concentrate on his passion for bowls and maintaining his reputation as a champion on the greens of his home town.

In 2009 the release of his autobiography, *Shooting Star,* brought the Stein story to a whole new audience. If you couldn't be there when the phenomenon was unleashed on the Rangers public, then surely reliving the glory days is the next best thing.

**MAGIC MOMENT:** The skipper came striding out into the Spanish sunlight to give the Bears the first sight of the continental prize they held so dear.

# JOHN GREIG
## *'THE LEGEND'* **1961-1978**

### GERS CAREER: Games 755; Goals 120; Caps 44

F OR A moment in time John Greig was the most stylish man on the planet, at least in the eyes of tens of thousands of Rangers supporters. Light three-piece suit, dark shirt and tie, thick-rimmed dark glasses and a goatee beard gave him the film star look. The expanses of a foreign airfield provided a stark and arid backdrop and in his left hand was the ultimate accessory – the European Cup Winners' Cup.

The iconic imagery of the captain in the aftermath of the Barcelona triumph is a timeless tribute to the club's finest hour in Europe, none more so than the pictures of the skipper on the tarmac at Barcelona airport en-route to the glorious homecoming. The sight of Greig with the elegant cup held aloft, surrounded by jubilant Gers fans, tells the story that a thousand words couldn't. Not just about the occasion, but about the man.

Greig is a legend, *the* legend at Ibrox but his status goes beyond that and surpasses even his momentous playing achievements. Over the years an aura accumulated around him and it has bridged the generation gap in a way few other players have done. His relationship with the lens has played a part in spreading the magic and still does.

Photographer Eric McCowat was the other half of the partnership that encapsulated a glorious era for the Light Blues, on duty in Barcelona in 1972. His archive from that period remains a regularly tapped resource.

The Glaswegian snapper, now based in Peebles, said: "I followed Rangers from pre-season in Sweden in the 1972/73 season and it was an eventful year. I travelled home and away with the team and got a real feel for the camaraderie there was. I'd started in photography in 1967, as a darkroom boy with the *Daily Mail*, so it was still early in my career. John Greig was the captain and a leader of men, that's for sure. He was hard, he had to be in his role, but what a lot of people don't realise is he was also a joker. Greigy did a great Shirley Bassey impersonation. He kept everyone entertained and I think he saw that as a vital part of his duties as the captain. It wasn't just about what happened on the park. Over the years I've watched him grow into a great ambassador for the club. All these years after he finished playing he still has a special attraction for the fans."

*Leadership is practised not so much in words as in attitude and in actions.*

**Harold Geneen**

McCowat was one of a select band of Scottish photographers who departed for Spain with the team in 1972. He returned with the valuable shots of the goals, of the premature celebrations and of the jubilant team leaving for home with the cherished prize. However, it's the one that got away that still plays on his mind.

McCowat said: "John famously vowed not to shave his lucky beard off until the run ended. Everyone wanted the picture of it coming off but Greigy had his head screwed on. It cost Eric Craig at the *Daily Record* £100 to get the picture."

Still, McCowat has the consolation of the striking departure pictures being locked away in his darkroom. He said: "I've been taking pictures for 40 years but the runway pictures in Barcelona must rank as my favourites. They captured the mood perfectly, not least because John had dressed for the occasion in the three-piece suit and dark glasses. The press had been bussed to the plane with the team and I had my camera ready to get pictures of him climbing the steps with the trophy. At that point the fans hadn't caught a glimpse of it because the presentation had been done in the ground, not on the pitch, and there had been no lap of honour. When the supporters got a sight of the trophy they dropped their bags and ran from their own planes to mob Greig, they were swarming all over the place. They were amazing scenes and made for great pictures. A lot of those images pop up on internet auction sites and for sale elsewhere, it's very difficult to keep on top of it even though I hold the copyright."

McCowat and his colleagues had unparalleled access to the squad in the run up to the final but even they did not uncover the club's best guarded secret. He added: "Of course we all know now that John Greig's foot was broken for the final in Barcelona but none of us had a clue at the time. Willie Waddell was determined not to let the press catch wind of the problem and made him go through all the training sessions that we attended."

The plan worked perfectly, Greig played on and the trophy was claimed. Then, and only then, the lucky beard could be consigned to folklore.

Greig himself recalled: "As we made our way to Ibrox, cheering fans began lining the surrounding streets about a mile or so from the ground. There were at least 20,000 inside the stadium as we made our way round the track on the back of a specially converted lorry. I was still sporting my beard and the supporters began chanting for me to 'get it off', but I wasn't daft. I had already arranged for a hairdresser in Edinburgh to do the needful and the *Daily Record* paid me £100 for exclusive pictures of me being shaved."

The thirst for a piece of Greig extends beyond photographs. In 2005 publisher Mainstream invested in the life story of a former pro, who had not kicked a ball in anger for well over quarter of a century, safe in the knowledge they were guaranteed a return. Greig was enlisted to undertake a book signing tour and was received with adulation at every turn, from his home town Edinburgh to the Glasgow heartlands and north to the Highlands and Islands. The 2005 DVD release *John Greig – Legend* was similarly well received.

Memorabilia of every shape and form is washing around the peculiar world of football collecting. Nothing with the great man's moniker is out of bounds, even letters sent as part of his office duties create a stir in auctions. If you want, you can get yourself your very own John Greig action figure.

A more imposing and permanent figure sits alongside the trinkets and photograph albums on the inventory of reminders of No.4, The Edinburgh-born star has not only been immortalised in black and white, sepia and glorious technicolour on film but also in bronze. On Edmiston Drive, in pride of place between the Bill Struth Main

Stand and the Copland Road end he stands towering over the fans who mill below on match days. With a ball in one hand and the obligatory captain's armband, the likeness is impressive. Greig himself agrees, although he is slightly bemused by the fact he is still alive to give the seal of approval since most sculpture tributes tend to be posthumous.

The Greig statue is, in fact, not just a tribute to the man but designed as a memorial to the 66 who died as a result of the 1971 Ibrox disaster. It was created by Maryhill sculptor Andy Scott and unveiled in 2001 to mark the 30th anniversary of the collapse of stairway 13. Greig had been captain on that tragic day and, with the rest of his team-mates, did all that he could to ease the pain of the relatives of those supporters who lost their lives following the team they cared so passionately for. The name of each of the 66 who perished is listed below Greig, standing guard.

The choice of figurehead for such a sombre and solemn purpose was not random, the supporters themselves had a role to play in thrusting Greig once and for all to the head of the pack of Ibrox legends.

In 1999, as Rangers embraced the hall of fame concept with a passion, Greig was installed as the official, undisputed 'Greatest Ever Ranger'. The cynic might suggest that the internet and phone polls, and the resultant gala dinners, that have become so prevalent in recent years are little more than a money maker for clubs turning clever marketing tricks. That may be true to an extent but to the men who are honoured the recognition is a humbling experience.

Reflecting on the 1999 coronation as Ranger supreme in his biography, Greig said: "I have always maintained that whle a player can con fans some of the time by kissing the badge on his jersey and declaring that he is playing for that jersey, you can't kid them all the time. They are the ones who judge a player's worth to the team and his feelings for the club and respond accordingly. Receiving the highest number of votes in a poll featuring so many great players meant an awful lot to me, considering how easy it is for the younger and middle-aged fans to forget those players from the past whom they never saw play. After all, the game is more about today and tomorrow than past successes. I was in my late fifties when I was named 'Greatest Ever Ranger' in competition with the current stars and other worthy candidates who came before and after me, but maybe, in a sense, I shouldn't have been all that surprised. I have never had anything other than the greatest respect for the Rangers fans and I think that respect has been reciprocated."

Fans not only voted with their phones and their keyboards in recent times but with their feet when Greig was drawing the curtain on his playing career in 1978. Rangers had never granted a player a testimonial up to that point but the Legend, as he was later christened by Graeme Souness, was the exception. A crowd of 70,000 packed into Ibrox to watch Rangers tackle a Scotland select in Greig's benefit match and show their appreciation for the service he had given and the dedication to the cause he had displayed.

The testimonial came on the back of Celtic counterpart Billy McNeill being honoured at Parkhead. The Hoops legend netted £40,000 from his game against Liverpool but Greig's committee trumped that well and truly and hauled in £75,000 in his benefit year. It was a huge sum in 1978, more than six-times what manager Jock Wallace was reputed to earn in a year. It was finance that opened the door to the manager's office for Greig, with Wallace taking the opportunity to double his money by accepting a £25,000 deal to join Leicester City. Would the same numbers turn out to roar their appreciation for any of the current players? The all-seated capacity of Ibrox means we will never know the answer but an educated guess suggests they would not. Greig then captured the imagination, he had and still has an x-factor that in truth is impossible to pin down. Commitment? Loyalty? Image? Media appeal? Perhaps a little bit of everything. Granted the concept of testimonials was still relatively rare but the lasting kerb appeal of the man ensures that if the exercise was repeated it would still pull in the numbers.

The turnout was confirmation of what everyone already knew, that the skipper had worked his way under the skin of the Rangers supporters. He knew that himself, aware that as a cult hero to Rangers supporters it would naturally make him a target for elements of the Celtic faithful. To combat that he kept his family based in Edinburgh, out of the full glare of the Old Firm spotlight. He valued being able to walk along Princes Street without being stopped at every turn, either by autograph hunters or aggravation seekers, and only moved west in 1979 when he got to grips with the manager's job.

His choice of home turf during his playing days also gave him breathing space from the fervent media attention that went hand in with his day job.

Greig's gruff persona did not prevent him from striking up a strong working relationship with the Scottish football press. They appreciated what he brought to the table and named him player of the year in 1966 when such honours were still in their infancy. Ten years later he became the first person to win the award twice. He was also awarded an MBE in 1977, so his performances had obviously reached an audience outwith the Scottish boundaries. In his brief break from Rangers, between leaving as manager and returning in a behind the scenes role, Greig jumped the great divide and joined the media corps as a radio pundit. He respected the media and in return the media respected him, not least because they knew how valuable it was to have Greig onside. Upset him and you risked alienating the entire Rangers support.

It was not all back slapping and mutual appreciation though. Greig is remembered as an all-star, yet his full-throttle style did not win universal praise. Here was a player who did not have the cultured touches of his contemporaries like Jim Baxter but he still won approval from the sprawling terraces because he had heart.

When he missed the 1970 League Cup victory against Celtic, a victim of flu, some media commentators even pondered if the loss of the dynamo had a positive impact on a side which produced an impressive footballing display. At the same time they acknowledged that the Ibrox captain was untouchable, if fit he would be in the team. It was an unwritten rule but one the management, players and fans throughout the 1960s and 1970s accepted.

He was backed to the hilt by a succession of team bosses, not least the legendary Willie Waddell. It was Waddell who thrust Greig into action on the biggest night in the club's history knowing he was not fully fit, preferring to go with his skipper in the European Cup Winners' Cup final in 1972 despite carrying an injury that transpired to be a broken foot rather than go into battle without him.

When Aberdeen-based journalist James Forbes launched an attack in print in 1969, Waddell made it his personal mission to take him to task. Forbes said at the time: "There is no harder player in the country than John Greig, skipper of Rangers and Scotland. He puts in every ounce of effort. But the more I see of him the more I get the impression that referees let him get away with murder. One wonders whether Greig will stay in the game when his playing days are over. It has been suggested that he take up refereeing, as he has had so much experience of being in charge of matches."

Just like Colin Stein, Greig was better with you than against you. He was notoriously tough and unforgiving but only sent off three times in a long and winding career at the highest level. Those red cards, one for every six years on the park, were according to Greig unmerited with one exception. He holds his hands up when it came to knocking out Aberdeen's Joe Smith with a single punch during a match at Pittodrie after a nasty challenge.

Greig said: "The facts bear out my contention that I was not a dirty player who set out with the express intention of injuring opponents. I played the game hard, but I also tried to play fair within the rules. I was capable of sorting out opponents who tried to do the dirty on me and I never shirked a tackle, but while I always played to win, I refused to do so at all costs."

As it happens, even his fiercest critic was eventually won over. In 1975, with Greig on his way to his second player of the year award, Forbes wrote: "In 1969 I was trying to point out that there were times when Greig was a little too boisterous with his tackling but there can be absolutely no doubt that he sets an example to his colleagues. If ever there was a player who had the will to win, it was John Greig – and he'll still have it next year."

The strong relationship with the media continued when he moved from the pitch to the dug-out, voted Scottish football's personality of the year by a panel of 22 sports writers in 1979 after winning a cup double. That appeal to the press was crucial in winning time and space as he embarked on what became a thankless task trying to turn around a lumbering ship that was beginning to lose its way. The judgements were reserved and when Greig's departure was finally confirmed there was a sense of mourning in the reports which followed.

Those troubled times as manager tested the resolve even of the Rangers support and some broke ranks. Greig the legend, the greatest Ranger, the cult hero. Even he was not immune to the wrath of a Rangers support who demanded success. Past achievements held little water and Greig remembers dark days towards the end of his tenure as manager. He said: "There was a spell when some fans began protesting outside the ground. Frankly, that situation broke my heart. I felt I was responsible for the team's poor performances and lack of results and, given my relationship with the supporters, it hurt a great deal that they obviously felt I was failing them.

"I was offered money by various newspapers to write stories about the club and had no difficulty refusing every one of them. Money has never been that important to me. It seemed far more important to me to leave with the same degree of dignity that I had displayed when accepting the role of manager of Rangers.

"I had offers of other jobs – Hearts had expressed an interest several times and Morton wanted me as manager – but I accepted that I had effectively put myself out of the game. Where do you go in Scotland after Rangers? Anyway, I could never have managed a team in opposition to Rangers."

He retired from frontline duties as a dyed in the wool blue, but it had not always been the case. Greig had been rejected by his boyhood heroes Hearts as a schoolboy but Rangers decided to take a chance. He had impressed the scouts as an inside forward, despite a lightweight frame. Despite worshipping the Jambos, the interest from Glasgow opened his eyes to an alternative football outlook and after going to watch his new team in action he was converted. The loyalty never wavered, even in the face of tempting offers from the likes of Everton in later years.

In 1960 he broke off from the sensible pursuit of an engineering apprenticeship to sign permanently with the Light Blues, accepting Scot Symon's offer of a £10 weekly wage. The gamble paid off several times over as he went on to carve out a long and distinguished career in the game, never needing to fall back on the safety net of a trade outside of sport.

By the age of 18 he was in the first team and made a dream start when he set the ball rolling in a 4-1 League Cup victory against Airdrie with the opening goal. By 1962/63 he was a permanent fixture in the side, helping his club to the championship and the Scottish Cup. By the time he was 21 his hat-trick was complete, with a League Cup win in the 1963/64 campaign rounding off the set of domestic honours. That was part of a treble for the all-conquering Rangers side of the era, a team which has gone down as one of the finest in the history of the club even if the man himself would argue it is impossible to draw comparisons between the star line-ups from decade to decade.

The following season the League Cup was claimed again and for Greig the captaincy was added to his list of honours. That, above all of the glittering silverware, confirmed his arrival as one of the big guns at Rangers. He did not need time to settle into his new role, always prepared to lead from the front and stick his head above the trench. Leadership came naturally, not least because of his willingness to take games, and team-mates, by the scruff of the neck and treat them with the same firm-handed approach as he did towards the opposition.

Greig was schooled in the traditions of the club he found himself leading, very much in the Struth camp. More of a Davie Meiklejohn or George Young than a silky skilled player in the Alan Morton or Willie Henderson tradition. His honesty was appreciated by the Rangers fans who could still relate to the old reliance on discipline and uniformity, even if Greig's tenure as on-field leader began in the Swinging 1960s. His qualities were an antidote to the excesses and eccentricities of Jim Baxter, Willie Henderson and Willie Johnston.

Greig joined an illustrious list of men to have captained Rangers and Scotland when he led the national team out on December 7, 1965, against Italy in Naples. The game ended in a 3-0 defeat but the consolation for the skipper was the fact he had enjoyed his finest hour and a half in Scotland colours against the Azurri. It was the Rangers man who scored in the 1-0 win against Italy prior to the Naples return leg, scoring with a classic strike from outside of the box to clinch maximum points in the World Cup qualifier a month prior to his appointment by Jock Stein as captain.

Despite his best efforts he never did play for Scotland in the final stages of the World Cup or European Championships, one of very few regrets from his playing days.

Greig had played his first game for the national team in a 1-0 win against England at Hampden in the Home International Championship, given his big break by former Ibrox mentor Ian McColl who had gone on to become Scotland's boss. He earned a further 43 caps over the space of 11 years, called upon by McColl as well as Jock Stein, Bobby Brown and Willie Ormond. He returned three goals and led the side in 15 games. The highlight was when he skippered Scotland to the unofficial world title, beating England in the famous Jim Baxter-inspired contest at Wembley.

With Rangers, he lifted his first coveted prize as skipper after the 1966 Scottish Cup final against Celtic, when Kai Johansen's goal was the difference between the sides, and went on to be named Scottish Football Writers' player of the year in both 1966 and 1976, adding another League Cup winner's medal in 1970 to keep the vault well stocked.

He endured the misery of the 1967 European Cup Winners' Cup final defeat against Bayern Munich but of course made up for that in Barcelona five years later when he dragged himself off the treatment table to take his place in the side.

Greig's favourite Barcelona anecdote, a close second to being stopped at customs for failing to declare the cup itself, relates to the fans. He recounts with vigour the story of the supporter who was woken the morning after the night before after sleeping off the excess in Manchester airport. The fan was stunned to find himself in Manchester, the policeman who prodded him asked if he'd got on the wrong plane and was met with the response: 'No, I drove to Barcelona.' Greig loved it, he loved the "fanatacism" of the Light Blue brigade.

More glory was to follow, much more. The Scottish Cup in 1973 was just the beginning, with his first championship as captain coming in 1975. The treble the following season was thrown in for good measure, a sweet moment for the Edinburgh boy done good.

Yet another League Cup success in 1976/77 was the solitary highlight of that season but Rangers and Greig hit back in style with another treble in what was to be the gritty veteran's swansong. He retired from playing at the age of 35, having been honoured with an all-star testimonial packed out by adoring Gers fans.

He put the boots away for a good reason, not just because of advancing years and tightening hamstrings. He quit playing to take over as manager in the summer of 1978 and despite not going down as the greatest coach Ibrox has ever seen he was not devoid of success.

It was a natural progression for the captain and it was big news. Once again, photographer Eric McCowat was at the heart of it as the country's newspapers tried to quench a seemingly endless thirst for news on the most famous of Rangers.

McCowat recalled: "Willie Waddell had worked for the *Daily Express* before returning to Rangers as manager and had tipped them off that he was preparing to offer John Greig the manager's job. The desk at the *Express* phoned me in Edinburgh and told me to get to John's house, I wasn't to let him out of my sight. I decided the best approach was to be straight with him, rather than hiding round street corners. I knocked on his door and told him he was about to be offered the job but he didn't believe me. He and Sandy Jardine went down to the Commonwealth pool for a sauna then out for lunch with their wives before the call eventually came to go through to

Glasgow to meet with Waddell. I was waiting for him when he got back home to Edinburgh to get a picture of him cracking open the champagne. It was May 24, 1978 when he got the job – my birthday, and I was supposed to be out that night. Instead I spent it camped outside his house but I got the picture in the end. It was the same day in 1972 that Rangers won the European Cup Winners' Cup, so I've spent a few memorable birthdays with John Greig."

He won a cup double in his rookie season as team boss and claimed another Scottish Cup in 1980/81 and League Cup the following term. For all the cup joy, league triumph proved frustratingly elusive for Greig. He attempted to inject some youthful enthusiasm, recruiting Ally McCoist and working with teenage prospects such as Derek Ferguson and Ian Durrant, but time was his enemy and he never benefited from the fruits of his labours on the youth team's training pitch.

In October 1983 he stood down from the top job, making way for the return of Jock Wallace, and left the Rangers payroll for the first time since he joined as a fresh faced teenager eager to prove Hearts wrong.

The absence lasted all of seven years. In 1990 Greig, who had ventured into the travel and hospitality business and dabbled in the media world, accepted an invitation to return in a public relations capacity during the Graeme Souness revolution, his special bond with the media important to smooth some of the rough edges the manager's abrasive style created.

One of the other key duties Greig was handed when David Murray brought him back to the club was strengthening bonds with the supporters' organisations at home and abroad. He went on to become honorary president of the North American Rangers Supporters Association.

In truth it was when Dick Advocaat took the helm in 1998 that the gnarled veteran really came into his own. He became minder, confidante and friend to the Dutchman and his guide to the minefield that is life in the Old Firm world. Advocaat's arrival came soon after Greig had given the Rangers family a startling fright, collapsing after suffering a heart attack in the gym at the ground. He was advised to ease his workload but soon threw himself into the new, enhanced role as part of Team Advocaat.

In 2003 the legend accepted an invitation to join the Ibrox board of directors, just as Alan Morton had done all those years before. His role now is more fluid, serving as an ambassador for the club and an inspiration to the young players he casts a knowing eye over at the Murray Park training complex most days. Greig is also on hand to lend his experience, wisdom and expertise to the parents of the next generation. His role is as much about marketing, selling the club and the Ibrox ethos that he himself benefited from when he took his first steps on the road to football stardom. As a captain all those years ago he led by example and that approach has carried forward now he holds the lofty position of director.

Greig said: "I think largely because of my loyalty to the club I have always enjoyed a close affinity with the fans. They appreciate that I chose to spend my entire playing career with Rangers when it would have been easy to have sought bigger earnings elsewhere. While money is important in terms of allowing you to enjoy a certain standard of living, cash has never been my God. I was also well paid by Rangers."

He won praise and favour more for his determination than outright ability on the football park. His loyalty was the other telling factor in his popularity with the supporters and his one club career earns him special status. He has, in time, become the godfather of Ibrox and Murray Park.

**MAGIC MOMENT:** A boy in a man's world, DJ
announced his arrival with a cup winning
goal against Celtic at the age of 16.

# DEREK JOHNSTONE

## 'DJ' 1970-1983 and 1985-1986

### GERS CAREER: Games 546; Goals 210; Caps 14

S OME STARS shine bright before disappearing without trace,
some linger on in the distance and others keep burning in full
view. Derek Johnstone falls distinctly into the final category.
Through radio, television, news-
papers and magazines he has
never once dipped out of the
public eye in almost four decades
of employment in football in one
guise or another.

Familiarity, it is only fair to say,
has bred contempt among
sections of the Rangers supporters who have tired of
Johnstone because of a media
career which keeps him central
to the game, particularly in
Glasgow. Yet for others he
remains a hero, preserved in a time
bubble that keeps memories of watching him grow up from boy to
man on the Ibrox turf fresh in the mind.

The fact he starred at Ibrox from such a young age was a huge part
of the appeal but his goalscoring record is another. Only Ally
McCoist was more prolific. Then there's the fact he was integral to

the club's one and only European success and the extrovert personality that reaches out to the man in the street.

Not only that but he was all things to all men in a Rangers shirt. The Ibrox supporters have a history of lavishing their affections on the big, bustling strikers who play with their heart on their sleeve. Look no further than the chapter devoted to Colin Stein. Derek Johnstone could play that role with the best of them, his powerful frame capable of bossing even the biggest opponent and dominating in the air.

But there's also a place in the hearts of the Gers fanatics for the cultured schemers in the Jim Baxter mould, even if nobody could ever match Slim Jim in their eyes. Johnstone could at least try to replicate that style, accomplished with the ball at his feet and as happy dribbling or splitting defences with a pass as he was battering through opposition defences.

They also appreciate raw characters, the cheeky upstarts in the Willie Henderson or Willie Johnston style. Johnstone, with his booming voice and love of the good life, had a touch of that about him too.

*To get back my youth I would do anything in the world – except take exercise, get up early or be respectable.*

**Oscar Wilde**

He had all the traits to earn cult status and he did, over and over again. He became an instant hero as an underdog when he won the cup as a teenager fresh out of school. He was a defensive hero in Barcelona when the European Cup Winner's Cup was claimed. He was a hero in the treble winning seasons of 1976 and 1978. Johnstone packed more into his career than some entire squads have done.

It wasn't just the supporters who took to Johnstone – he won over team-mates, fellow players, managers, the media, chairmen and his future employers and did it not solely on talent. Character has played as big a part in the Johnstone success story.

David Francey, the golden voice of football broadcasting for decades, watched Johnstone grow and mature as a player before following his own footsteps into broadcasting. He regards Johnstone as a friend, not just an associate, and that is a mark of the way DJ broke down the boundaries between the media and football inner circle.

Francey, who first began commentating for the BBC in 1940s, was at the height of his own powers when the Ibrox idol was at his playing peak. The broadcaster, who retired in the late 1980s after a remarkable career spearheading the corporation's radio coverage of the Scottish game, was on hand to witness all of the major moments in Johnstone's career: the cup final winner as a teenager, success in the European Cup Winners' Cup final and his prolific 1978 season.

Francey said: "Playing as a teenager for either one of the Old Firm was never easy, it took a certain type of player to handle it. I'll always remember Bobby Brown, the Rangers goalkeeper, coming into the side for his first game when he was 17. A ball came into the box and Bobby jumped to clutch it confidently – he opened his eyes to find himself in the back of the net with Johnny Vigurs beside him. Johnny turned and said to him: 'You don't catch those ones Bobby, you tip them over the bar'. I know he never forgot that throughout his whole career.

"When Derek arrived in Glasgow for his trial with Rangers as a schoolboy he asked two men at the station 'how do you get to Ibrox?' They looked him up and down and one replied: 'With a lot of practice son, with a lot of practice.' As it happened Rangers were very fortunate to have found him young and he was a big success very early in his career.

"The fans took to him straight away. It helped that he was a likeable big lad but more importantly he was a very good football player. With time it's easy to overlook the fact that Derek Johnstone was one of the finest players of his generation. He had skill, power and he also had a great deal of pace. Derek was the complete package and that was why he was so versatile."

That versatility extended beyond the confines of the football pitch. Johnstone's dramatic entrance on the Scottish football scene created a stir and from day one he was in demand, at times his personal life reaching the front pages just as his football life hogged the back page headlines. He soon became media savvy, as Francey recalls: "He was always very good with the media so we should have had an inkling as to what path he would take when he finished playing. He was somebody who always answered your questions well. That might sound obvious, but not every player came across well in interviews or was comfortable speaking when a microphone was placed in front of them.

"I eventually became very good friends with Derek through broadcasting. Every time I bumped into him he'd break into a commentary, he always likes a laugh and a joke. I think that's something supporters can relate to and appreciate. These days too many professional footballers see the press as adversaries."

Francey, who combined his part-time radio commitments with his full-time job with the electricity board, is now into his 80s and enjoying his retirement in Newton Mearns but the memories are still vivid.

He also left a lasting impression on those who faced him on the football pitch over the years. Amongst his peers, Johnstone was popular. In 1978 the Scottish Professional Footballers' Association launched its own player of the year award. The union's members put their expertise to good use to vote for the man among their number who had excelled and Johnstone romped home to gain the inaugural prize.

The SPFA awards have come to be dominated by Old Firm players. Since Paul Elliot in 1991, there have been a further 15 successive winners from Rangers and Celtic. But it has not always been that way. In the early days Glasgow's finest had to work hard to win approval from their colleagues in the Premier Division. Between Johnstone's triumph in the first vote in 1978 and Elliot's tide turning 1991 win, there were just four other Old Firm winners in 12 end of season polls. All four were Celtic stars, Johnstone was the only Ranger to etch his name onto the roll of honour until Ally McCoist repeated his achievement in 1992.

His fellow professionals appreciated his bravery, his ability in the air and his composure on the deck. They also knew at first hand how infectious his personality could be and even today he still has a magnetic pull to his one-time team-mates and former opponents when in the company of those who graced Scotland's pitches at the same time. I have seen the way a room lights up when he walks in to an old boys' reunion and that was reinforced in 2007 when the stars of past and present turned out in force to lend their support to a black tie dinner staged in Glasgow to honour DJ. Tables were snapped up by eager fans in double quick time.

Johnstone's character, star status and presence also made him a big hit with the fairer sex. His reputation as a ladies' man has led to many brushes with the tabloids over the years but that never detracted from his appeal to the fans on the street. If anything, it made him even more like one of the lads. One of their own.

The fact he has maintained his place in the public eye well after kicking his last ball in anger has ensured DJ remains fresh in the minds of supporters young and old. Rangers supporters can hang on his every word in print or over the airwaves – and the current stars know it. Sometimes it hurts.

Johnstone's role as a media figurehead has put him at loggerheads with some of the players who have tried, and failed, to match his achievements in light blue. In 2006 he became embroiled in a public spat with Peter Lovenkrands, famously claiming the Dane was "pants", amongst other things.

The striker hit back with a vital goal against Inter Milan and blasted Johnstone with both barrels post-match. Lovenkrands raged: "It's not only me who gets criticism but I have been getting stick even from Rangers legends who don't have a clue what is going on behind closed doors at Ibrox. They think they can go on the radio and talk a lot of rubbish. It doesn't help the players and it doesn't help the team. If you're a Rangers legend you should be supporting the team and the players. I think it's unprofessional and I don't think it's fair on the team and the club to criticise a player who is playing for them. It doesn't show much of a heart for the club. The person I'm talking about knows who I'm talking about and hopefully that will shut him up now."

As it happened, Lovenkrands was soon on a fast plane heading for Germany after six years at Rangers which promised much but in reality delivered nothing in comparison to Johnstone's contribution in his years on the playing staff. While the Danish international questioned his Scottish critic's professionalism, Johnstone views it completely differently.

He has built a career as an analyst by pulling no punches, whether be it Rangers, Celtic or any other club who are on the receiving end.

He is not just an old pro turning up to top up his pension. Johnstone has embraced the media world that has become his own, an accomplished presenter as well as seasoned match analyst. Indeed, his 2002 radio documentary "It's a money old game" was highly commended at the Sony Radio Academy Awards. He had writing credits as well as fronting the show, just one example of the depths of his talents as a broadcaster. Of course his ability to provoke debate and at times controversial opinions are the main lure for Clyde, a station who recruited him untried two decades ago when they gambled on his star billing pulling in an audience. It proved to be a shrewd move and with columns in the *Evening Times* in Glasgow and regular contributions to the Rangers News, his portfolio of outlets has grown steadily.

Football has been good to Johnstone and nobody knows it more than the man himself. Between leaving school and the present day he has had less than a week of unemployment, a record he cherishes. For all he enjoys the good times his status has afforded him, he prides himself on grafting to stay at the top of the game across four decades, reinventing himself between the 1970s, 80s, 90s and past the Millennium.

Johnstone was just a boy of 16 when he bounded onto the first team scene on September 19, 1970. The fresh faced rookie bagged a double as Cowdenbeath were dumped 5-0 at Ibrox after being trusted with the No.9 shirt by Willie Waddell.

Scoring goals had been the biggest downfall for Rangers in the lean years that had preceded Johnstone's debut. Strikers came and strikers went but by the time Johnstone was deemed ready for action the club was on the back of the lowest return of goals since the mid 1950s.

The Dundonian had a weight of expectation on his shoulders but he carried it like a man. He was not the biggest in the world, an inch short of six feet, but was powerful and athletic. Johnstone played the game with an ease that belied his youth, comfortable in every part of the field even as a teenager. Not just that, he had self confidence in abundance and those factors were not lost on Waddell. Within a matter of weeks they also became crystal clear to the supporters as they cast their eyes over the new kid on the block and discovered they liked what they saw.

Mind you, scoring the winner in an Old Firm final did not do his chances any harm when it came to the Light Blues legions. He became an overnight sensation and lapped up the role without any complaints.

Playing the main striking role in the League Cup final on October 24, 1970, was a boy who had been a trainee just weeks before and a schoolboy prospect less than a year earlier, making regular trips from his home on Tayside to train with the Rangers kids. The response was phenomenal and 106,000 fans witnessed the dramatic arrival of one of Scottish football's most colourful characters. Almost four decades on he remains a key personality in the game.

Back to *that* game. Willie Henderson picked out Alex MacDonald in midfield and in turn he sent Willie Johnston scampering down the right wing to cross for DJ to power home the only goal of the game by beating Jim Craig and Billy McNeill to the crucial header.

Johnstone recalls: "I wasn't expected to play in the final, everyone thought Willie Waddell would go with the more experienced players. He took me into the boot room on the Friday before the game and said 'here's half a dozen tickets, get some friends and family along. You're playing'. That was all the ceremony he needed. I was glad he had told me in advance because it meant I could go away and prepare myself for it. As a boy you lay in your bed at night dreaming of scoring the winning goal in a cup final – the next day I woke up and did it. It took a bit of beating."

At the end of his first full season as a Rangers first team player Johnstone's versatility became clear. During a pre-season training camp on the continent he dropped back to central defence and even won comparisons from Waddell to the legendary John Charles. High praise indeed, but in time-honoured fashion the young protégé took it in his stride.

He flitted from attack to defence and back again throughout the remainder of his career. In many ways his adaptability became a cross to bear, with nobody sure of what was his best position or sure whether to class him as a goalscorer or a stopper. Had he been allowed to ply his trade in one or other of those positions he may even have hit headier heights, a bold statement considering everything Johnstone achieved in the game.

Johnstone, like a clutch of fellow Rangers cult heroes, planted himself into Ibrox folklore in 1972 with his telling contribution to the European Cup Winners' Cup campaign. For him the adventure began in Turin when he helped his side to a 1-1 draw against Torino and kept his place for the 1-0 return win against the Italians in Glasgow. He was even more important in the two semi-final games against Bayern Munich, keeping the highly fancied Germans at bay as Waddell's side moved through to the final with a 2-1 aggregate win.

Colin Jackson's cruel injury on the eve of the final in Barcelona guaranteed Johnstone a defensive berth for the showdown with Dynamo Moscow and he did not look out of place at Europe's top table. Johnstone breezed through the game, galloping forward to supplement the attack when his side were on top and lending his enthusiasm to the frantic shut-out operation after the Russians pulled it back to 3-2 in the second-half.

He admits: "I didn't realise how big it was until I started to look back in later years at all the great Rangers teams that haven't been able to win in Europe. In this game you can never say never, but who knows when it will happen again? Now the bigger clubs are getting richer and Rangers and Celtic are struggling to keep up."

A Scottish Cup winner's medal in 1973 made it a trophy treble, Johnstone setting up Tom Forsyth for his famous tap in to win the game against Celtic 3-2. In the 1973/74 season he scored 15 goals to help the club on its way to the championship but his striking ability was even more crucial in the domestic treble in the next term, not least his title clinching goal against Dundee United at Tannadice in the final month of the season. He was the Premier Division's top scorer and also on target in the 3-1 win against Hearts in the Scottish Cup final.

His most prolific spell came in the treble winning 1977/78 team, with the ratio of 25 goals in just 33 league games and another Scottish Cup final goal, in the win against Aberdeen, to take his tally to 38 in the league and cups.

That return made him the automatic choice as Scotland's player of the year and Johnstone's stock was rising all the time. It was expected to shoot through the roof in Argentina when he took his place in what was supposed to be an all-conquering Scotland squad. Funny how things never work out the way they're supposed to when the national team is involved.

Johnstone didn't feature in the chaotic World Cup campaign but returned to home soil to take his place as the new Ibrox captain, replacing John Greig following his move into the manager's chair. When asked about the honour, DJ's stock reply is: "The captaincy didn't matter too much to me, it was bad enough looking after myself never mind the rest of the team."

The fact he did not play in Argentina is difficult to comprehend when you study his form going into the tournament. He was a player at the height of his physical powers, with confidence brimming to overflowing. He was Scotland's newly coronated player of the year, the country's leading club goalscorer after a momentous season in which his side had won every domestic honour. For Scotland he had scored against Northern Ireland and Wales in two British International Championship matches before the send off for the 78 World Cup.

That did not seal the deal when the team plane landed in Argentina. Kenny Dalglish and Joe Jordan were the partnership

MacLeod put his faith in, with the duo playing together for 260 minutes of the 270 minutes played. Joe Harper was the only other striker to get a look in, earning 10 minutes of action against Iran. The results, and ridicule that followed, did not vindicate MacLeod's approach with the embarrassing 3-1 defeat against Peru and 1-1 draw against Iran only countered by what proved to be a hollow 3-2 victory against the Netherlands. Jordan scored against Peru, Dalglish against the Dutch. Johnstone kicked his heels on the touchline.

It was a bizarre end to what, in club terms at least, was Johnstone's most productive. Winning the European Cup Winners' Cup win of 1972 as a rookie is naturally a personal highlight of his, but in 1977/78 he was very much the main man.

The season started for Johnstone on August 24 in the League Cup, having missed the opening two league games. Both had ended in defeat, against Aberdeen and Hibs, as Rangers supporters braced themselves for another long hard year after the disappointment of a trophyless campaign in 1976/77.

Johnstone made his entrance in time to start allaying those fears, bagging a double against First Division side St Johnstone in the first leg of a double header in the second round of the League Cup. Days later he made his first Premier Division appearance of the season, helping his side to a 4-0 win at Partick but failing to hit the net. It proved to be a rare blank for DJ that term as he embarked on a spectacular streak of form.

His first league strike was in the 3-2 Old Firm victory in Govan on September 10. The train was back on the tracks and Johnstone was in the driving seat as it steamed majestically through the season sweeping up every award along the way.

He scored the first of two hat-tricks in a 4-1 win at Motherwell on October 15, with the other treble falling in a 5-0 win at Ayr on November 26. By then Rangers were through to the semi-final of the League Cup and Johnstone had taken his tally in that competition to three goals in six ties, including one in the 3-1 quarter-final second leg against Dunfermline. The first two months of 1978 were red hot for the purposeful striker. The year began with a goal in a 2-1 win at Partick on January 2. In six Premier Division matches in January and February he scored seven times, only shut out by Celtic in that period but still playing a part in a 3-1 win against the Hoops.

January and February also brought two Scottish Cup ties and three goals for Johnstone, a double in the 4-2 third round win at Berwick and the only goal of the game against Stirling Albion in the fourth round. In two months he had played eight games and been on target in seven of them, scoring nine goals. April and May were almost and as impressive, with seven Premier Division games hauling in seven goals as Rangers pipped Aberdeen by two points to win the league and the Scottish Cup semi-final, against Dundee United, and final, against Aberdeen, featuring a Johnstone goal. His record in the Scottish Cup that term was perfect: played five, won five and scored six with singles strikes in four games and a double in one.

In the eyes of new manager John Greig the season had been a roaring success for Johnstone. The football writers agreed. Although some voted for Aberdeen and Scotland goalkeeper Bobby Clark as player of the year, the journalists in the main plumped for Johnstone on the back of his truly inspirational form for Rangers. Yet as far as the national team was concerned, it wasn't enough.

At Ibrox he was appreciated though. Greig's first major decision as boss in the summer of 1978, in the aftermath of Jock Wallace's departure, was to decide who would inherit captain's duties in his own absence from the first team. Sandy Jardine, model professional and epitomy of consistency, a Scotland regular and international skipper, was the brutally obvious choice. Greig chose a more unorthodox approach and instead opted for a far less safe appointment in the shape of Johnstone. It was a surprise decision, but an idea Greig had in his mind from 1970 when the Dundonian burst onto the stage as a teenager.

In later years, Greig mused: "Even at that tender age I spotted something in Derek that suggested to me that he possessed the qualities necessary to one day become captain of Rangers. Sandy Jardine was the obvious candidate to eventually succeed me as captain at that point, but I felt that Derek would be a more beneficial choice in the long term and I began sharing a room with him on trips, so I could pass on the benefit of my experience."

Greig got the chance to put his theory into practice in 1978. The gamble, in his opinion, did not pay off. He said: "I made a mistake in not appointing Sandy captain, but I felt that his best years were behind him and that Derek's were ahead, so it would be better if a younger player took over from me. On reflection, I should have stuck with Sandy."

Johnstone collected his first trophy as captain in the 1978/79 League Cup final and scored twice in the 3-2 win against Hibs in the Scottish Cup final replay to bag another. The 1981 Scottish Cup, courtesy of a 4-1 replay win over Dundee United, and the League Cup the following season made it 14 trophies as man and boy in Govan.

In the summer of 1983 a £30,000 bid from Chelsea took Johnstone to London and England's Second Division. Injury prevented him from playing a major part in the Stamford Bridge side's promotion winning season, even returning to Scotland for a loan stint with boyhood heroes Dundee United late in 1983. Arsenal and Spurs had both been interested in Johnstone at his peak, when he was Scotland's player of the year in the late 1970s, but he opted against moving and he would be the first to admit his introduction to football south of the border came too late for him to do his reputation justice.

The escape route was a familiar one, leading right back to the main door at Ibrox. Jock Wallace parted with £25,000 to take the idol back to Glasgow at the beginning of 1985 but, a little over a year later, a line was drawn under a glittering career. After his swansong in April 1986 in a 2-1 defeat away to St Mirren he departed with 546 appearances and 210 goals to his credit, a tally surpassed only by Ally McCoist.

Johnstone has always believed he could have done even better. He said: "I became a utility player and in many ways they took the rise out of me. I would be playing centre-half one week, up front the next and in midfield the week after that. I never got a run in one position. I played something well over 500 games and I would say a third of those were at the back. I never took penalties or had a good run as a striker, so to be the club's second highest scoring player of all time is something I'm proud of. I never tire of telling Ally McCoist that I would have beaten him if I'd been playing up front regularly."

The next chapter was bizarre for Johnstone, with the Chelsea connection handing him an unexpected managerial break. Blues chairman Ken Bates bought a controlling stake in Partick Thistle and put his former striker in charge in time for the 1986/87 season, hoping to use the Jags as a nursery club for some of the Stamford Bridge young guns.

His celebrity and cult status in Glasgow appealed to Bates, one of football's more flamboyant characters. Partick directors arrived at a city centre hotel to complete the sale of the club, passing DJ on his way out. After completing the deal Bates told them: "By the way, I have found a new manager for you." Bates was told they already had a manager but replied: "I know you do, but this is a really good one. It's Derek Johnstone." Bates was instantly reminded he had always maintained he would not interfere, hitting back with: "You didn't believe that did you?"

The form was steady but unspectacular and Johnstone parted company with Partick after less than a season. It turned out to be his lucky break, paving the way for his entry to the media world with Radio Clyde, who snapped him up just five days after his managerial career had ended, and launched him headlong into a profession which has given him the type of stability his peers who have followed the coaching path have never enjoyed.

**MAGIC MOMENT:** Mesmerised Celtic
defenders trailed in his wake in 1979 as
Cooper scored his most memorable goal.

# DAVIE COOPER
## *'MOODY BLUE'* **1977-1989**

### GERS CAREER: Games 540; Goals 67; Caps 24

O N MARCH 23, 1995, at Glasgow Southern General hospital two consultants made the decision which plunged Scottish football into mourning. When Davie Cooper's life machine was switched off, it became clear football fans often don't know what they've got until its gone.

Cooper was cherished by the Rangers support in his prime but it took his death to ram home the message of just how important he had been to the club. When he departed for Motherwell in 1989 there were no effigies of manager Graeme Souness being burned in the streets. He slipped quietly away as attention turned to the new wing king in Govan, Mark Walters, just as Willie Henderson before him had been allowed to drift through the exit.

Yet Cooper's shock passing six years later united supporters, not just of Rangers, in their appreciation of his talents. To recount a well worn tragedy, Cooper collapsed while filming a children's football coaching demonstration at Broadwood Stadium in Cumbernauld on March 22, 1995. He was alongside Celtic striker Charlie Nicholas and Scotland under-21 coach Tommy Craig at the time. The stricken veteran was rushed to Monklands hospital before being transferred to Glasgow. After a night in intensive care he was declard brain dead and the decision was taken to switch off the ventilator which had prolonged the inevitable. A brain haemorrhage was identified as the cause.

Cooper was used to playing to the crowd and the theme continued following his death. A staggering 9,000 people turned out to pay their final respects, many in tears as they lined the streets of Hamilton to watch the funeral procession.

A floral tribute from rock star Rod Stewart was among those laid on the grass outside Hillhouse Church. The message from the musician, a staunch Celtic fan, read: "One of Scotland's greatest." Representatives from each of the 40 Scottish league clubs at the time joined the great and good of the game along with celebrities from the worlds of music and media.

The Reverend Jim Mackenzie described Cooper as a true gentleman who inspired love and affection in everyone who knew him. Walter Smith, then in his first spell as Rangers manager, told the mourners: "Somebody once said simplicity was genius and Davie Cooper's football was touched by genius. God gave him a great gift and I don't think he can be disappointed about the way he used it. Rangers have had many great players over the years but there are very, very few of them who reach legendary status like Davie Cooper."

Ally McCoist added: "I watched, listened and learned from Davie. I also learned the importance of strength of character. He was single-minded and determined." Celtic's club wreath came with the message: "Your ability, your friendship and your honour will be sadly missed." Tommy Burns, manager at the time, described him as a national treasure while braveheart Alex McLeish broke down in tears as he attempted to read a tribute to his former Scotland team-mate in the aftermath of his death.

Scottish Football Association secretary Jim Farry hit the mass appeal on the button when he said: "Davie Cooper was a great player who brought joy to hundreds of thousands. He was also one of the few players to bridge the gap to gain the admiration of supporters of opposing teams as well as those who followed the clubs he played for."

Sandy Jardine, a man who knows a thing or two about Rangers stars, said at the time: "I put Davie on a par with Jim Baxter when it came to pure, natural ability."

More than a decade has passed since Cooper died but the name still looms large in Scottish football, kept alive by dedicated supporters. Stephen Pollock is the epitome of the Cooper devotee. He worshipped the winger as a player and is committed to keeping his memory alive. Pollock founded the www.daviecooper.com website in honour of Coop and happily devotes his spare time to maintaining it.

The fascination began at an early age. Pollock said: "I guess it all started in the mid-80s when my uncle took me along to Ibrox to watch Rangers. I remember the hum of anticipation that reverberated around the stands when Cooper got the ball. He was something special and could seemingly conjure up magic at will. It was playground football on a grand scale. Ever since then I've been hooked on his talent."

One of the most popular parts of Pollock's tribute site is the video section, with glorious clips of some of Cooper's finest moments. He is well placed to judge the affection the late great is still held in by Rangers fans of all ages, with his decision to set-up the site well received.

Pollock, a software developer from Glasgow's south side, knows a bit about performing. He's a drummer in a band, The Shone, and also plays piano and guitar. The webmaster added: "I was searching for 'Davie Cooper' on the internet and was surprised at the lack of information available. Aside from a small biography on the Rangers website and a Wikipedia article there was very little to look at. I thought it was about time somebody created a tribute site for the great man, so I started doing some research and it all snowballed from there. What strikes me is the depth of emotion that Cooper's name still arouses amongst football supporters, especially Rangers fans. I get loads of e-mails from folk saying how moved they were by watching his goals again and reading about his life. There's something about the man which strikes a chord in people, it's hard to put your finger on it but it's there.

*Laziness is nothing more than the habit of resting before you get tired.*

**Jules Renard**

"Fans admire his loyalty. I receive a lot of messages from fans raving about Davie's loyalty to Rangers football club. They regards Davie as a 'true blue' – a childhood Rangers fan who signed for the club of his dreams and stayed with them through good and bad times. It's a terrible cliché now but he did really play for the jersey. As one fan described it in an e-mail to me: 'He's in the heart and soul of the club'. Supporters put him up there with John Greig and Ally McCoist in terms of club legends.

Pollock is not blind to the failings of his hero. Just like Willie Johnston and Jim Baxter before him, Cooper was not perfect. That, after all, was part of the appeal. He said: "I've always been intrigued by football's flawed geniuses – Best, Baxter, Gascoigne. To me Cooper fell under that category. Although with Coops it wasn't booze or birds, it was his laziness and, on occasion, petulant attitude towards authority figures. We forgave him because he was an unassuming footballing genius who could turn a game on its head in seconds."

The fans also forgave the lean years, when Rangers struggled and Cooper was dragged down with them. The arrival of Souness brought a rebirth. Pollock said: "Every fan loves a great sporting comeback and Cooper didn't disappoint. In 1986, he performed the footballing version of the rope-a-dope. For years he had been pinned to the ropes and subjected to a battering by an indifferent manager, mediocre playing staff and, at times, by his own questionable attitude. In the twilight years at Ibrox, under Graeme Souness, he staged a dazzling comeback and played some of the most electrifying and consistent football of his career."

To stage a comeback you have to have hit the heights in the first place. Cooper did that very early in his Gers career. Pollock said: "My favourite Cooper goal has to be the one he scored in the Dryborough Cup final in 1979. Only maybe Pele or Best in their prime could have pulled off something like that. To do it against Celtic in a cup final makes it even more special. I never tire of watching it and delight in the close control and composure Cooper showed that day. If professionally shot footage of this goal existed I'm sure it would feature in the top 10 goals of all time programmes. Sublime."

Cooper had grown up as a goalscorer, cutting in from wide to put his deadly accuracy to good use. He did not specialise in tap-ins, preferring the dramatic to the understated finishes. Two of his goals have gone down in fan folklore as among the finest ever scored by a Gers player, in fact one of those has been voted the greatest ever scored by the club.

That came in the 1979 Dryburgh Cup final and it was a goal more befitting of a European Cup final. The ball was chipped in from the right flank, Cooper took the ball on his chest inside the box and did a couple of keepy-ups while holding off his marker, let the ball bounce and flicked over the head of his minder and turned inside. By now he was dead centre in the Hoops penalty box, deep in enemy territory, but had the presence of mind and strength of character to throw in another couple of keepy-ups to leave not one but two more defenders stricken. Another keepy-up took a fourth stopper out of the equation before he killed it on his chest and calmly slotted it under the keeper.

His strike in the 1987 League Cup final rivalled it, a very different production. This time he was 19 yards from goal with a five man Aberdeen wall between him and Jim Leighton's* goal. A left foot rocket left the wall watching and Leighton stranded, almost ripping the roof of the net out as it flew into the top left hand corner. Free-kicks were as a good as a penalty with Cooper on the park, he didn't often miss the target with them and it was the same story when he was on penalty duty. Unlike so many wingers, Cooper had a ruthless streak to match his artistry.

The footage of those moments may be grainy, but the talent was brought into sharp focus when Cooper died. Pollock, like so many others, made the pilgrimage to Govan. He added: "I'll never forget the scenes outside Ibrox after Davie passed away. The stadium gates were transformed into a tapestry of red, blue and white scarves. The pavement below was covered in pictures, programmes and tributes to the great man. I remember going down there with one of my mates to pay my respects. It was all very sad and I felt totally numb afterwards."

The temporary shrine to Cooper in the days and weeks following his death grew and grew. A carpet of fresh cut flowers sat beneath a wall of colour, and not just red, white and blue. Woven into the collage of Rangers scarves and jerseys were Celtic mementoes tied to the railings by Hoops fans. For a time at least a city was united in grief. That moving tribute marked the full stop to a wonderful career that had started in Lanarkshire in the 1970s.

Cooper first caught the attention of senior clubs as a teenager turning out for Lanarkshire juvenile side Hamilton Avondale. Crystal Palace and Coventry City were keen on adding him to their youth ranks but the young Scot was not tempted to move south, he could not even be persuaded to leave Hamilton when Motherwell and Clyde expressed an interest. His determination to stay in his home town led him to drift out of the game after leaving school but eventually Clydebank took him under their wing.

Even before his 20th birthday he had become a star, the Bankies leading scorer in their Second Division title success of 1975 with 22 goals from his beat on the right wing. He was just three goals off the league's golden boot that term.

A string of big name English clubs began to circle around Kilbowie. Manchester United, Leeds United, Derby County, Leicester City, Norwich City and Sunderland were all avid followers of his progress. They were wasting their time, as Aston Villa discovered when they lodged an offer of £65,000 in 1976.

Explaining his decision to stay put at the time, the humble winger said: " I know I'm 20 and shouldn't really be wary aout moving to England, but I'm a home-bird at heart and I'd have to think very seriously about going. I like Hamilton, where I live with my parents, and I like the club, my mates and the general set-up."

Even with the benefit of glorious hindsight he never regretted rejecting the English overtures. He was one of those infuriating all round sportsmen, handy with a snooker cue and a talented tennis player as well as a horse racing tipster of some repute in football circles. When it came to his career he refused to gamble.

He later remarked: "Money was never my motivation. You can only live in one house at a time and eat three square meals a day, it was always more important that I had my family and friends around me." His brother John had been a promising player before Davie shot to prominence, snapped up by Hull City as a 16-year-old but soon returning to Hamilton Accies after being struck by home sickness and retiring through injury at the tender age of 22.

The kid brother, the Clydebank star attracting a frenzy of attention, waited a full year before finally spreading his wings, even if it was just a short hop to Govan. Jock Wallace was prepared to equal the club's transfer record and pay £100,000 for a talent being heralded as the finest prospect in Scotland. It helped that the target had spent many happy afternoons at Ibrox as a boy, cheering on his Rangers heroes.

By the time of his short hop to Glasgow in June 1977, at the age of 21, he had been fast tracked from the Scotland under-21 side to the full international squad.

It left Clydebank manager Bill Munro cursing his luck. He said: "Sadly, football is a bit of a vicious circle. Players are brought on as entertainers, they attract the crowds then you have to sell them."

Wallace had not only secured himself a winger and a creator but got a goalscorer into the bargain, one proven at the top level. Cooper had scored 18 times for the Bankies in the Premier Division prior to his big money move.

Cooper cherished the possibilities that were stretching out in front of him. He slipped the No.11 shirt over his shoulders for his competitive debut in a 3-1 defeat at Aberdeen on August 13, 1977, and made a place on the team-sheet his own. The youngsters missed just a single game in his first season and bagged half a dozen goals as Rangers beat Aberdeen to the Premier Division title by just two points. He was an ever present in the victorious Scottish Cup campaign, which culminated in a 2-1 win over the Dons, and played every game of the League Cup run on his way to scoring in the 2-1 victory against Celtic in the final. One season, three trophies ... the new boy was off and running.

It was a big occasion and it required a song, with the fans duly obliging with a catchy number that did exactly what it said on the song sheet.

> We've got Davie, Davie, Davie, Davie Cooper
> On the wing, on the wing
> We've got Davie, Davie, Davie, Davie Cooper
> On the wing, on the wing
>
> Davie, oh, Davie Cooper
> Oh, Davie Cooper on the wiing
> Davie, oh, Davie Cooper
> Oh Davie Cooper on the wing

In his second season a cup double was again inspired by Cooper's promptings and he was on target in the 1981 4-1 Scottish Cup final replay triumph over Dundee United.

Cooper was a big game player and the vital goals kept on coming, netting again in the 1981/82 League Cup final. Again Dundee United were on the receiving end, beaten 2-1. There was a three year gap for further honours, the drought broken by a flood of Ally McCoist goals, Super Ally's hat-trick earning a 3-1 win against Celtic in the League Cup showdown of 1983/84 as Cooper picked up another winner's medal to match the one which followed the next season.

It was not all plain sailing for Cooper and Rangers throughout his stay. In 1985 he found himself at loggerheads with the club over the re-signing terms on the table. Cooper took the unprecedented step of speaking out against the rumours of the package he had rejected, acclaiming the only way he could meet the quoted figures of £100,000 over three years was if he helped the team to win the Premier Division and European Cup every single season. He was adamant he was not being unreasonable at a time when Rangers were notoriously budget conscious and eventually an agreement was reached to keep him on the staff.

The cup success of the previous years was not enough for the Rangers board or the fans and Graeme Souness knew he had to make sweeping changes when he took charge in 1986. Cooper was one of the few survivors but he did more than just cling on; he flourished. The manager later admitted he really had not realised just how good his former Scotland team-mate was, claiming Cooper would have been a hit in Italy's Serie A if he had been charitable enough to tip off his former clubs on the continent. Souness never did make the call, he wanted to keep his cultured winger all to himself.

In 1986/87 the Souness-inspired side were back on top of the tree and Coop missed just two of the 44 games as the title was finally reclaimed, having scored the winner against Celtic in the League Cup final that term from the penalty spot.

The next season he bagged Rangers' opener in the League Cup final, which ended locked at 3-3 with Aberdeen before a 5-3 penalty victory.

There was one final medal at Rangers, a Premier Division gong in 1988/89 by virtue of nine starts and 14 appearances from the bench. By that time Mark Walters was the man in possession of the No.11 jersey and the writing was on the wall. A return to Lanarkshire was imminent.

It was in August 1989 that Cooper finally left Rangers, despite expressing his desire more than once to see out his playing days in Light Blue. Tommy McLean, a former Rangers team-mate, spent £50,000 of Motherwell's money and every penny would later be justified. He joined a colony of Gers FPs at Fir Park with McLean joined on the coaching team by Tom Forsyth and players Craig Paterson and Bobby Russell in the dressing room to greet him.

With Well there was a renaissance, playing 150 games in just four years and masterminding the campaign which ended with the glorious 4-3 Scottish Cup final success against Dundee United in 1991. For a player who thought his trophy winning days were behind him, it was a sweet moment.

As it happened, Souness may have been premature in allowing Super Cooper to leave the building. In 1991 he was pipped by a single vote as Dundee United's Maurice Malpas won the Scottish Football Writers' Association player of the year award.

Just as he had been at his two previous clubs, Cooper was a massive hit with the Steelmen. The pace was beginning to fade as he entered his 30s but the brain was as sharp as ever and that was put to good use when he moved in from the wing to adopt the role of playmaker for Well. In the summer of 1993 he was appointed to the Lanarkshire side's coaching staff, combining his duties with playing, and he relished the opportunity to work with a crop of talented young players who were coming through the ranks at that time.

Within months he had transferred those coaching skills to Clydebank as the 37 year-old went back to his roots fully 16 years after departing from Kilbowie. He craved regular football and that was behind the decision for one last fling with the Bankies. He had always looked after himself physically and was still turning out in the Scottish Football League at the age of 39 before his tragic death on Clyde's pitch. Those who worked with him on the training ground predicted a bright future on that side of the fence for a player with a wealth of experience at club and international level but he never had the opportunity to prove them right and Scottish fans never had the chance to see if he could bring the same entertainment from the touchlines as he had as a player.

When he returned to Clydebank in 1993 he did so as a first choice player, even though age was beginning to take its toll on a player who had never been blessed with lightning pace in the first place.

Bankies chairman Jack Steedman hit the nail on the head when he said: "The legs had gone a bit, but nine minutes of Coop was like 90 minutes from someone else."

Many managers agreed, particularly when it came to Scotland. Cooper first tasted international football when he was invited to join Ally MacLeod's squad for a South American tour in 1977. It was when Jock Stein took over that he made his debut, earning his first cap in a friendly against Peru in 1979. He was 22 when he helped the national side to a 1-1 draw, playing alongside future manager Graeme Souness in a team that also featured club captain Sandy Jardine and Kenny Dalglish. Asa Hartford was on target.

A further 21 caps followed under Stein, Alex Ferguson and Andy Roxburgh while with Rangers and Motherwell but he will always be remembered as the player who kept his cool to send Scotland on their way to the 1986 World Cup finals in Mexico. In the decisive qualifying game it was Cooper's penalty equaliser with nine minutes to play against Wales in Cardiff which won a place in the play-offs, the jubilation turning to despair when Stein collapsed and died.

The show had to go on for Scotland, despite the sombre mood in the squad. Cooper scored the opener in the 2-0 play-off win against Australia which secured a place at the world's top table and dedicated the victory to the memory of Stein.

He was used sparingly by Ferguson in the Mexico finals, with two appearances from the bench proving to be his only experiences of a major competition.

His international career appeared to have ended when he played in a 2-0 defeat at the hands of Brazil in the Rous Cup at Hampden in 1987. With his club fortunes fading, the winger looked to have bowed out.

His revival at Motherwell prompted a change of heart from Roxburgh, who pencilled the veteran in for a place in his 1990 World Cup squad and fielded him in friendlies against Norway and Egypt in the build-up. That game against the North Africans in May, 1990, proved to be his last in dark blue as injury scuppered his hopes of joining the World Cup party in Italy.

He did not always win favour in the corridors of power at SFA headquarters in Park Gardens, always making it clear that he put his club paymasters at Ibrox before country, but that attitude did not prevent him from serving Scotland with distinction. The blazers may have had concerns, but a succession of managers did not.

Roxburgh said: "Football is not about robots or boring tactics. It's about excitement, emotion and individual flair and imagination as shown by Davie Cooper."

Excitement and flair were a given when it came to the Rangers and Motherwell star and emotions naturally followed, usually in the form of frustration and deep displeasure. Apart from the obvious and effective Super Cooper, there were a few more tongue in cheek nicknames applied to the winger. Albert was one, after the *Coron-*

*ation Street* character Albert Tatlock. The Corrie man spent his life moaning, just like Cooper.

Graeme Souness claimed he knew if his star man was due an above average performance by the level of complaining in the build-up to the match. The more grumbles there were, the bigger the threat there was to the opposition.

To the media he became known simply as Moody Blue. He was a shy character, particularly as a young player, and uncomfortable with life in the spotlight. His introverted traits did not endear him to the press but his performances on the park made up for his reluctance to wax lyrical off it.

The BBC's Chick Young summed it up perfectly when he said: "Davie Cooper's worst injuries were usually huffs. And that can be a serious problem for a player."

The Moody Blue tag stuck throughout his career, even though with age and experience he began to play the media game more cleverly. He was even called upon as a pundit on television and radio as he moved into the veteran stage of his playing days, something that would have been unthinkable when he first arrived at Ibrox as an evasive and reluctant hero.

The trappings of success were not Cooper's motivation. Team-mates remember a modest man and his star billing after his record transfer to Ibrox made him feel awkward. He didn't even drive in his early days a professional, preferring to take the train to work. There were no flash cars for him.

His style of play made him the centre of attention but a boyish shyness that followed him in the first decade of his career ensured he never exploited that in the way Jim Baxter or Willie Henderson had done in the 1960s and 1970s.

In the years leading up to his death Cooper began to open up to the media and those closest to him in football saw a dramatic change as he finally began to accept his place in the public eye.

His biography, *True Blue*, in 1987 gave an insight into the man behind the public persona and supporters an idea of what made him tick but such opportunities were rare. He preferred to keep his private life private, never easy for a player in the Glasgow goldfish bowl.

A very reserved man whose chosen career forced him to live his life in the public eye as a cult hero and he remains prominent. Cooper's image, just like John Greig, will never be allowed to fade.

In his beloved home town, at the Hamilton Palace sports ground, a bronze statue has been erected in his honour. Unveiled in 1999 to mark the fifth anniversary of his death, Ally McCoist was called upon to perform the ceremony. Fittingly McCoist was accompanied on the day by his baby son Argyll, the son he had bestowed with Cooper as a middle name.

An even more conspicous tribute stands in Motherwell, where the main stand at Fir Park has been named in his honour and a variety of suites and sections of the stadium are laden with the tag in a shrine to a veteran who lit up the early 1990s at the club.

Soon in Clydebank another building with the same famous name should begin to take shape. The Davie Cooper Centre is scheduled to open in the next two years. It will offer play and recreational facilities for children and young adults with learning difficulties, physical disabilities, behavioural or emotional problems.

The charity behind the centre was launched in 2005 and includes former Clydebank Football Club chairman Jack Steedman on its board of directors. It was Steedman who first tempted Cooper into the senior game, waiting outside the factory where the apprentice printer was working with an envelope of used notes. Legend has it Steedman had been so determined to clinch the deal that he had emptied the Bankies social club's fruit machine the night before to give him the necessary collateral.

The travelling from Hamilton every day put Cooper off the move initially but eventually he gave into the pressure and the two men struck up a strong and lasting relationship.

Steedman had planned to build a new stadium for Clydebank FC and name it after the club's brightest star. When the club folded, he agreed to lease the land to the charity to ensure the Cooper name could at least be put to good use in another form. The Rangers Supporters Assembly has already donated funds to the project, which has already attracted lottery support. In 2009 an outdoor activity centre should be in operation with an outreach programme in place the following year and a respite facility constructed by 2011. The plans have the full support of Cooper's family and are gathering pace and enthusiasm as the deadlines begin to loom.

The charity's launch in 2005 coincided with the 10th anniversary of the player's death, the same year in which his former clubs Motherwell and Rangers met in the League Cup final just three days before the anniversary. It became the Davie Cooper Final, with his image adorning the tickets and proceeds from programme sales going to the charity funding the creation of the Clydebank centre.

In another 10th anniversary tribute, supporters launched a fundraising campaign to foot the bill for a giant banner depicting Cooper in a typically stern pose. The coffers were full to overflowing in double quick time and the pictorial memorial was unveiled before a match against Motherwell on December 27, 2004. There's a concerted campaign among the fans who watched him play to ensure the next generation are educated about a past master, desperate to ensure that the fact he is no longer around does not mean he is forgotten.

**MAGIC MOMENT:** Ted left clutching the man
of the match award after tying Dundee United up
in knots in the 1986 League Cup semi-final

# TED McMINN
### *'TIN MAN'* **1984-1987**

**GERS CAREER: Games 65; Goals 5**

MEIKLEJOHN, MORTON, McPhail, Young, Baxter, Henderson, Johnston, Greig, Stein, Johnstone. Legends, one and all. Those 11 men form a team steeped in the glory of success after success, thousands of appearances between them. Ted

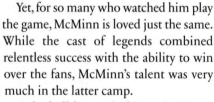

McMinn, on the other hand, amassed the paltry tally of 37 Premier Division starts for Rangers and three league goals.

Yet, for so many who watched him play the game, McMinn is loved just the same. While the cast of legends combined relentless success with the ability to win over the fans, McMinn's talent was very much in the latter camp.

It had all begun in his native Dumfriesshire as a talented schoolboy but his path to the top was not direct. He went the roundabout way, as he so often did on his mazy runs, starting out with Glenafton in the juniors before being picked up by Queen of the South. At Palmerston he became a favourite, a crowd pleaser, an entertainer. He was playing Second Division football, providing some light relief from the grind of the bottom rung on Scottish football's ladder and soon established himself as a first choice in the Queens team. His intriguing displays on the flank, doing his best to replicate his idol Davie Cooper despite a notably different build, sparked interest and it was no surprise to the Dumfries club's fans when he was plucked from relative obscurity by one of the big guns.

He arrived at a time when Rangers were at one of their lowest ebbs, without a league title for six years when the Castle Douglas born winger hung his kit in the Ibrox boot room. Jock Wallace was in his first full season of his second stint at the helm when he targeted the Queen of the South talent.

As anyone who has travelled around the area will testify to, the region is one of Scotland's great outposts. Far less remote than the Highlands yet oddly isolated, the south west stomping ground of McMinn is not renowned as a hotbed of football talent. Yet he made the breakthrough and he made it big when he eventually caught the eye of Wallace.

It was an unlikely marriage. Here was a manager who appeared to put work rate and discipline above all else in hot pursuit of a player who could hardly be considered to be one best suited to fitting into a set game plan. Yes he was a team player, but McMinn was not the type who could be slotted into a team and tasked with following a set of detailed instructions. Expecting the unexpected was par of the cause. Wallace, however, was willing to bend his principles now and again. In McMinn's case he did it again and again, buying him not once but twice. What the player did have in his favour was a determination, a spirit and a courage that carried him through his career and beyond. If he took a knock he came back brighter, if he fell backside over elbow he bounced up again and had another go.

*The measure of who we are is what we do with what we have.*
**Vince Lombardi**

Wallace, no doubt, approved of that attitude. The veteran manager needed all the help he could get when he first went after the rangy winger. They were grim times, make no mistake. Attendances in the face of indifferent performances were alarming, dipping as low as 7,500 at Ibrox for the latest in a string of meaningless league matches when Dundee United visited in May, 1984.

McMinn arrived the following season but the fans remained to be convinced that the side was heading in the right direction, despite setting the league woes to one side to win the 1984 Scottish Cup.

Fourth place behind Aberdeen, Celtic and Dundee United had been the outcome of the 1983/84 season following the turmoil of John Greig's departure and Wallace's re-appearance.

There were signs of a revival at the beginning of the following season, the first eight games of the Premier Division push passing without defeat. McMinn was introduced to the Premier Division in the 10th game, on the back of a 1-0 defeat against Hearts, and came on from the bench to help his new side to a 2-0 win at St Mirren. He was propelled into the starting 11 the following week, replacing Bobby Russell. His first goal came in a 4-2 win against Dumbarton at Boghead, when he scored direct from a corner. Welcome to Ted's world everyone.

The new boy dipped in and out of the team throughout the 1984/85 season, too late to play a part in the League Cup final win and unable to help Rangers avoid a repeat of the fourth place finish from the previous term.

He came into a team not overflowing with players who could set pulses racing. Yes, Davie Cooper was in attendance but he was enduring something of a dip in form in the pre-Souness days. Yes, Ally McCoist was on the staff but, as ridiculous as it now sounds, the jury was out on his contribution. The team for McMinn's first game featured Peter McCloy, a stalwart and European hero who was winding down, in goal. The defence comprised Dave McKinnon, John McClelland, Craig Paterson and Dave McPherson. It was a workmanlike unit but devoid of a dominant character, Terry Butcher was a distant dream while John Greig had long since gone and even Tom Jaws Forsyth had left the building. McMinn came into the midfield at No.11 with Cooper on the opposite flank and the journeymen Ian Redford and Cammy Fraser through the middle. No Alex McDonald, no Paul Gascoigne or Barry Ferguson. In attack McCoist partnered Iain Ferguson, a committed and dependable striker but one not likely to trouble Bob McPhail, Colin Stein or Mark Hateley in a debate over the best forwards the club has ever seen.

In short, McMinn landed in a struggling team devoid of real outstanding characters. He brought a touch of colour to the party, even if he sometimes got it wrong he at least had the guts to try and do something out of the ordinary. The new kid on the block could not lift the gloom permanently but at least temporarily there was a silver lining to the cloud.

The attraction boiled down to the whole winger affair. From Morton to Laudrup, a wide man worth his salt has been able to earn a special place in the opus of Ibrox. Mind you, even when the good times did begin to roll there was not universal love for the big man, who stood 6ft tall and weighed in at just under 13 stone in his prime. Rangers fans were often divided about the merits of such an unorthodox player, a mould breaker in every sense, and Scotland's managers shared the same opinion. There was no room for this joker, and his foibles, in the international deck despite his value to Rangers, Seville, Derby, Birmingham and every other club he turned out for.

Mind you, he had it all to do to persuade the punters in his Gers days as well as the coaches. Supporters remained non-plussed by Wallace's attempts to spark a revival, with 8,424 rattling around a sparsely populated Ibrox to see their men beat Dumbarton in March of that year.

Fans desperately wanted something to cling to, some signs of encouragement. In a young striker called McCoist and gangly winger named McMinn, or the Tin Man, they had at least two crumbs of comfort. What would the crowds have been without those green shoots of recovery?

Jim Jack, a lifelong Rangers supporter who was born and bred in Arthurlie Street, just a hop and a skip from Ibrox, was among the hardy souls who clung to the hope which sprung from McMinn's marauding runs. Jack said: "I was working overseas in 1984 and came back to find the football wasn't great, to say the least. I stayed in Cardonald and at that time you certainly didn't need a season ticket to guarantee you would get in, you could leave the bars at 2.45pm and still make it in for kick-off.

"Ted McMinn didn't play a lot of games or score a lot of goals but he was an industrious players and the fans will always give their support to a player who is giving their all, that is what we all want to see from everyone who wears the jersey. Of course it was Jock Wallace who took him to Ibrox and you could trust his judgement.

"Ted was a Dumfries lad but even at Ibrox he was considered one of us. He always spoke about coming up to watch Rangers and idolising Davie Cooper, you could imagine Ted standing beside you on the terraces. He gave the impression he was in awe when he first walked through the dressing room door, whereas so many players puff out their chests and expect to be the centre of attention from day one.

"There was no doubt he was ungainly – so often he would get to the by-line and go to cross with one foot but end up touching the ball away with the other before taking a fresh air swipe. We've all done that, and the supporters never got on his back even if things were going against the team when it happened. They could laugh along with Ted when it went wrong because it was so good when it went right, sometimes he just tried to be too clever."

Jack believes it was McMinn's bouncebackability that made him so endearing, not just to the Rangers fans. He added: "On my travels I made a point of getting down to Palmerston recently, simply because it was a ground I hadn't been to for many years. Speaking to the Queen of the South supporters in the bar afterwards, they still remember Ted McMinn fondly. He's one of those players who sticks in the memory when so many come and go without any impact. The Spaniards must have wondered what they had signed when he arrived at Seville but he never failed to win a set of supporters over, probably because he was prepared to sit and have a beer with the fans rather than standing apart from them."

Jack, now based in Aberdeen but still following his team home and abroad with the Fraserburgh-based Dave Smith Loyal, was brought up watching some of the club's legendary wingers. He holds McMinn up alongside the great names of the past, despite the player's occasional disciplinary lapses. He said: "I was born in 1952 and have been watching Rangers for as long as I can remember. I've used to be lifted over the turnstiles or wait until they opened the gates 20 minutes from the end to run in and collect beer bottles on the old grass hill to take to the off-licence for money for sweets. Alex Scott was in his prime then, before he was replaced by Willie Henderson. On the left there was Davie Wilson, one of my favourites, and then a succession of other great wingers. A player who can beat a man is always going to stand a good chance of endearing himself to the people in the stands, football is about entertainment after all.

"Ted had his fall-outs with Graeme Souness, there was the apocryphal tale of the time he infuriated the club by getting new windows in his flat but went to one of the rivals of the sponsor CR Smith. He was never one to conform. Even after the fall-outs he actually went on to play his best football in his last season. People often talk about Ted McMinn's virtuoso performance against Celtic in the first Old Firm game of the 1986/87 season, when Ian Durrant scored the winner, but I remember his performance in the League Cup semi-final on a wet Wednesday night against Dundee United just as well when he scored one and laid on the other for Ally McCoist. United just couldn't get near him that night, he would take the ball to defenders and go past them with a trick or a flick, rather than using his physique to knock the ball past them and chase it and was man of the match by a country mile."

The Tin Man was indeed a one off. Incidentally, the origins of the Tin Man tag are a mystery, even to the man himself. After all, he's watched the Wizard of Oz and astutely points out the Tin Man never ran – so that comparison doesn't hold water. Could it be simple rhyming slang or did the Rangers fans feel he didn't have a heart? Nobody knows, nobody really cares. Maybe the Wizard of Oz does hold the key, despite McMinn's protestations to the contrary. His straight-legged adventures down the wing had a metallic quality right enough. There's a more definite story behind his real name, Ted. Except it isn't his real name. Kevin Cuthbert McMinn actually picked up his new Christian name at school because his peers, showing observational skills beyond their years, noticed he ran as though he had a teddy bear under his arm. And perhaps a defender in his hip pocket.

His style of play and appearance had never been seen before and, in all likelihood, will never be seen again. He was at his bounding best when running at a vulnerable full-back, with his akward gait disguising an ability to bamboozle defenders and his inimitable style proving impossible to second guess. Mind you, sometimes defenders didn't have to second guess him because he would bamboozle himself.

McMinn claims his unpredicability was not unique to him. He said: "There's not one player in the world who knows what's going to happen. There was a time I miskicked the ball and ended up flat on my face and 40,000 people stood up and cheered. I won the fans over because they wanted something different."

According to McMinn, he nutmegged Celtic's Derek Whyte 15 times in one game. A bit of poetic licence undoubtedly, but not beyond the realms of possibility where the Tin Man was concerned. Supporters still talk about the day Whyte, who was Celtic's next great thing at the time, was torn to shreds. The ball didn't just go through his legs, it went round him, over him and every other way in a merciless performance from Rangers' on song king of the wing.

Moments like that left a lasting impression, at the root of a unique relationship as far as an Ibrox player and his supporters are concerned. Rangers is different to most other clubs. Up and down the land players earn cult status for their individual attributes and personal efforts but at Rangers that rarely counts for anything unless accompanied by a healthy dollop of success. McMinn is one of the few to have left with little in the way of precious metal while still managing to win a place in the bosom of the Gers faithful.

His promotion to regular starter coincided with a horrendous period for the club, with bad result after bad result plunging him and his team-mates to sixth in the top flight in 1985/86.

The depth of the problems at that time intensified the desire for individual heroes among the fans. Starved of a team effort, it was all they had in that difficult era. Average attendances slumped to an all-time low of 25,000 in 1985/86 and a group of fans who had been spoilt in the past were going cold turkey. In the 1970s there was a galaxy of stars but in the transitional period that followed the occasional twinkle in the distance had to suffice.

The board responded by replacing Wallace with Graeme Souness and the Scotland star found it difficult to accommodate a player who was as far removed from the stylised approach of his new manager as you could imagine. If Souness looked like a Rolls Royce on the park, McMinn was the football equivalent of a Reliant Robin with his awkward look – but under the bonnet he had the engine of a Ferrari and the handling to match, capable of tearing up the wing and meandering through defences in his own chaotic style.

It was, however, Souness who provided McMinn with two winner's medals to mark his time on Glasgow's south side, with nine starts and six substitute's appearances in the Premier Division title win of 1986/87 and a place in the starting 11 for the 2-1 League Cup final win against Celtic. Then he was gone.

In the end it was not style or ability that cost him a place in the Souness masterplan, it was discipline. The breach of curfew was followed with an incident on a night out in East Kilbride, which led to a court appearance and a two week suspension by his club late in 1986. In January 1987 Wallace returned with a second bid for his protege, having failed with a £200,000 offer previously, and his promise of £225,000 of Seville's cash swung the deal. From Castle Douglas beginnings, he was going global. Spain didn't know what was about to hit it.

As it happened, Souness did afford him the chance to go out on a winning note with an appearance from the bench in a 5-0 win against Clydebank at Ibrox. The starting 11 that took to the pitch that day illustrates just how marked the transformation had been at the club. Instead of McCloy, England star Chris Woods wore the No.1 jersey, Graham Roberts had arrived from Spurs to take his place in a defence featuring England skipper Terry Butcher alongside Dave McPherson, a fellow survivor from McMinn's league debut. Souness was adding his own steel to the midfield, with young Derek Ferguson earning rave reviews, Davie Cooper back at his best and Ian Durrant establishing himself as one of the country's most cultured prospects. Robert Fleck and Ally McCoist were in devastating form, with Fleck bagging a hat-trick in McMinn's swansong and McCoist contributing two. Times were changing, it was survival of the fittest and for McMinn it was time to spread his wings.

Jock Wallace took him to Seville and the ungainly Scot became an unlikely hit in La Liga. Jaime Bogus Figmento, a writer with the Spanish sports paper *Los Cojones*, was called upon to assess the chances of Jose Antonio Reyes transferring his talents to Arsenal. He credited two unusual sources for the inspiration behind the Reyes X-factor.

Figmento said: "The Sevillians say: 'Jock taught us; Ted inspired us'. With his inelegant Tin Man running style, erratic crossing and unquenchable zest for lager, he was the soul of football. The Seville orange is a bitter fruit, but the Scots turned it into a delicious conserve, at once sweet and tangy, that is a fixture of breakfast tables across the globe. So it was too that Wallace and McMinn took the unpalatable and sour football of our region and with their tartan magic transformed it into something delectable and desired the world over. Before they came we were inhibited, defensive, obdurate, dull. With their relaxed, easy-going Calvinist attitudes they put us in touch with our emotions and taught us how to embrace joy."

Joy is exactly what McMinn brought to tens of thousands of supporters every week, at every port of call along his voyage through British and European football. It was the surprise element that provided the excitement, that drew gasps of disbelief and astonishment from the fans. Sometimes they were positive gasps of wonderment, other times they were the type of gasps more normally reserved for occasions when a disaster is imminent. His meandering runs could go any one of two ways, very well or very badly.

The Spanish sojourn was short but it did afford the opportunity to prove he could live in exalted company in one of Europe's toughest leagues. Fans in Seville still talk about one particular occasion when he teased Atletico Madrid before tearing them apart, playing the role of matador and bull in one day.

Seville was an intriguing stop for the lone Ranger. As the Spaniards found out, he is not the type of player supporters forget. The club has, in recent years, gone from strength to strength with two consecutive Uefa Cup final appearances in 2006 and 2007. The latter showdown, against Espanyol, was hosted by Hampden Park. The prospect of a trip to Glasgow, the spiritual home of the Tin Man, brought the memories flooding back. Even Seville chief executive Jose Cruz name-checked McMinn in the preview press conference. Two decades on, he still has a hold on a set of supporters who have a history of lavishing appreciation on players out of leftfield. The most loyal followers call themselves Biris – after the Biri-Biri nickname given to Alhaji Momodo Nije, a Gambian import who was mercurial and unpredictable but touched a chord like no other player had done before. The ultras in the steeply banked stands of the Ramon Sanchez Pizjuan stadium loved him and revelled in his talents throughout the 1970s. In McMinn they had an heir apparent.

Maybe it shoudn't have been a surprise that McMinn caught the attention of the Spaniards. Just as he had been at Ibrox, he was something completely different. The emotions he provoked were greater than any other player of his generation, with the mix of intrigue and frustration coupled with excitement and expectation. Wallace used him in La Liga not just as a winger but occasionally from deep in midfield, where he could run at full tilt at startled opponents and cause a whole different set of problems than he could from his posting on the flank.

Wallace soon departed the land of oranges and McMinn was not far behind, with Derby County splashing out £300,000 to spark an endearing love affair between a club, a winger and its fans. Arthur Cox was the manager behind the neat bit of business, as the new man's performances propelled him to the verge of the Scottish national side as the World Cup finals in Italy in 1990 loomed large on the horizon as a shining target. A knee injury late in 1989 cut McMinn down in his prime, spending 14 months on the sidelines as he worked back to full fitness and blowing his World Cup dream into tiny pieces.

When he returned in 1992 it was if he had never been away. The Derby fans had their idol back, even it was only temporarily, and he was named the club's player of the year in 1991/92. McMinn, whose wife is secretary at Derby County, is among the most loved players in the history of the Rams despite staying for only a couple of eventful years.

In 1993 he switched to Birmingham before a spell with Burnley and then Joondalup City in Australia. In 1996 Australian sports journalist Mel Moffat, reported: "Ted's proving to be a big hit. He's only been playing a couple of weeks but everyone's impressed with him, particularly the fans, who seem to adore him." Spot the trend?

McMinn returned to England to move into coaching as assistant manager to former Rams colleague Mark Wright at Southport, Oxford United and Chester City. More recently McMinn has served as a summariser on BBC radio, covering Derby games.

All of his on-field achievements and off-field endeavours have, of course, been put in the shade by his battle against illness. The problems began to surface in July, 2005, when McMinn developed a limp during a round of golf. Having suffered from gout previously he was unconcerned but his condition worsened in the days that followed, struggling to walk and unable to stomach food or drink. Hospitalised due to dehydration, three days of tests revealed a vicious infection which began to kill the flesh on his foot. Three operations to try and combat the infection failed, surgeons recommended amputation of the leg below the knee. At McMinn's request they attempted a compromise but the outcome left the patient unable to walk properly and eventually he decided to accept the advice and agree to the amputation. Two days after the major surgery he discharged himself from hospital, way ahead of schedule, and rejected the suggestion he should confine himself to a wheelchair in favour of more physically draining crutches. When his prosthetic limb arrived, he went against the advice to use it for 20 minutes at a time to allow it to bed in – keeping it on for painful 12-hour stints as he learnt to walk all over again. Doctors cannot be certain where the infection stemmed from, theories include a scratch or bite while on holiday or the outcome of the countless painkilling injections he endured as a player.

McMinn appreciates he should not be portrayed as an angel struck down by cruel misfortune. Married four times, he was no stranger to living his life on the edge and enjoying some wild nights out. One of those included the breach of curfew that did not endear him to recently appointed manager Graeme Souness. He played few games after that incident as Souness adopted a hardline approach to his first job in management.

With typical spirit he fights on in the face of adversity, determined not to let disability become an insurmountable obstacle.

Over time he built up the strength and confidence in his limb to return to action on the golf course but finding something to get his teeth into outside of sport has been more difficult. Retired footballers tend not to be in huge demand for run of the mill employers and disabled ex-players are even less sought after. McMinn's response, in February 2007, was to decide if you can't join them then try and beat them. He founded Advent Couriers, a delivery and taxi service, and has thrown his heart and soul into building the business in and around his adopted Midlands home at Ashton on Trent.

There has also been time for charity assignments and he even embarked on a gruelling charity bike ride shortly after the operation, fittingly crossing the start line outside Ibrox before pedalling south on a 300 mile journey home to Derby accompanied by his wife Marian, former Gers team-mate Dave McKinnon and a group of friends as they embarked on a fund-raising drive for Derbyshire Royal Infirmary and the Murray Foundation, which supports Scottish amputees. Ted's Big Adventure, as it was tagged, was delayed by an hour due to a clamour for autographs.

The Rams played host to an all-star benefit match for McMinn in 2006, featuring a Derby select against a Rangers legends side. Ally McCoist and Gordon Durie, with a double, were on target in a 3-3 draw.

The result was immaterial, what was noticeable was the response from supporters. They travelled from across Europe and as far afield as North America and Australia to attend, in Britain they came from Thurso in the north to Taunton in the south. For a man who had been far from the public eye in the years preceding the game, it was an astonishing turnout. The Pride Park attendance record was shattered as 33,475 packed in to pay tribute to the man at the centre of all of the attention. The figure included 10,000 Rangers supporters and provided a glaringly obvious message, as if it was needed, that the Tin Man still has a place at Ibrox.

If anything the illness and disability has galvanised opinion. Previously there were two distinct camps, the pro-McMinn side balanced by those who failed to see the attraction. Now there appears to be unity, McMinn is one of their own and the Rangers supporters have rallied around him. In fact fans of all persuasions have rallied round, the messages of support that flooded in share some wonderful memories – from the Queen of the South fan who claimed McMinn, his club's "greatest ever" player, was the one man who could take a corner and still make it into the box to get on the end of it to the Rangers supporter who revelled in his tormenting of Old Firm foe Derek Whyte or the Falkirk supporter who just marvelled from afar at the talents of a player who could not be copied, no matter how many schoolboys tried to.

His struggles in later life have brought him back into the limelight and in return sent his popularity soaring. But McMinn is desperate not to play the sympathy card, understandably determined to stand tall in the face of adversity. He took knocks as a player, a man pursued by growling defenders for a living let's not forget, but nothing to compare to those in more recent years. Just as he did as a player, McMinn has picked himself up, dusted himself down and got on with the game. This time it's the game of life.

**MAGIC MOMENT:** The Souness era hit full flow when the inspirational skipper popped up with the goal to clinch the 1986 league title.

# TERRY BUTCHER
## *'CAPTAIN COURAGEOUS'* **1986-1990**

### **GERS CAREER:** Games 176; Goals 11

CULT STATUS can be a peculiar thing and lead to odd situations. In November 1990, with Butcher locked in dispute with Graeme Souness and destined for the exit door at Rangers, an audacious transfer swoop was launched. It wasn't AC Milan or Barcelona who had the recently retired England skipper in their sights – it was Inverness Clachnacuddin.

The Highland League side needed a defender after all, having conceded a record breaking 151 goals in the previous season. The recently retired England captain fitted the bill and the biggest name in British club football had him on their radar.

With Butcher kicking his heels in the reserves, Rangers supporting Clach chairman David Dowling made his move but had his hopes of a transfer coup dashed, albeit politely, by the Ibrox hierarchy. It left Dowling to reflect at the time: "Nothing ventured, nothing gained. People will laugh but the fact was Terry hasn't been playing and we thought we would take a chance."

The 20th anniversary of that cheeky attempt to do business has passed and the Highlanders could be forgiven for raising a glass in Butcher's honour. It certainly put them on the map.

Dowling remains convinced the unthinkable could have happened. With a skip in his voice, the Inverness businessman recalls what could have been his finest hour with affection.

He said: "We came in to take over the club in 1990, that was my first involvement, and not long after it became well publicised that Terry Butcher had played his last game for Rangers. We reasoned that it would probably take a few weeks for him to get everything ironed out at Ibrox to allow him to move on and thought in between he could come and play for us. The rule in the Highland League at that time was that you could loan players for up to three weeks, so it all fitted.

*There is no greatness without a passion to be great.*

**Anthony Robbins**

"I made the call to Campbell Ogilvie, who was secretary at Rangers at that time, to make the offer. Campbell politely declined but it was a serious approach from us. I think it was viewed as a publicity stunt at the time, probably by Rangers and everyone else, but that wasn't the case. I reckoned that Terry Butcher would have added at least 1,000 to our gate so even if I had to pay a couple of thousand a week to cover his wages it would have been worth our while.

"Terry was a massive player for Rangers a huge personality in Scottish football, not to mention an England captain. I've no doubt people would have turned out in great numbers if we had managed to take him up to Inverness. If Rangers had come to us with a financial package I would have matched it but it didn't go that far."

Dowling insists his affinity to Rangers did not cloud his judgement when he swooped for Butch. Instead he had his business head on, swayed by the huge pulling power of a personality of the magnitude of Butcher.

He added: "Clach were a bit of a laughing stock. In the season before myself and my fellow directors came in they had played 34 league games, losing 31 and getting draws in three. My kids were getting teased at school because their dad had bought a club in such a bad way and we wanted to send out a message. Terry Butcher would certainly have done that. If it had been a publicity stunt then it would have been one of the best ever. The story just ran and ran at the time and Clach were in the headlines for the first time in a long time. There is still that was carried in the papers hanging on the wall at the club.

"Terry was a great, great player for Rangers. His signing put a few thousand on the gates at Ibrox because people wanted to see what all the fuss was about and I'm sure it would have done the same for us at Clach."

Years later Dowling finally got to meet the man he had admired from afar and the experience did not leave him disappointed, with the Ibrox hero filling the role admirably.

The Clach chief said: "Terry did end up at Grant Street Park eventually, a few years ago when he was scouting. We took him into the boardroom for a dram and he was a great man, everything you would expect. I only wish we could have had him on the park instead of in the boardroom.

"When we tried to sign him we were away to Cove Rangers in our next game and I still remember their manager coming out to meet the bus – just in case Terry came walking off with the rest of the players."

Mind you, the Clach manager at the time was just as intrigued by the prospect of pencilling the name Butcher onto his team sheet. Boss Roshie Fraser found out about his signing target when his sister-in-law saw a report on television. Fraser said: "I honestly couldn't believe it. Can you imagine what my reaction would have been if I got off the bus at Allan Park to find Terry Butcher sitting outside the ground in his car with his boots in his hand?"

They weren't the only minnows to chance their arm either. In 1994 Ross County tried to lure Butcher even further north after he had been sacked by Coventry while Clydebank were also circling round Glasgow's big fish and Dumbarton attempted to tempt him with the manager's post in 1995. Long after his Rangers days had ended, he was still a big name and a big pull for fans. Clubs knew it, and beat a path to his door even when he entered his veteran years.

The defender almost never got that far though. Terry Butcher, honorary Braveheart, almost quit football when he was 18. The reason? Not injury, not lack of form but because he wasn't tough enough. By his own admission, as an 18 year-old he was scared to hurt opponents and took pelters from the Ipswich coaching staff for his perceived dearth of tackling ability and lack of aggression. His dad talked him out of it and Rangers fans should all raise a glass in his honour. Butcher, born in Singapore to a naval family, gradually became accustomed to fighting his corner and became a bruiser in the old fashioned way, a fearsome figure thanks to his 6ft 4inch frame but a gentle giant when extracted from the heat of the battle.

He and Graeme Souness did not always see eye to eye but even after dropping his captain from a cup semi-final the manager leapt to his defence, claiming: "It is the biggest decision I have made in my four years as manager at Ibrox. He has been the most important single factor in anything we have achieved. It was a momentous decision for me to take."

The image of Butcher, blood soaked and battered and bandaged in his England kit, is one of the football classics. He bears more scars than the average player, suffering a series of horrendous injuries in his quest to keep the ball out of his own net. He broke his leg in 1987, shattering the bone, but it was with Ipswich that his commitment almost cost his life. In 1982 he broke his nose and was hospitalised for five weeks, told by doctors that the blow had been near fatal as the broken bone had severed an artery. Did it impact on his approach to the game? Not in the slightest, as anyone who watched him charge in to challenge after challenge with apparent disregard for life and limb would testify.

He always wore his heart on his sleeve and let emotions run loose. In one League Cup final he stunned the crowd, and officials, by hurling the ball at the referee and in Aberdeen after one stormy encounter sparked a police investigation when he took his frustrations out on the referee's room door at Pittodrie. He would kick anything that moved to secure full points for Rangers, even if it did move courtesy of a pair of hinges.

That passion drew a thin line in the turf. Famously it catapulted Butcher and his team-mates from the back pages to the front pages of the national newspapers in 1988 when they stood trial following the Old Firm war at Ibrox the previous year. Butcher, Chris Woods and Graham Roberts joined Celtic striker Frank McAvennie in the dock as the central characters in the most high profile court case Scottish football has ever seen. Butcher and Woods were both found guilty of breach of the peace, fined a total of £750, while the charge against Roberts was found not proven and the Hoops star was found not guilty. They appeared at Glasgow Sheriff Court as the result of a melee which police and prosecutors claimed could have sparked a riot. The fracas had been started by a collision between McAvennie and Woods, resulting in a red card for the Rangers goalkeeper. Butcher was also sent for an early bath later in the match,

The court action was the fuel for a massive debate about police involvement in football matters but was deemed necessary to quell rising Old Firm tensions.

It became front page news but by that stage the England skipper was already used to his role as fodder for headline writers in Scotland. Before the ink had dried on his Rangers contract he became a massive character in the game north of the border and the supporters could not fail to be swept along. They had a new hero.

Butcher's arrival in the summer of 1986 was a major coup for Souness and the club. It was a notice of intent, the £750,000 signing of the Ipswich and England star proving Scotland was no longer going to be a football backwater. Rangers were back as a force.

It cost £725,000 to take Butcher north, a deal which took the total spending for the close season to £2million. It was a staggering spree and one that left the Rangers fans giddy as the new season loomed.

There have been more expensive signings, there have been more controversial signings and there have been signings that in the long term have been more beneficial. But, when it comes to sheer impact, the arrival of Terry Butcher wins the day.

In one fell swoop, Graeme Souness sent out an emphatic message of intent. It was delivered to the media and the opposition but most importantly to the supporters who had suffered through a torturous period of underachievement. If any group had a right to be sceptical it was the fans but any lingering doubts about the direction Souness would take the club were swatted away on August 1, 1986.

Butcher's big money move was part of £2million spree by a determined Rangers board, aided and abetted by a manager who had the bit between his teeth.

Souness himself had cost £500,000 from Sampdoria in Italy and he quickly invested £600,000 in England goalkeeper Chris Woods from Norwich and £175,000 on Watford striker Colin West. The £725,000 spent on Butcher came on the same day as £75,000 was handed to Israeli side Macabi Haifa to land Avi Cohen. Quicker than you could say 'we are the champions', millions had been emptied from the Ibrox coffers.

Rangers had to bid high for Butcher, who was allowed to move on by an Ipswich side who had been relegated from England's top flight.

Continental clubs, who had already lured the best of British in the form of Ian Rush, Gary Lineker and Mark Hughes, across the channel were on the scent but the stiffest competition came from Tottenham. The Rangers offer blew all of the competition out of the water and they got their man, leaving Souness to confirm: "Terry is exactly the type of player I want – the best of his type."

Butcher, who was paraded for the first time in front of an expectant Rangers support in a friendly against Bayern Munich at Ibrox in early August 1986, had already won 45 caps and proved he could live in exclusive company during the 1986 World Cup finals.

He took his competitive bow in Edinburgh on August 9 that year in a 2-1 Premier Division defeat away to Hibs at Easter Road. It was one of only six league defeats the Light Blues would suffer that term and Butcher was a bedrock for that success, missing just a single game in his maiden season in Govan as his side beat Celtic to the title by six points and was an ever present in the League Cup run which culminated in a 2-1 win against the Hoops in the final. To cap it all, the skipper scored Rangers' goal in the 1-1 draw against Aberdeen at Pittodrie, the penultimate game of the season, that clinched the league. It was a satisfying start to his career in Scotland, although he almost missed out on the chance to see the league flag unfurled when he was invited to play for a Rest of the World select in the English Football League's centenary celebation game at Wembley in 1987. Suspended from club football, Butcher could play no part on the field on the day the ceremony took place but Souness refused to let him travel to London for the glamour game under the twin towers – Butcher was his captain and he wanted him to lead the celebrations at Ibrox. There were no arguments from a man who was lapping up the taste of victory he would soon become accustomed to.

Speaking during his playing days he said: "Graeme Souness told me he wanted to build the best side in Britain and I wanted to be part of it. What I did not realise was the enormous pressure there is in the game in Scotland. My wife and I have been made very welcome but sometimes the attention of the fans is overwhelming and you are very much aware of the fact that Rangers are expected to win every game." Butcher was not one to shirk that responsibility, he could hardly hide given his stature in any case. He grew to accept and love the part of Rangers hero and even after his managerial sojourns back home in England it was always Scotland that he returned to when employment did not dictate otherwise, he enjoyed being part of the Rangers family and now retirement did not take him out of that. It merely moved him back a step and let him enjoy it even more. Butcher came to call Scotland home and one of the proudest Englishmen in history found a home in Scotland, making a mockery of the Auld Enemy divide.

With his stock rising week by week in the eyes of the supporters, disaster struck just four months into his second season when he broke his leg in a game against Aberdeen in November 1987. It was a cruel blow for the player but perhaps a blessing in disguise for the club, who were bracing themselves for a £1million bid from Manchester United when injury struck. Instead Sir Alex Ferguson turned to Gary Pallister.

Without their inspirational skipper Rangers faltered in the league, finishing third behind champions Celtic and runners-up Hearts. They did win the League Cup in Butcher's absence but were back at their mean spirited defensive best in time for the start of the 1988/89 season, in which Butcher led them to a Premier Division and League Cup double.

It was the start of the nine in a row journey, the first building block towards a piece of history.

The six point advantage they had carved out over Aberdeen by the time they lifted the trophy in May 1989 was stretched to seven the following year. In each of the two campaigns Butcher missed just two games. At times he was prone to calamitous errors and dramatic own goals but in the main he proved to be a formidable addition to the Rangers squad, both on and off the field.

His international commitments dovetailed, in the main, with his club success. Butcher was already an established international when he arrived at Ibrox, that was a major part of the appeal for Souness. However, his promotion to the role of his national team's captain dovetailed with his glory years in Glasgow.

He had a cupboard full of caps to his credit when he was recruited and was the lynch-pin around which the England team of the late 1980s revolved around. The leg break which kept him out of the 1988 European Championships was a crushing blow for his country, who fell apart defensively in that tournament.

Bobby Robson had hoped to have his defensive rock at the heart of his push for international honours, planning to pin his hopes on a Butcher and Tony Adams partnership. Intensive treatment at the

Lilleshall rehabilitation centre in a desperate attempt to avoid the inevitable failed to speed him back to full fitness.

Butcher had skippered England for the first time in a European Championship qualifier against Yugoslavia in 1986, just months after joining Rangers as club captain.

He had to wait almost three years to be handed the armband again, replacing Bryan Robson as the Manchester United midfielder's injury problems intensified. Peter Shilton, who had rejected the captaincy once before, was bypassed as Bobby Robson headed straight for his former Ipswich protege. The manager's justification was simple: "Butcher is a great player and the others respect him. That's a great asset. He is a good talker and motivator as well as being a commanding figure."

He also had experience, having amassed 64 caps by the time he took on the responsibility permanently in 1989, in time for the 1990 World Cup finals in Italy.

Those factors were not always enough to win favour with the notoriously demanding and fickle England fans. In 2007, when Frank Lampard was booed by his own country's fans for his contribution against Brazil at the new Wembley, it brought the memories flooding back for Butcher, who had himself been targeted by the Three Lions brigade. He always felt his club ties, both during his time with Ipswich and Rangers, had been the root cause of the indifference. Had he been an Arsenal player, according to Butcher, there would have been no such problems but his allegiances somehow made him inferior to rivals such as Tony Adams in the view of Joe Public. The criticism from the stands simply strengthened Butcher's resolve to prove his detractors wrong and he came so very close to doing that in the most impressive way imaginable.

Everyone remembers how it ended but, long before the agonising semi-final defeat at the hands of Germany in the famous penalty shoot-out, the campaign had begun in very different circumstances.

Butcher and his team-mates bowed out as the gallant losers, undone by the lottery of penalties. They left Italy broken hearted but with pride intact.

When they had arrived for the start of the tournament they had been written off by their own country's press as no hopers.

Butcher, who had experienced the full force of the media scrum at the 1986 World Cup finals in Mexico and in 1982 in Spain, was prepared to take a battering and determined to prove the detractors wrong. He played the part of Captain Courageous to a tee, with the image of his blood soaked shirt and bandaged head from the Italy finals capturing the moment forever. He led by example, never afraid to stick his head in where it hurt. Sometimes hurting heads too, with his confessions of deliberately head butting a Tunisian opponent in a 1990 finals warm-up game causing a storm after his retirement from the national team.

The World Cup semi-final against Germany proved to be his final appearance on the biggest stage of them all, on the back of his only defeat as England captain. After 10 years and 77 caps he brought the curtain down on a distinguished career on the international stage. Bobby Robson had departed, Graham Taylor had been appointed and Butcher felt it was time for a changing of the guard on the playing front too. At the age of 31 and entering the final year of his contract with Rangers, he declared his intention to devote himself to his club side.

That was no more than Souness demanded, with Butcher later admitting that the Govan gaffer had on several occasions used bogus injuries to excuse his players from international duty with Scotland and England. Rangers were the cash cow and Souness expected a suitable return for that investment, including devotion.

Butcher may also have felt he had to prove his worth to the hard task master in the Rangers dug-out after four trophy filled years with the club. His fifth season proved turbulent, to say the least and it all came to a head on September 26, 1990, when Rangers ran out at Hampden for the League Cup semi-final against Aberdeen.

The Light Blues in the crowd were stunned to see the side take to the field without its captain. Butcher, along with fellow star Mark Hateley, had been bombed out.

The defender had suffered the unexpected fate after faltering in a 2-1 league defeat against Dundee United in the previous game, the first loss of the Premier Division campaign.

With his 32nd birthday looming, Butcher had undergone a knee operation after the World Cup finals and, by his own admission, had struggled to get back to full fitness in time for the new season.

For the semi-final it was John Brown and not Terry Butcher who filled the No.6 shirt that had, up to that point, been his sole property.

The defeat to Dundee United proved to be his last appearance in the jersey of the club he had taken to heart but the controversy raged on long after he had trooped off the pitch at Tannadice after that disappointment.

Butcher decided not to attend the semi-final after being dropped, with the decision hitting him like a punch to the gut. Despite public protestations that there had been no fallout, it was common knowledge that the relationship between manager and captain had been strained at various points. They were two similar characters, committed beyond the point at which most people would draw the line, and it inevitably led to heated moments.

The atmosphere became bitter towards Butcher's final days with the club. Souness delivered what he considered to be an ace as the conflict moved to a tie-break after verbal volleys in both directions, calling a press conference at Ibrox to reveal that his captain had refused the offer of an olive branch. Souness told a stunned audience that he had asked Butcher to play in the League Cup final against Celtic but the player had declined. Souness, the master spin doctor, had piled the pressure on a player who had been granted his transfer request after being dumped into the reserves alongside the Rangers kids and had become deeply unhappy. The manager used the press conference to claim Butcher had refused to play in the final, which Rangers went on to win 2-1, because he had lost his feeling for Rangers and had his heart set on a move away. It was a clever move by the coach, aware that the tide of public opinion could quite easily turn against him if he did not dampen the grass root support for the captain.

The revelations quelled any fears Souness had of a revolt from the supporters who had been concerned about the treatment of their hero. Instead, Butcher's departure became accepted and the club moved on.

In time those revelations have been forgotten, they never damaged Butcher's reputation beyond repair, even if some in the Light Blue legions have never quite been able to look at him with the same affection.

The Butcher-Rangers divorce became official in November, 1990, when the worst kept secret in football was confirmed. Coventry City manager John Sillett was out, Butcher was in as player boss. Butcher was just 31 but having watched Souness embrace his dual role at Rangers with purpose, he was hungry to do the same. Success was not quite as instant for Butcher as it had been for Souness and his managerial career was a slow burner to say the least. Dismissed by

Coventry in 1992, he took over at Sunderland in 1993 but struggled to waken the sleeping giant.

He returned to embark on a career in the hotel trade in Scotland in 1994, rejecting a succession of offers to return to management in the lower leagues until answering a call from Dundee United to join the coaching staff. Even after leaving Ibrox he knew how to win favour with the fans, laying on a nine course banquet at his Bridge of Allan Hotel to mark the nine in a row celebrations in 1997. He had after all led the club to the first two of those historic title wins.

His football rebirth at Tannadice in turn led to his appointment as manager at financially stricken Motherwell, where the Rangers hero came into his own as he rallied a youthful Well squad and turned them into a competitive force in the SPL. A big money move to Sydney United in 2006 did not work out, with Butcher returning to British football with Brentford in 2007 after a brief stint helping neighbour Jimmy Bone on the Partick Thistle coaching staff.

The managerial chapter in Butcher's life story is intriguing. Here is a man who as a player was one of the game's great captains, he led by example with fearless and courageous performances and was a supreme organiser. It appeared at times that Butcher's arms did almost as much work as his legs, pointing and waving with ferocity as he cajoled his team through every match. The fact he went about his business with an honesty and integrity, despite the ruthless streak of a natural born winner, made him a Rangers captain in the traditional mould. He was made for the job, although the fact he was also picking up trophies with impressive regularity made the appointment all the more acceptable to the man on the street.

Yet as a manager he struggled. He had every component a chairman would pick when preparing the blueprint for the coaching machine to take any club to the next level but at both Coventry and Sunderland it simply did not click, as so many of the game's great performers have found.

The renaissance came with Motherwell when most, maybe even the man himself, must have thought his hopes of ever managing at the top level again were long gone. With the Steelmen he found himself in what turned out to be the ideal scenario to ignite the embers which had been burning since his Sunderland demise, with his back against the wall and seemingly no way out of the plight the club found itself in. Well, a club in administration, had no money and seemingly no hope but Butcher used that as a tool as he rebuilt from the bottom up and constructed a young team full of the type of desire and never say die spirit that had formed such a large part of his own playing career. Taken out of that environment and thrust into the more glamorous setting of Sydney he once again struggled to set the managerial heather alight, with underdogs Motherwell he had found his forte. For his next assignment he chose Brentford before hooking up with George Burley on the Scotland coaching staff. He finally made it to the Highlands when he took charge of Caley Thistle in 2009, decades after Clach's failed bid to land the big man, and led the north men to the First Division championship the following year.

Whether based in Lanarkshire, Sydney or the Highlands he will always be a huge figure in the history of Rangers, in at the start of the Souness revolution and in place for the early steps of nine in a row. Yet, Butcher actually only played three full seasons for the club. That relatively short stop is out of sync with his standing in the eyes of the fans, his achievements in a short space of time, and part in restoring the club to the top of the tree, responsible for knocking the normal rationale out of kilter and earning him legendary status. Think Rangers under Souness and automatically you think of Terry Butcher.

**MAGIC MOMENT:** Walters completed a
five-star performance with the fifth goal
in the 5-1 win against Celtic in 1988.

# MARK WALTERS
## *'THE TRAILBLAZER'* **1988-1991**

**GERS CAREER:** Games 144; Goals 52

NYONE IN this game who wants to be at the top has got
to realise that along the way the disappointments can be
greater and the criticism even
worse. With those words, Aston Villa
manager Graham Taylor sent Mark Walters
off to Rangers primed and ready to bring
Scottish defences to their knees.

Taylor's worldly wise words came in
response to concerns that Walters would
find his path to success in Scotland
blocked by racism. He made an almost
casual observation as his protégé prepared
to join the Graeme Souness revolution,
claiming: "Obviously Mark could come in
for some insults because of his colour." As
any football fan knows, Graham Taylor is
a man who loves to be right. On this one
occasion he must have yearned for the chance to be proven wrong.
Unfortunately for Scottish football, the assessment hit the target. It
was 1988, not 1908, but attitudes were stuck in the past.

Walters had to develop immunity to the vile hatred which spilled
from Scotland's terraces in his early days north of the border.
England had at last started to make headway in banishing racism

from football and Aston Villa had been pushing back the waves for years, although Walters was no stranger to racial tension despite the city's reputation as a cosmopolitan centre. From a young age he grew up in the troubled Lozells area, which developed a reputation as an area blighted by conflict. Those difficulties were overcome and the experience would stand Walters in good stead in football. It was as a pupil at Holte Comprehensive in Lozells that the raw talent began to be nurtured but the social lessons outside of the game were as valuable in the years ahead as any coaching session. At his old club Walters had followed in the footsteps of those who broken down the boundaries but at Rangers he filled the role of pioneer.

As he ran out at Parkhead for his debut he was greeted by the sight of Celtic fans decked out in monkey suits, with bananas littering the track throughout the game as the new boy was targeted by the fans of his new Old Firm rivals. At Tynescastle just 14 days later there were similar scenes, with bananas

*Fans don't boo nobodies.*

**Reggie Jackson**

again hurled in his direction by Hearts fans and allegations of verbal abuse from the opposition team. It forced the SFA to launch an investigation but it was not just Celtic and Hearts fans who found themselves in the dock.

Rangers also had to root out a supporter who had turned on the club's own player during a game against Morton inside the first three weeks of his stay in Glasgow. An Ibrox season ticket holder was banned indefinitely as the then head of security Alistair Hood promised to get tough on any fans who dragged Rangers into the racism row that was proving to be a scar on the face of Scottish football.

Labour MP Brian Wilson bucked the trend of outrage, calling for calm in the aftermath of the shameful scenes that greeted Walters in Scotland. Wilson, who at that time was the parliamentary adviser to the Scottish Professional Footballers Association, claimed the minority of hard core racists would exploit the publicity their actions were generating.

Wilson said: "Almost exclusively the banana brigade are daft boys and social inadequates who, having been confronted with something unfamiliar, have reacted in a crass, copy-cat fashion. But let's not box them into that corner by condemning, without any attempt to reform. The obvious irony of Rangers' own position in these matters is, itself, bound to cause many old prejudices to be reassessed."

Wilson claimed the fact Ibrox fans were being forced to address the thorny issue of racism might in turn lead them to grasp the nettle of sectarianism. He acknowledged the Rangers faithful had decided the "colour didn't matter" and used the issue as a platform to call for religious differences to be cast aside in the same manner.

Unfortunately, just as sectarianism will linger on in the murky backwaters of the game, racism will survive in football for as long as it forms part of society. Walters and his enigmatic performances in light blue helped enormously in shaping attitudes amongst Rangers supporters. He ceased to become the first black player to turn out for the club and instead became a star in his own right. His race became irrelevant, not least to the tens of thousands of impressionable youngsters who spent hours attempting to perfect his distinctive double shuffle in playgrounds and parks up and down the country. I should know, I was one of them.

Celtic's own supporters received a similar wake up call when Paul Elliot arrived in Glasgow soon after. He may not have boasted the same skill or ability as Walters but he still won a place in the hearts of the Hoops fans and became Scotland's player of the year in 1991.

Yet, almost two decades since Walter blazed a trail at Rangers, the ignorant minority continues to grab headlines all too frequently. In 2006 a group of Airdrie United fans turned up at Gretna wearing white hoods in a chilling message aimed at young opposition player Matthew Berkeley. In 2007 St Johnstone striker Jason Scotland was on the receiving end of verbal abuse from the stands in a Scottish Cup tie at Motherwell. Any notion of smugness surrounding Scottish football and racism can be banished quicker than a Walters turn.

The fight has to go on, with the Show Racism the Red Card campaign targeting primarily the up and coming generation of supporters. It is a long term strategy with a long term goal, one that has to be attacked with tenacity if repeats of the most high profile incidents are to be avoided in the future. The SRTRC campaign is not giving up on offenders as lost causes, with coordinators insisting "mindsets" can be changed. The main stick to attack the problem is publicity but a crop of homegrown ethnic players would surely do far more than any poster campaign.

Only one Scottish-born non-white player has ever been capped by his country, a staggering statistic. Andrew Watson, the first black player to wear the dark blue jersey in the 1880s, was in fact born in the British colony of Guyana. Paul Wilson, a Celtic player of mixed-race descent, was capped in the mid-1970s but since then the progress has been painfully slow.

Rangers did have high hopes for Jaz Juttla, born in Glasgow of Indian descent, but he has drifted down to the junior ranks. The club still actively scouts the Asian leagues on their patch for new talent with the hope of breaking the mould, just as they did when Walters was recruited. Seeds are being sown and when the crops begin to bear fruit the minority in the crowds could find themselves even more isolated.

The recruitment of Walters all those years ago made a statement about the determination within the new management team at Rangers to break down boundaries where prejudice was concerned but the football message it sent out cannot be underestimated. There was a political element to the decision by Graeme Souness to pursue Walters but it was based purely on football pedigree.

It is easy to make the assumption Rangers made Mark Walters but his pre-Ibrox career cannot be overlooked. Born in Birmingham, he joined boyhood favourites Aston Villa straight from school and was just 17 when he was promoted to the first team by manager Tony Barton in 1982.

Villa stood on the brink of greatness as a teenager laden with tricks and brimming with enthusiasm was unleashed on England's First Division. Less than a month after Walters took his bow, his club became European Cup winners. Victory over Bayern Munich, when Peter Withe scored the only goal of a tense final in Rotterdam, put the Midlands side on a pedestal. Their rookie winger did not play on that famous night but he was knocking on the door and the fact, despite his inexperience and tender years, he was capable of forcing his way into arguably the best side in Villa's history speaks volumes for his ability.

Walters earned his first winner's medal when he lined up for Aston Villa in the European Super Cup final of 1983, when the Birmingham side humbled Barcelona 3-1 over two legs to be crowned undisputed kings of the continent. The Englishmen were defeated 1-0 at the Nou Camp but the return match followed a different script. With the Spaniards reduced to 10 men early in the second half, Villa took charge. A Gary Shaw goal took the game into extra time and Walters found himself playing a key role in the comeback, taken down in the box after coming on as a substitute to earn the penalty that led to Gordon Cowans putting the hosts 2-1 ahead on aggregate. A Ken McNaught goal clinched a famous victory and a European double.

Domestically life on the claret side of the city's divide was more frustrating for Walters, coming into a side that enjoyed success on foreign soil in his first season but could not break free from mid-table in the First Division. For all the euphoria of the win against Bayern in the Netherlands, the harsh statistics tell the story of a club on the slide.

In 1984, at the end of Walters' first full season as a professional, the club finished respectably in sixth place. Two 10th place berths followed before a drop to 16th by the summer of 1986. Worse was to follow, with Walters suffering the indignity of playing in the side which surrendered top flight status by finishing rock bottom with just eight victories in 42 games in the 1986/87 term.

He at least played a part in regaining a First Division place, with Villa bouncing straight back by finishing runners-up to Millwall in the Second Division. Midway through the season he was propelled from England's second tier to Scotland's leading league when Rangers came in to tempt him away from the club that had given him his big break.

Mark Everton Walters was hot property in the closing months of 1987. Aston Villa were in the Second Division but were flying high and the winger was attracting a string of admirers. Everton looked to lead the chase but they failed to meet the Birmingham club's £500,000 valuation. Rangers displayed far less hesitancy and blew the competition away with the personal package on offer.

Villa boss Graham Taylor did not want to lose his talented winger but said: "I knew that would be it the minute he walked into Ibrox to talk terms with Graeme Souness."

On top of a reputed £50,000 signing on fee, Walters was reported to have had a £2,000 weekly wage lavished upon him. As odd as it sounds now, with that type of money just as easily lost behind the sofa of most Premiership stars, he joined an elite band of players earning a six figure salary. Newspapers at the time ran wage comparison tables. His cash-laden contract was big news, outstripping the Prime Minister by more than £40,000 and the chairman of British Rail by more than £20,000. It highlighted just how far Rangers were prepared to go in the club's pursuit of success, coming at the time the club had tested the water with a £750,000 offer for St Mirren midfielder Ian Ferguson.

The signing took the Souness spending spree to a staggering £5million in the space of just 18 frantic months in the transfer market. Taylor, who went on to cap Walters for England, added: "Managers like Souness and Kenny Dalglish seem to stand in front of a shop full of players and simply point to the man they want."

Not that the winger's manager grudged the move, with Taylor admitting: "Mark has got the kind of gifts that make him something special. Now he has got the platform at Rangers and is surrounded by so much talent. If he does the trick then the world's his oyster."

The praise heaped on Walters before he had even kicked a ball whetted the appetite for a support hungry for another feast of flank trickery as the deletion of Davie Cooper from the Ibrox menu loomed large. Cooper, who was struggling with injury when his heir apparent rolled into town, would soon be on his way to Motherwell. The fact Walters was quick to prove his ability to fill his boots made the transition painless for fans nervous about the loss of a veteran who had been their darling. Walters, a bundle of energy and livewire from the first whistle to last, was a different player but had the same ability to thrill. Taylor even hailed him as the next John Barnes but Walters arrived with different hopes. He harboured ambitions of a central role for Rangers, claiming that was his most effective position, but it was out wide that he sparkled for Souness and brought misery to Scottish Premier Division rearguards.

The Englishman arrived eager to get started, already well briefed on what lay in store. Neale Cooper, a team-mate at Villa, had told him that the Birmingham city derbies were like a reserve match compared to the Old Firm rivalry and the new recruit soon found that out for himself.

His debut would be at Parkhead just two days after his Hogmanay arrival in 1987. He had barely had time to catch his breath when he plunged head first into the deep end of Glasgow football life.

From a side struggling to break free from the Second Division, Walters found himself parachuted into a team still basking in the reflective glory of the previous season's Premier Division and League Cup double. The scent of silver polish was thick in the air at Ibrox but the new boy would have to wait, having arrived too late for the League Cup triumph that brought the campaign's sole trophy.

His introduction in the Old Firm game on January 2, 1988, ended in a 2-0 defeat despite the promptings of a new attacking weapon who showed in flashes the sharpness that would prove fatal to Celtic in years to follow. Despite the intimidation off the park and the traditional cut and thrust of the Glasgow derby on the field, Walters showed composure on the ball and a willingness to run at opponents with pace and poise.

Casting the rose tinted glasses to one side, not every one of the frequent Souness cross-border raids was a roaring success. For every Terry Butcher there was a Mel Sterland, for every Ray Wilkins there was a Mark Falco. Which camp would Walters fall into? Decidely the former, he went into the side at Parkhead and couldn't be shifted for the remainder of the season. He was signed as a creator but also discovered a scoring touch within weeks of signing on at Ibrox, with seven goals in the final 12 league outings.

By the time his first full season rolled around, in the summer of 1988, Walters was acclimatised to the Scottish game and ready to hit the ground running. He missed just six league games as Rangers beat Aberdeen to the title by six points and became an accomplished big game performer, not least on the Old Firm stage. He scored in three of the four Premier Division encounters with Celtic in the 1988/89 campaign, most notably in the 5-1 win at Ibrox and a double in the 4-1 canter in the second home game.

The 1988/89 League Cup had the mark of Walters stamped all over. He was on target in the 3-0 win against Clyde in the opening game, had the net bulging in the 6-0 rout against Clydebank, scored again in the 4-1 quarter-final win against Dundee and grabbed a double against Hearts in the 3-0 semi-final success to put his club on the road to a 3-2 final victory against Aberdeen.

He attacked 1989/90 at full pelt, again an integral part of the Souness masterplan as the early rounds of nine in a row developed. The league was again in the bag, this time the margin over Aberdeen stretched to seven points. It was a team packed full of strong characters but Walters had the mental resolve to match anything Chris Woods, Gary Stevens, Terry Butcher, Richard Gough, Ray Wilkins, Ally McCoist , Mo Johnston, Trevor Steven or any of the other international stars brought to the table. Souness admired his ability to keep his cool, to live in the pressure cooker. Indeed, Walters was quickly put on penalty duty by a gaffer who knew a thing or two about the big occasion.

He was dependable from the spot but ironically it was when strikers McCoist and Johnston took on that burden that he went on to enjoy his most prolific period, in goalscoring terms at least. The 1990/91 season would be the swansong for the man who lit up Scottish football with his razor sharp skills and it was a fitting one.

The league was won in the most nerve wracking of manners, with victory on the final day of the season against Aberdeen securing the prize and the nine in a row tower began to take shape. Walters was architect, project manager and builder rolled into one. He was the schemer behind so many of the goals from the Mark Hateley, Ally McCoist and Mo Johnston striking department but he actually emerged from the title race as the club's leading Premier Division scorer with 12 goals to his credit and one better off than either Johnston or McCoist and two ahead of Hateley. As usual, he scored freely against Celtic and Hearts – the two teams who had given him such a painful introduction to Scottish football suffered most.

In the League Cup, the other trophy the club picked up in his final year, he put the Hoops to the sword once again as he and Richard Gough did the damage in a 2-1 win. It was another sweet moment in a sugar-laced Ibrox career.

For those who swayed with every twist and turn from their seats in the Ibrox stand, the England career of a Rangers hero is one of the great mysteries. Walters played for his country at every level, capped as a schoolboy while trying to carve out a place for himself at Aston Villa and again for the under-21 team after making the breakthrough in the club game.

He had a long wait to complete the set, aged 27 by the time he made his full England debut. That came in 1991 when he played his part in a 1-0 win over New Zealand in Auckland. Bobby Robson, a regular spectator of Rangers games as he kept tabs on his national skipper Terry Butcher and Chris Woods as well as the rest of the English contingent in Govan, had studiously ignored the undoubted talents of Walters.

It was Graham Taylor who gave the Midlands man his shot at international glory but he proved to be a one-hit wonder, with his appearance against the Kiwis proving his one and only senior appearance with the Three Lions on his chest. Just weeks later Walters became a Liverpool player but the familiarity of playing in the English league did not enhance his prospects. Again it was John Barnes who proved a thorn in his side, an impossible obstacle to shift in his quest for international opportunities. The 1991 chance came as

Taylor looked for a deputy for the injury blighted Barnes, with Walters joining John Salako as well as Andy Sinton and Tony Daley in staking a claim for the berth.

It also came at a time when Walters was winding down his Rangers exertions and readying himself for an all new challenge. Graeme Souness was a huge admirer of the winger he had plucked from the backwater of the English Second Division. He had given the Birmingham-born star his chance to shine on the Old Firm stage and gave him another huge platform when he returned from his new base in Liverpool to hand over a cheque for £1.3million in 1991 to haul him back south of the border to Anfield.

Whisked away from his adoring Ibrox public, Walters received a more mixed reception on Merseyside after his early promise failed to materialise into a concerted period of good form. He played his part in two successful runs to FA Cup and League Cup success, in 1992 and then 1995, but was restricted to a watching brief from the bench in both finals. The departure of Souness did not boost the winger's chances, with successor Roy Evans adopting a more measured and defensive approach in his attempt to bring league glory back to the expectant Kop fans.

His cause was not helped by the fact he was taken in as a replacement for a fading John Barnes. A tough assignment and an unforgiving one. In the end it was Steve McManaman who emerged from the considerable shadow cast by Barnes to become the new darling of Anfield.

Walters, despite highlights including the winner in a 3-2 aggregate win against Auxerre in Europe after his side had trailed 2-0 following the first leg and a hat-trick against Coventry in the league, found himself drifting down the pecking order and was sent out on loan to Stoke and Wolves before joining Southampton early in 1996.

To class the Liverpool career of Walters as a failure would be as big a mistake as to forget his Aston Villa shift. He played 115 more games in the famous jersey than most ever manage and knocked home 19 valuable goals over the course of five years on the Reds' payroll.

In the summer of 1996 he moved on to Swindon Town and spent three productive years with the club before switching to Bristol Rovers, where he again proved a big hit over a three year period. In 2002, just over a month before his 38th birthday, the winger called time on a career of more than 20 years.

Since then he has been taken full circle, back where it all began at Aston Villa where the under-14 side at the club's academy benefit from the experience of a man who combined skill with commitment throughout his playing days. The Villa academy is one of the most succesful in the Premiership, churning out first team players roughly 10 times more frequently than the average club in the English top flight. The task for Walters is to keep that rate going and it is one he is attacking with relish. Dion Dublin, himself a former Villa star, used a BBC documentary to point the finger at clubs for failing to offer black coaches an opportunity in the game, a big factor in what he viewed as continued institutional racism in the sport, but that is not something the Midlands side can be accused of with both Walters and fellow flying winger Tony Daley both enlisted and highly valued. In fact, when rookies Ashley Young and Gabriel Agbonlahor were unleashed on the Premiership in 2007 they drew inevitable comparisons with the Daley and Walters dream team of yesteryear.

For Walters the club coaching commitments have been combined with a day job as a PE teacher. While he finds himself in the grip of Midlands life his connections to Glasgow remain strong, still finding the time to turn on the style of the Rangers veterans in the Sky Masters exhibitions and looking as fit now as he did in his prime, still as athletic and energetic as he ever was and still producing moments of match changing skills even if it is on a smaller stage.

He had the ability but Walters also had the physical strength to live in hurly-burly of the game. Had he not been lured south by Liverpool, he would surely have remained key right through to the climax of nine in a row. To watch him in Masters tournaments turning on the style in light blue once again, it looks as though he has never been away with the trademark balance and reflexes not dampened by the mists of time.

He also holds a more official post in the Rangers heirarchy, appointed the first honorary member of the Rangers Supporters Trust when it was founded in 2003 in a mark of the respect he is held in by the fans he left with so many glowing memories in Govan. Just like Ted McMinn his stay was relatively short in duration, at least in comparison to a John Greig or David Meiklejohn, but he used his time to good effect and gave his all for the cause whenever he ran out with the Rangers crest on his chest.

**MAGIC MOMENT:** The original Golden Balls became the club's undisputed goal king in 1996 when he surpassed Bob McPhail's achievements.

# ALLY McCOIST
## 'SUPER ALLY' 1983-1998

### GERS CAREER: Games 581; Goals 355; Caps 61

CHRIS WOODS, Ally Dawson, Stuart Munro, Graeme Souness, Dave McPherson, Terry Butcher, Bobby Russell, Colin West, Ian Durrant, Ted McMinn, Derek Ferguson, Robert Fleck, Jimmy Nicholl, Cammy Fraser, Davie Cooper, Hugh Burns, Nicky Walker, Scott Nisbet, Dave McFarlane, Dougie Bell, Craig Paterson, Graham Roberts, Neil Woods, Jimmy Phillips, Billy Kirkwood, John McGregor, Avi Cohen, Robert Falco, Ian McCall, Trevor Francis, Richard Gough, Ray Wilkins, Mark Walters, John Brown, Jan Bartram, Iain Ferguson, Gary McSwegan, Gary Stevens, Kevin Drinkell, Ian Ferguson, Andy Gray, Eric Ferguson, Neale Cooper, Tom Cowan, Mel Sterland, Mo Johnston, Bonni Ginzburg, Davie Dodds, Stuart McCall, Nigel Spackman, Chris Vinnicombe, Mark Hateley, Peter Huistra, Terry Hurlock, Oleg Kuznetsov, John Spencer, Brian Reid, Andy Goram, David Robertson, Trevor Steven, Alexi Michailichenko, John Morrow, Dale Gordon, Steven Pressley, Lee Robertson, Paul Rideout, Ally Maxwell, David Hagen, Neil Murray, Steve Watson, Fraser Wishart, Charlie Miler, Colin Scott, Gordon Durie, Craig Moore, Basil Boli, Brian Laudrup, Alan

McLaren, Brian McGinty, Gary Bollan, Alex Cleland, Billy Thomson, Neil Caldwell, Paul McKnight, Stephen Wright, Gordan Petric, Oleg Salenko, Paul Gascoigne, Derek McInnes, Peter Van Vossen, Erik Bo Andersen, Theo Snelders, Greg Shields, Jorg Albertz, Joachim Bjorklund, Steven Boyack, Scott Wilson, Seb Rozental, Andy Dibble, Darren Fitzgerald, Barry Ferguson.

Every single one of those players had a part to play in nine in a row, whether a single substitute's appearance or a barrage of goals. Many were little more than support crew but the majority have a decent claim to go down in the proud history of Rangers Football Club as heroes. Some were elevated beyond that, woven into the very fabric of the institution. That is where Ally McCoist, the one name missing from the roll of honour above, enters the equation.

*Choose a job you love and you will never have to work a day in your life.*

**Confucius**

McCoist is set apart from the bread and butter nine in a row men. He was in at the start and he was there at the finish, in between he shattered almost every conceivable goalscoring record as he rampaged through the historic seasons with deadly accuracy and a neat line in cheeky banter. Super Ally, the ultimate hero.

So when did it happen, when did the kid from East Kilbride find himself rocketed into the company of the Ibrox immortals? Certainly not during his first season, the 1983/84 campaign, when he struggled to get into his stride. His return of eight goals in 29 starts, which included a penalty and three against his old club St Johnstone, did not convince the paying public that the saviour had arrived.

It was difficult to judge. Here was a young striker who was plunged into a struggling team with obvious creative deficiencies. Everyone knew he had potential but the £200,000 question was whether he would fulfil it. Then it happened, with a bang. Ally McCoist arrived as a Rangers goalscorer and with it came the swagger and the confidence which was at the heart of everything good he did on a football pitch.

In February 1985 McCoist was a Premier Division striker who had returned two goals in 16 appearances for the once mighty Glasgow Rangers. He was foundering but before his dream job met a rocky end he was afforded one last opportunity to prove he had what it took. Nobody could argue with the outcome.

On March 2, 1985, Ally McCoist bagged a double in a 3-1 win at home to relegation threatened Dumbarton. Next time out, against St

Mirren, he scored again. Then a week later he did it again, this time against Dundee. A fortnight later he scored his first hat-trick in Rangers colours in a one man assassination of Morton and a week later it was Hearts who were picking another McCoist goal out of the net. Then he scored against Celtic, and in the next game against Dundee United. It was a sensational burst of goalscoring form with 10 strikes in the space of nine games. The most amazing thing about it was that it came from a player in a losing team, with Rangers winning just three of those nine fixtures.

As the tide began to turn in favour of Rangers the waves of goals became more and more frequent. He had finished up in 1985 with 17 league and cup goals to his name, the next year it was 27 and after that 36 and 35 in 1988. The goal machine was going from strength to strength and his club were reaping the rewards with prize after prize landing in the previously dusty trophy cabinet.

Fast forward to 2007 and McCoist could be forgiven for feeling a sense of de ja vu. As assistant manager to Walter Smith he found himself joining a club in decline, lacking direction and in desperate need of success. Just as he had when he signed as a player all those years ago. The difference this time is the benefit of vast experience that he can use to guide his charges and shape the future.

His return to the club coincided with the year in which the 10th anniversary of nine in a row was celebrated. Oh how the underachieving class of 2007 must have hated the tales of those days when silver dripped from the Ibrox shelves. Except they were being spared of the bragging, the new model McCoist is a more reserved and modest character than the gallus striker brimming with confidence. Well, maybe not but he's at least making an effort to keep the boasts to a minimum.

McCoist said: "I wouldn't want to listen to stories about nine in a row if I was a player right now. They will know about it because its part of the club's history, but they don't need to be told about it. It's very difficult to compare teams in different eras. Our lads just now have been fantastic in what they have achieved in qualifying for the Champions League, they have done everything we have asked, but to compare them to the team we had is virtually impossible."

The Ibrox assistant looks back on nine in a row with nothing but fondness but has the sense to acknowledge that it would be folly to aim for a repeat now he has swapped the penalty box for the dug-out.

ALLY McCOIST

That will not prevent him from trying and his analysis of where to begin is simple.

He said: "Our team was unique. We all had one aim. When I look back at some of those characters – Brian Laudrup, Davie Robertson, Andy Goram, Richard Gough – and think that to have so many different attitudes and complex characters united was the greatest achievement. With that group it was a special time in my life. I don't think I ever belonged to another group like that – you would have walked to the end of the world for any of them, knowing they would have done the same thing for you. Without that I'm not saying you won't win anything but it makes it a whole lot harder."

He and Walter Smith quickly pinpointed the players who can help them in their quest to find a similar mix to the 1990s group who etched their name into football folklore, winning back to back titles in 2009 and 2010. The recruitment policy has had a strong tartan look to it, although McCoist is quick to dismiss the notion that all-Scottish is the way to go.

He said: "It's important for your supporters to have a spine and a good base of Scottish players. I always feel our own fans can relate to them a bit more. We had a Scottish team with players like Andy Goram, Richard Gough, Stuart McCall and myself through the core – but we also had Brian Laudrup, Pieter Huistra, Alexi Mikailach-enko and others. They came into our squad and adapted to us, we didn't have to adapt to them."

McCoist of course spent his time between playing and the recent return to club football with Rangers on the other side of the fence, analysing the game in minute detail in his television role. As well as the technical fine details, he also took the opportunity to assess shifting attitudes in the game.

He added: "I would take the spirit and camaraderie from that squad and try to build it. I don't think you see it as much now as you did then – I look at some of the Celtic teams that we beat and they had it. Tommy Burns' team was one of the best I played against and it's a shame for them that they aren't remembered for what they had, but they were up against something that was a little bit special."

That special package took a lot of careful crafting to get it to the stage when domination domestically was a given for the best part of a decade. McCoist's own journey to the start of the nine in a row adventure was not straight forward.

Ibrox legend John Greig had publicly stated that McCoist would never play for Rangers when his career was in its infancy in the early 1980s. The claims from the then Ibrox manager were made after the young prospect had turned his back on the Light Blues in favour of a move to Sunderland when St Johnstone decided the time was right to cash in. Greig failed to get his man but speculation continued to link him with the striker even after his move south, prompting the then manager to lay it on the line to the media – McCoist's boat had sailed as far as Rangers were concerned. As it happened, his ship actually did come in and it docked in Govan. Greig was successful at the second attempt when he finally signed McCoist in 1983 and insisted his protestations that the new recruit would never wear the famous jersey were merely a smokescreen designed to put the media off the trail. Fact or fiction, it really doesn't matter. The all important thing is McCoist did eventually wind his way through the front door.

It was in August 1981 that Rangers first attempted to lure the East Kilbride prospect to the club. Just 18 at the time, McCoist had been a huge hit at St Johnstone with 28 goals in his first season in the Perth top team. Greig had offered £300,000 to dwarf the record haul Saints had ever brought in for a player, which stood at £70,000 for John Connolly from Everton. Sunderland turned out to be even more determined, weighing in with a £400,000 bounty and winning the bidding war before persuading the teenager England was his promised land. Black Cats manager Alan Durban insisted McCoist was "one for the future", that he would have to serve an apprenticeship at Roker Park after committing to a five year contract. If his Sunderland stint was to be classed in that way, it is safe to say McCoist left without a recognised trade.

His St Johnstone manager Alex Rennie had hailed his protégé, who won 10 youth caps while at Muirton Park, as the best in his age group in Scotland, as a natural goalscorer who had the ability to also turn out as a top class central midfielder. In England he was neither, with just nine goals in two seasons during a disappointing period. A cut price £200,000 deal ended the association and finally took the player to Ibrox in the summer of 1983. It would turn out to be a marriage made in heaven but not before a testing spell.

It took two years for him to become established and prove to the Rangers faithful he belonged, bouncing back after being dropped by Jock Wallace in 1985 to establish himself as one of the greats.

McCoist had been a Rangers supporter as a boy, he knew what made the fans tick. He arrived during a barren spell but was under no illusions about what was required, admitting: "I'm only too aware of what the fans expect from us, even when there's no trophy at stake they give us the will to win."

Within his first two seasons at Rangers, McCoist began to show himself to be a media savvy young man. He was eloquent and articulate. Whisper it, here was a Scottish footballer who spoke with intelligence and authority despite his tender years.

He was also proving to be a useful striker and Graeme Souness needed little convincing, lassoing his man with a four year contract in 1986 with his reign in its formative stages.

Mind you it was not all back slapping and mutual appreciation, with McCoist famously winning the nickname the Judge after being relegated to the bench for the bulk of the 1990/91 season by Graeme Souness. It was a seminal moment in his relationship with the fans, with the striker jettisoned from the team but never dislodged from the hearts of the Bears who still chanted his name even when it had to be directed at the bench rather than the penalty box.

He kept smiling, kept working and came back stronger. In 1992 McCoist, who had sailed past Derek Johnstone's post-war scoring Rangers scoring record of 131 goals the previous year, was named Scottish Football Writers' Association player of the year to cap a memorable season in which he had been Europe's leading league scorer as his club clinched its fourth successive title. He had bagged 39 goals, 34 of those in the league, in 45 starts as well as four for Scotland, Not that the achievements won universal approval, with French magazine *l'Equipe* threatening to withdraw the Golden Boot award it ran in conjunction with Adidas because it considered Scottish football too inferior to merit one of its players winning the prize. Adidas went ahead with the presentation and repeated it the following year when 34 league goals again put McCoist at the head of the striking class.

Disaster struck in April 1993 when McCoist broke his leg during Scotland's 5-0 humiliation against Portugal in Lisbon, forcing him to miss his own testimonial match against Newcastle United later that year. Even with the star turn relegated to the touchline, more than 42,000 turned out to provide him with a £500,000 pay day. It eased the pain of the leg injury, which kept him out for six months, with the testimonial year estimated at the time to be worth £1million to him. Financially McCoist was the most marketable player Rangers had ever had. On top of his bumper wage and bonus package at Ibrox he had a lucrative boot deal and was in huge demand for personal appearances up and down the country, the fans just couldn't get enough. As early as 1993 his agent was working towards establishing the star client as a television personality, with Neil Hobday claiming: "Ally could front anything from chat shows to fashion programmes, news, current affairs, kids' shows and anything involved in footall. He's a natural."

In 1994 the goalscoring king got the chance to visit the home of the Queen, awarded an MBE for his services to football at the end of his testimonial season, receiving his gong from the Prince of Wales and wore Rangers tartan for the occasion. He labelled it: "My biggest ever honour – by miles."

McCoist broke down the barriers with widespread and all encompassing appeal. He even ventured into varsity life after cornering the student market, awarded the first ever honorary blue St Andrew's University had dished out.

On the international stage he won the affections of the Tartan Army with some crucial goals, none more so than his dramatic appearance from the bench in a qualifier against Greece leading up to Euro 96. Absent from the Scotland team for 28 months following his leg break in Portugal, McCoist had not even been named in Craig Brown's initial squad but he was drafted in and came on to score a crucial winner with only his second touch of the ball to put his country on the road to the finals in England, where he rounded off his season's work with the winner in the European Championship group match against Switzerland. The enthralling comeback led Brown to proclaim: "Every supporter of every club likes Ally. The Celtic fans will have been as pleased as the Rangers ones to see Ally make his fairytale comeback. That takes a lot of doing. Ally has won everyone over through the years by the way he plays football for the fun of it. Even when he scores against other clubs, Ally is rarely treated as an enemy. He breaks the great divide between the Old Firm because both groups of fans agree he is one of the most talented strikers this country has ever seen. The same measure of respect is given to Celtic's John Collins. The Rangers fans admire his talent, regardless of the colour of his shirt. Ally is also genuinely likeable and steers away from some of the sillier antics that we have seen from some Rangers and Celtic players in the past. There are individuals in both camps who could learn a lot from his example."

The death of Diana, Princess of Wales proved an unlikely test case for his popularity among Scotland fans. When McCoist refused to play for Scotland against Belarus on the day of the high profile funeral his stance won universal approval from the Tartan Army as well as his team-mates, with the SFA eventually bowing to the public pressure his views created and postponing the game by 24-hours. The fact he was such a dependable goalscorer, with a respectable ratio of close to one in three for Scotland, lifted McCoist above the usual club loyalties. Capped 61 times and with 19 goals to his credit, it was his club form that truly made it impossible to argue with his status as the country's main man.

It was in 1996 that he shattered Bob McPhail's all-time best tally of 231 Rangers goals but 13 years earlier he had signalled his intent. On 25 March 1983 a special thing happened. Rangers won the League Cup, okay nothing new there. Rangers beat Celtic, certainly not for the first or last time. On the scoresheet was the name McCoist and next to it in bold type was a number … 3. It was the first Super Ally hat-trick, a landmark occasion.

They just kept coming. In the league Morton suffered at the hands of McCoist triple three times, Falkirk twice, Dunfermline twice and Motherwell twice in the space of just two months in 1992. Other top flight hat-tricks came against Dundee, Hibs, St Mirren, Hearts and Raith Rovers. Not to mention the four goals he fired past helpless Falkirk in 1992.

He didn't keep the triple salvos for the league alone. Cup hat-tricks came against Celtic, Dunfermline, Arbroath, Raith, Stranraer, old club St Johnstone, Alloa Athletic and Falkirk.

That's before you even get started on the doubles. McCoist was a goal machine of the type Scottish football has never see before, he hurt teams and did it with a smile on his face.

It was in the last month of 1996 that the most momentous record tumbled at the boot of McCoist, with Gordon Wallace's Scottish league tally of 264 goals bettered in a 4-3 win against Hibs. In 1997 a double in the Champions League against GI Gotu took his continental total to 20, beating the record by Celtic and Hearts striker Willie Wallace. Later the same year he breezed past the Scottish Cup record of 51 goals which had been held by former Aberdeen and Rangers forward Jim Forrest.

His goals were crucial to the success his club enjoyed during his purple period. So what did he win? The League Cup of 1984 was just the start, with another one the following season and another seven besides those two. The first league title fell in 1987 before the nine in a row run began in May 1989. For good measure the Scottish Cup fell into the arms of McCoist, just the once though. That solitary win to complete the domestic set did not come until 1992 when he and Mark Hateley were on target against Airdrie to end a frustrating wait in the national cup competition.

Europe was the only box not ticked for Super Ally, even though he was no stranger to the continental game even before he arrived at Ibrox. As a teenager at St Johnstone he had turned out as an unofficial trialist for Benfica after befriending Portuguese defender Frederico during a holiday on the Algarve. In typical McCoist fashion, he scored.

Competitively, the closest brush in many campaigns famously came in 1993 when he and his team-mates were within an ace of reaching the European Cup final. The Battle of Britain against Leeds was won in no small part thanks to the contribution from East Kilbride's most famous son, with a goal in each of the 2-1 wins at home and away. McCoist played in nine of the 10 ties that season as Rangers finished their Euro campaign unbeaten but knocked out at the group stage as Marseille edged through to the final by virtue of a single point.

And so a European medal proved illusive and at the age of 35 the McCoist era ended. The swansong came on 16 May 1998 at Celtic Park, of all places, in the Scottish Cup final. There was to be no fairytale ending to the striker's career or manager Walter Smith's first stint at the helm. Hearts failed to read the script, scoring twice to cancel out McCoist's obligatory goal and deny him one final moment of glory.

He left Ibrox behind but did not stray far from his roots, making the short journey to Kilmarnock in the summer of 1998. Not unexpectedly the Killie days were not as prolific, with McCoist's role to bring experience as much as goals to a side who had been punching above their weight by holding their own in the top half of the Premier Division. He stayed for three seasons, finally calling it a day at the age of 38 in May 2001. He made just 32 league starts, scored only nine top flight goals, but his contribution was still valued.

A full-time career in television was beckoning, with McCoist taking to the small screen like a fish to water. From the early chat show days of McCoist and McAulay to *Question of Sport* captain and key part of ITV's Premiership coverage, the retired striker attacked television with the same force as he launched himself at crosses. It wasn't all serious business mind you, as anyone who has seen the Question of Sport out-takes will know. A show far better than the sugar coated prime-time version.

Nobody really saw McCoist the coach coming. When he linked up with Walter Smith in the Scotland set-up it was seen as a motivational gimmick, a short term fix to lift squad spirits after the dark depression of the Berti Vogts reign. It turned into far more than that, with McCoist becoming touchline enforcer and orchestrator for Smith and a key ally on the training field.

His contribution to the Scotland cause did not go unnoticed. Dunfermline and Livingston both tried to tempt him into the club game in a coaching role, Inverness Caley Thistle went one step further when they offered him a crack at SPL management. The offer from the Highlanders was considered before being rejected on the grounds of distance from his Glasgow home. Astutely he also rejected strong overtures from under-pressure Alex McLeish at Ibrox who wanted back-up, cleverly keeping his Rangers coaching copybook clean until the really big break came with Walter Smith's recall to the dug-out early in 2007. With McCoist as his assistant, the nine in a row gaffer looks like he might just be able to recreate some magic but the pair would never promise a repeat of the end result.

McCoist said: "At the time of nine in a row you didn't spend a lot of time looking below you, even though you were aware of those who were putting pressure on you. I wasn't aware of anyone who was going to stop us because I felt that squad of players all knew what was required. In actual fact the anticipation levels were not as high as they were for eight in a row, I don't know why. I felt we were going to do nine in a row when we got there but felt there was more pressure for eight.

"I can't believe it has been 10 years. It has absolutely flown in. My greatest memory is Brian Laudrup scoring the header. It was an absolutely tremendous goal and the scenes of celebration were tremendous. It was actually more relief than celebration when we got the result. Make no mistake, if we hadn't won it we wouldn't have been the team that won eight championships – we would have been the one that lost nine in a row. There was massive disappointment that we didn't do 10 but there would have been more if we hadn't done nine.

"I can remember coming back down on the bus after the game and it was one big party, magic. They are memories that will be with me for the rest of my life. It was a period of your life where you don't really appreciate it or think about savouring it. Now I look back with great pride. You keep going and trying to achieve things but I'd be very surprised if I could top that. For a team to do that in this day and age would be an incredible achievement."

**MAGIC MOMENT:** In 1993 the ultimate Ibrox
shot-stopper became the only Rangers goalkeeper
ever to win Scotland's player of the year prize.

# ANDY GORAM
## *'THE GOALIE'* **1991-1998**

### GERS CAREER: Games 260; Caps 48

I AM not a bigot. It is one of the opening gambits of Andy
Goram's after dinner routine and seen as a necessary precursor
for a player who has been dogged by sectarian accusations and
suspicions for almost as long as he has been connected to Rangers.

The Bury-born goalkeeper does not
shy away from the issue, instead he
now earns a living poking fun at
the religious tensions that sur-
round the game in Scotland.

His routine is close to the bone,
taking the audience into the
future when Goram jokes about
the day he and Donald Findlay
rule the roost at Ibrox and back to
the past when he became
embroiled in highly publicised
spats with Celtic opponents, most
notably Pierre Van Hoojidonk. At
the same time Goram claims he cannot possibly be bigoted, having
had three Catholic wives. Then pours over the three divorces which
followed.

His stand up act is designed to be taken with a pinch of salt, as a
piece of comedy rather than an exercise in social commentary. The

sensitivities in Scottish football have ensured it is not always received in the spirit it is intended, I have witnessed the jeers and cheers for myself. One dinner date in Ayrshire in 2007 went beyond verbal sparring and ended with the Goalie being attacked by an irate guest who claimed his speech had been littered with offence and sectarian jibes.

Goram, despite providing headline fodder for years, does not court media attention yet on this occasion he felt moved to defend himself by giving a rare tabloid interview in an attempt to clear his name and safeguard his lucrative new career on the after dinner circuit.

He said: "There are people who will have a go at me just because of who I am. I'm just trying to make a living and I'm not having some clown leading people to believe I'm some bigot. I admit I've done daft things in the past but this is my livelihood we're talking about. I'm not going to put that at risk by making stupid anti-Catholic jokes. Hundreds of people have heard my after-dinner talks now and they'll all tell you the same thing. I don't make sectarian comments, I don't talk about terrorists, I don't use the word 'Fenian' and I don't get steaming drunk. I have plenty of witnesses who will testify that I didn't make a single remark which could have caused offence. I'm sick of being called a bigot for no reason."

Goram is a self-proclaimed Rangers fanatic. To this day he still travels the world attending conventions and supporters gatherings and reaching out to those who idolised him. During his playing days the approach was no different, perfectly prepared to live the high life with Rangers fans in Scotland and Ulster as well as overseas.

He said: "We were punters ourselves, we drank in Duke Street or on Paisley Road West. We used to drink, play dominoes and have a carry on with them but they respected that come Saturday we would knock our pans in for them on the pitch. We were no different to them."

That willingness to welcome every Rangers fan with open arms and typical enthusiasm in turn led to Goram finding himself the subject of unwanted headlines and in some dubious situations.

In 1998, the keeper found himself in the firing line when he wore a black armband during an Old Firm game after the murder of Loyalist terrorist Billy Wright. He claimed it was in memory of his aunt, who died four months earlier, but the following year was again forced to deny links to terrorist groups when a picture surfaced of him in front of Loyalist flags in a pub. He later admitted it was not until after he had finished playing that he realised the implications, pleading naivity in response to the charges levelled against him.

Little did he know the experiences, tough as they were at the time, would provide him with cannon fodder for a burgeoning new career as an entertainer dressed in a shirt and tie rather than gloves and boots.

The fact he's able to treat the religious divide with contempt underlines his determination to avoid getting caught up in the serious debate again – he knows he cannot escape it, so instead is using it to his own advantage. Even after all these years he still knows how to push the buttons of the Rangers supporters and, just as it did in his playing days, that often provokes a response from Celtic quarters. He still revels in his ability to do that, and in his role as self-proclaimed Rangers fanatic, but has become more acutely aware of the responsibilities that go with his place in the public eye. Indeed, in 2007 he was one of the professionals shouting from the rooftops about the need for an end to sectarian songs and chants as the issue again began to take hold.

But the "daft things" he claimed to have done earlier in his career have stuck against his name, as he found out when he encountered Ireland's most famous footballer and a future Celtic star during his short stop at Manchester United well after his Gers days. Even with distance between The Goalie and Ibrox there was no way round the issue.

*Concentration comes out of a combination of confidence and hunger.*

**Arnold Palmer**

He said: "I went down, met all the Manchester United players but there was one I never spoke to – Roy Keane. With him being a Celtic boy and me a Rangers boy it was an obvious thing. We never spoke for two months. It didn't bother us, although we had a couple of pops in training. We had one when he was on my side in an eight-a-side game, I got the ball and gave it to Luke Chadwick who put it over the bar. Keane had a right go at me, telling me to give him the ball. I lost the plot, do I have to give him the ball because he's Roy Keane? Coming off the pitch one of the boys said to me 'we don't speak to Roy Keane like that'. I just said 'there's going to be changes then'. A few of them were scared of him, which I found strange because at Rangers there was nobody above anyone else. If they were they got brought back down pretty quickly. Don't get me wrong, Roy Keane was a fantastic player but we didn't knock it off. He had his beliefs and I had mine."

The devotion to the Rangers cause led Goram into choppy waters in and out of the game but that was also part of the attraction to the supporters who grew to love him. He came from a Rangers family and made no secret of the fact he was living the dream of playing for his boyhood heroes. He revelled in the Old Firm environment, not least because he helped defeat Celtic so often in games he considered to be the height of his football life.

"My dad was a Rangers man but I never thought I'd get there. It's just a shame he never saw it.", said Goram, who arrived at Ibrox in 1991 in a round-about-fashion having served a long and distinguished apprenticeship with Oldham Athletic and Hibs before winding up at his spiritual home following the death of the man who had inspired him in the game.

He quipped: "Like any son, I wanted to do what my father did. My father was a goalkeeper at Hibs from 1948 to 1950 and then Oldham, where I grew up. You want to do what your father did – I'm just glad he wasn't a ballet dancer."

At 5ft 11inches he was no Peter McCloy but he had the spring and agility to compensate for his relative lack of height. It was his shortage of inches that led West Brom to release him as a teenager and that early rejection remained a motivator throughout a senior career that outlasted all of his contemporaries.

He could have chosen county cricket ahead of football but turned his back on that to follow his heart. He did resurrect his bat and ball career when he moved to the Premier Division, becoming the only other man besides Scot Symon to earn a Scotland cap at both football and cricket, and dabbled again when he eventually retired from football.

The fear of failure drove the player on , both personally because of his early treatment at the Hawthorns and in terms or his team thanks to his passion for the Rangers cause.

Goram said: "To get told at such a young age that you're never going to make it is sickening but you want to prove them wrong and I did that. I was only 17 when I played in the first team at Oldham, Jimmy Frizell gave me the last three games of the season. I got battered – I had no size and no frame but it was a good education. It was also a big lift after being released by West Brom.

"Joe Royle came to Oldham the next season and was looking for an experienced goalkeeper. He brought Martin Hodge in but he took ill, with a chest infection I think, and Joe had to play me. I kept my place – to be fair to Joe, he could have brought somebody else in but he kept faith in me and gave a young kid the chance of a lifetime."

That chance of a lifetime led to a seven year spell with Oldham which brought his first Scotland cap. He was an Englishman with an English accent but his father had been born in Edinburgh and had brought his son up as a Scot. There was no hesitation in accepting the chance to play in front of the Tartan Army. In time the accent faded, but the lingering reminders of his roots will never be disguised as he flits between a broad English twang and gruff Scottish brogue without even knowing it.

Goram came home when switched to Hibs in 1987 to try and enhance his international prospects under Andy Roxburgh. He had spoken to the national coach and been told that playing for Oldham made it difficult for his performances to be monitored in any great depth and that a Scottish club would be a better idea. Easter Road braced itself for the arrival of one of the game's great prospects.

He could not help the Hibees win silverware but did play a part in taking them into Europe and, with his reputation growing with every passing week, it was only a matter of time before the Old Firm sat up and took notice and there was no question where he would end up. Walter Smith moved to take the international keeper to Glasgow in 1991. The recruit went on to endear himself to the Rangers crowd but he still remembers the difficulty he faced in replacing the dependable and popular Chris Woods in the No.1 jersey, with a defeat against Hearts three games into his new life in Glasgow hitting him hard. Goram regrouped, took a sharp intake of breath and vowed to work harder than ever to win over his fellow fans.

He added: If I'd have gone straight from Oldham to Rangers I think I would have struggled more than I did. I wouldn't have known any of the players I would have played against or the ins and outs in Scotland. I was so lucky in that everything panned out for me at the right time. I had seven years at Oldham learning my trade, four years at Hibs enhancing my reputation and then on to Rangers. My dad was a Rangers man but I never thought I'd get there. Its just a shame he never saw it. I never won a medal in my first 11 years in football so to go to Rangers excited me. To replace a fans' favourite is not very good. The start I had was not the greatest at Rangers and Walter took me up the stairs for a good chat. That one conversation was the change for me."

Trophies flowed thick and fast for a top quality operator who had been starved of success with his previous two clubs. He won a league and Scottish Cup double in his maiden campaign and five further Premier Division winner's medals to see the club up to the magic nine figure. He added two further wins in the League Cup and a couple of extra Scottish Cup badges for good measure.

Those prizes included the 1993 treble, a defining season for Goram as he was named Scotland's player of the year in recognition of his consistently brilliant performances that term. More recently he has been voted the best ever Rangers goalkeeper.

During his time at Ibrox the keeper admits his attitude changed for the better, revealing: "When you are young all you want is personal glory, you want to make a name for yourself and make saves. The older you get the more you realise it's for the team."

Nobody who saw Goram throw himself at the feet of forwards would argue against the fact that he was a big part of the Rangers team. He became adept at spending large periods of games inactive as his side dominated only to spring into life with a world class save, many of which translated into valuable points.

The well worn Tommy Burns line that he would have "Andy Goram broke my heart" inscribed on his headstone summed up perfectly the influence The Goalie had on the nine in a row run, not least the final two seasons when Celtic under Burns were coming back strongly and had the club's best side in more than a decade. They were met with stubborn resistance in the crucial Old Firm derbies, frustrated by a solid defensive unit and behind it a little goalkeeper who appeared to be made of rubber. Goram's gravity defying saves became a hallmark of the close run game which Rangers developed a habit of winning by the odd goal.

He was untouchable at club level under Walter Smith with never even the hint of a threat to his No.1 jersey thanks to his peerless displays of the art of goalkeeping. That's not to say that Goram did not know what competition was all about.

His contribution to the Scotland cause was also significant but he faced a battle with Jim Leighton for the No.1 jersey throughout his international career. That fight did not prevent Goram from notching 43 appearances for Scotland between 1985 and 1998. His big stage experience came in Euro 92 and Euro 96, when it was a goal he conceded rather than one he prevented that put him in the spotlight. It was an unusual situation for Goram, who loathed being beaten, but when it came to team-mate Paul Gascoigne's stunning strike for England, when he flicked the ball over the advancing defence before hammering a sublime volley past the keeper, he was prepared to view it from both sides.

Goram and Gascoigne were used to high jinxs at Ibrox but the international head to head was approached in a different frame of mind. Goram said: "Only Gazza could have scored that goal. You could see it coming – a surreal moment and probably the best you'll ever see at Wembley. I'd rather he scored it than anyone else. I never had the luck to play with Davie Cooper or Jim Baxter but Brian Laudrup must be the best I played with, Gascoigne a close second. Certainly Gazza must be the best I've played against. He was a special talent, there's one of them every decade as proved by Baxter and Cooper. We'd already said before the game that we'd swap shirts after the game. As I walked along he was coming towards me with that big daft grin – I looked at him and I think he got the message, if he'd have said anything I would have belted him."

The Scotland career drew to a close when Goram stood down from international duty in 1998, just weeks before the World Cup finals in France. Rangers, right back to the days of Graeme Souness, had been viewed as holding a disregard for Scotland action due to regular call-offs and that may have been a factor in the reaction to Goram's decision. The response still irks him, one decade on.

He said: "Jim Leighton and I were big rivals – we trained hard and pushed each other to the limit. There was only one place to play for. We weren't similar characters – Jim was the wild man and I was the quiet family man! We never really got on that way but in training we worked well together. It was a healthy rivalry, we wanted to show one another who was the best. We trained how we played.

"We were in America two or three weeks before the World Cup in 98. I was told at the training camp I wasn't going to be playing at the World Cup and I'd just left Rangers. I was clubless and knew that even if I wasn't playing I could still go to France and break a leg – it was my livelihood, it paid the mortgage. I'd been told by two different coaches that I wasn't going to be playing so there was no point at 36 going to sit on the bench. I'd rather a young lad came in so I took the decision and retired. I thought I was good enough to play in France, but that was just a personal thing.

"The press took it that 'Goram walks out on Scotland'. I gave the SFA a letter, there was no nastiness about it, three weeks before the

World Cup. Jim Leighton did the same thing two days before a game yet he 'retired', the press took different angles because I'm who I am, brash and confident. The sickening thing was the two of us did exactly the same thing but were tarred with two different brushes. The press were never going to get the right side of the story because of Craig Brown's way and Scotland's way. Watching it on television, that's when you think 'I wish I was there' but I did what I thought was right at the time. You're dealt a set of cards in your life and it's how you deal with them."

Goram's intriguing thoughts and his sensitive nature were revealed in a radio interview with former players Gordon Smith and Murdo MacLeod, allowing the ex-professionals rare access to his inner thoughts. Having featured on the front and back pages for more than a decade, he is guarded in his dealings with the media as I have discovered both during and after his playing days.

The pressures of life as a hard living Ranger in the public eye taught him to be that way, pressures that were relieved in 1998 when the new broom of Dick Advocaat swept clean. A former international by that stage, Goram was in jeopardy of going off the rails and prepared to drop down the leagues to stay in employment as he faced up to life after Ibrox. It was a prospect that filled him with dread but football would be a saving grace.

He said: "I was training at Ayr United, had a good week and had come to an agreement for me to sign. Then Motherwell came along and, with them being in the Premier League, I felt I had to speak to them, I signed for two years and was given the responsibility of the club captaincy straight away. Billy Davies is a clever boy and his idea was to give me the captaincy, it worked because I had two good years and enjoyed it. The captaincy and Miriam kept me on the straight and narrow, I could have gone down a stupid road but we went and got a pub in Lanark and I had that stability. I played on for five years after that and Billy Davies did me a great favour."

Then comes one of Goram's favourite anecdotes, the day Manchester United signed an ageing old keeper with dodgy knees in a move that shocked world football. It is one of the facets of his after dinner routine, one of a string of belly-laugh inducing recollections of a weird and wonderful career.

He said "With two months to go on my contract at Motherwell I was told I wasn't getting a new one. I was going into training one morning and I got a call from Ally McCoist, which was strange because he never calls you in the morning. He's usually just coming in. After training I got another call, this time from Walter Smith. He told me to keep my phone on because somebody would be calling. I knew something was going on, McCoist in the morning and Walter in the afternoon. I thought it was a wind up, so when the phone went and a voice said: 'It's Alex Ferguson, Goalie we've got Bayern Munich on the Wednesday, Fabian Barthez and Raymond van de Gouw are injured and I want you to come down and cover for the next two months. I said 'Coisty, get lost', or similar less complimentary words, and put the phone down. Two minutes later the phone went again, it was Sir Alex again and he said 'Goalie, you've got 10 seconds to decide'. That's how I ended up at Manchester United. It was a ridiculous turn of events. I gave up one of my signing on fees from Motherwell to go there but it was worth every penny."

After answering the SOS from United, Goram returned to Scotland to play out his days with Queen of the South and briefly under former Rangers team-mate David Robertson at Elgin City in the Third Division. His dalliance with perennial strugglers Elgin is another rich source of humour from a man not afraid to raise a laugh at his own expense.

Speaking is becoming a forte but Goram remains a football man. He is hoping a coaching role may open up, having served as a specialist with both Dundee and Airdrie United briefly. The assumption is that he is being picky about employment in the game but the truth is nobody has asked Scotland's finest exponent of goalkeeping to lend his experience. If nobody takes the gamble, the Goram tricks of the trade could be lost forever.

That troubles Goram, as does the fact he was not afforded an opportunity to say a proper goodbye to his friends in the stand when he played his final Rangers game, which was a 2-0 win over Celtic in April 1998. He said: "It was a bad year. We won nine in a row then the year after we won nothing – then to be told you're going to the World Cup to sit on the bench. It was a year to forget. At Rangers it was hard to take because we'd had so many good years. It was a special bunch of boys, everyone knew we liked a laugh and a carry on. We had such a good time – I think that's why they brought the DVDs and videos out, so we could remember what had gone on. We were very close.

"During the 1997/98 season Walter knew there was going to be something in the paper about him leaving, so rather than anything nasty appearing he came out and admitted it. We knew there was going to be big changes at the club. Dick Advocaat came in and got rid of virtually every Walter Smith player. I think nine of us left. For people to say we didn't try in that last season is ridiculous. You want to go and win for the gaffer more than ever, to go out on a high. I've seen players come and go since then, the likes of Lorenzo Amoruso and Tugay, doing a lap of honour round the park after their last game at Ibrox. We didn't have that chance to say goodbye that way, which was heartbreaking."The intermittent decline in fortunes 'his' club has suffered since his own departure has been another painful experience for The Goalie, or the Flying Pig as he was latterly known. That tag was one Brian Laudrup was particularly fond of and the pair, something of an odd couple, struck up a lasting friendship. Goram is in no doubt about how Walter Smith and Ally McCoist should set about rolling back the clock – by calling for bona-fide Rangers men.

He said: "A lot of players came in and didn't care, they just picked the money up. It is still happening. Brian Laudrup, Jorg Albertz, Pieter Huistra and the English lads like Mark Hateley and Dale Gordon. Alexi Mikailichenko, Rino Gattuso they all did their bit – they are not foreigners to me, they're one of us because of their attitude and the way they play. That's the biggest compliment you can pay them. Certain foreigners you wouldn't class as Rangers men. The ones that came to the club, that picked up money and did little in return. Walter has started bringing in young Scottish lads and from day one there's been a massive difference. They know what the club is about, they are Rangers fans at heart and will give that extra 10 or 15 per cent."

**MAGIC MOMENT:** Charlie Miller's cross, Brian Laudrup's thunderous header and the nine in a row dream became reality.

# BRIAN LAUDRUP
## *'THE GREAT DANE'* 1994-1998

### GERS CAREER: Games 150; Goals 45; Caps 75

FANTASTIC PLAYER? Without question. Loyal and committed servant? Undoubtedly. Cult Hero? Oh yes. Laudrup was a star, blessed with talents that have not been seen at Ibrox since his departure. He breathed new life into Scottish football at a time when it needed it more than ever and even more crucially put wind into the sails of the ship sailing towards nine in a row.

What he did not have was the edge of some of the cult heroes from days gone by, or indeed his contemporaries. While a Willie Henderson or Willie Johnston brought an element of intrigue and surprise as fans tried to second guess their next move on and off the park, with Laudrup you knew exactly what you would get. Exemplary, consistent and effective wing play. Hand in hand with that was an unassuming manner, a sophisticated charm and a softly spoken voice that brought calm to every situation.

None of those factors can be construed as criticisms, all are endearing in their own way. But it does bring into sharp focus what exactly makes a cult hero. Is ability alone enough? Or does a cult hero need a rough and ready edge to truly connect with the man in the street?

Brian Laudrup was perhaps more far removed from the Govan hardcore than any of the players on this list of 20. For a start he was parachuted in from overseas without any knowledge of the culture or politics surrounding his new club. He was also free of any of the blemishes, quirks or imperfections that so often prevents the 'them against us' line developing between players and fans. He seemed almost too good to be true. He wasn't a rogue in any sense, there were no apparent flaws to his football genius unlike so many of those who melt the hearts of Joe Public. In his spare time, he enjoyed wine collecting and reading – poles apart from the stereotypical football player as you could get.

> *Success is simple. Do what's right, the right way, at the right time.*
>
> **Arnold Glascow**

But a cult hero he is and always will be thanks to a confident nod of his head, thanks to that hair's breadth. When the Dane crashed home the header to clinch a 1-0 win against Dundee United on 7 May 1997 at Tannadice the nine in a row dream turned to shining reality for the Rangers following. In that split second Laudrup grasped the holy grail that had been chased since Celtic's record breaking run of the 1960s and 1970s. That goal, that collector's item of a Laudrup header, will forever be replayed and held up as the symbol of Rangers' historic run of title victories. Laudrup will forever be a hero.

From day one he had to live with huge expectations from a fan base built up into a frenzy by the media scrum surrounding their new man.

Here was an international star with a big reputation, a big name thanks in no small part to his international exploits and the superstardom of his big brother Michael, who was ready to turn his back on one of Europe's most glamorous leagues to decamp to Scotland just as he was about to hit his peak years. Laudrup was just 25 when he moved to Ibrox but throughout showed a maturity beyond his years to handle the peculiar pressures of his new job.

After all, he had plenty of experience of the big occasion. Laudrup, born in Austria but a proud Dane, made his international debut at the age of 18 in 1987. Five years later he was part of the squad which shocked world football by winning the 1992 European Championships in Sweden. The Danish team edged in after

Yugoslavia had been expelled, rushing from their beach holidays to assemble for the tournament and sweep to an unexpected victory. Germany were overcome 2-1 in the final and young Laudrup was living the dream, finishing fifth in the voting for the world player of the year.

It was not just at international level that he was a winner, savouring league and cup success with Brondby and twice named Denmark's player of the year before his switch to Italy.

For him to wind up in Scotland was an intriguing story, an almost unbelievable tale, but it was true. Walter Smith had pulled off an unexpected and audacious managerial move for the AC Milan man. In fact Laudrup was at the San Siro on loan from Fiorentina, the club with which he first proved his ability to hold his own in Serie A. With Milan he not surprisingly had his work cut out to carve out a regular niche in the first team but the fact he made it there at all was a glowing endorsement of his playing credentials.

The son of Danish international Finn Laudrup, who had been capped 21 times, began his own journey with Brondby in his home country. Germany was the first port of call on a trans-continental adventure when Bayer Uerlingen splashed out £650,000 on Denmark's latest hot young talent. Bayern Munich went further, investing 2million to lure him to the Olympic stadium before he crossed to Italy in another £2 million deal bankrolled by Fiorentina. The Tuscan club were relegated from Serie A during Laudrup's time, leading to his loan spell at Milan and ultimately his shock switch to Scotland.

Chairman David Murray insisted the deal was worth significantly less than the £3.5million being quoted by the Italians, with the Ibrox club preferring to put a figure of £2.2million on the deal. It made it even more of a bargain than it already sounded.

It was not a lightning strike by Rangers but a carefully considered and painstakingly executed exercise. Walter Smith and Archie Knox had begun scouting the Danish national team after several players in the side had been recommended to them, Brian Laudrup was not on their list of targets. The Serie A star was viewed as outwith their reach, even though it was he and brother Michael who shone brightest every time Smith and Knox watched the Danes in action. Then a funny thing happened, Smith received a call to say Laudrup was unsettled in Italy and that Fiorentina might be tempted to sell. He was, they were and the rest is history.

The classy midfielder was taken to Scotland for a weekend stay, wined and dined by David Murray and convinced that his future was blue. It took two weeks to conclude the negotiations, with financial settlement between the player and his Tuscan club the main stumbling block, but Rangers were prepared to tread carefully to get their man.

Deportiva La Coruna in Spain attempted to hijack the move but he was a man of his word and packed his bags to head for the west coast, eager to take advantage of regular European football. He left behind an AC Milan side who had won the league and the European Cup, although the Dane had not featured in that final the experience had lit a burning desire to succeed in the club game's biggest competition.

Playing in continental competition year in and year out was part of the appeal but there was more to Laudrup's decision than that. He said: "I was impressed by the club. I've never been in a place where there is such an atmosphere and history. I knew after two hours of arriving at Ibrox that I would sign for Rangers. I was impressed by everything about the club."

Smith was not fazed by Laudrup's lofty perch in Italy and persuaded him to swap Europe's fashion capital for Govan by promising a life free of the tactical shackles of Italian football and a licence to express himself. Italy had been an experience but not the one he had hoped for, with Fiorentina's fall through the trap door exposing Laudrup to the ugly side of the game. The club's players had to be smuggled away from the ground in the boots of cars to avoid the baying fans waiting to vent their spleen outside. With that behind him, the strains of the Old Firm way of life were second nature and he slipped into the side as if he had been born to wear light blue.

Peter Huistra had revelled in the creative role before Laudrup, as had Alexi Mikhailachenko. Both had worn the No.11 shirt to good effect and had threatened to establish themselves as favourites without ever really fulfilling their undoubted potential.

Laudrup had a chance to put that right. He promised much and delivered even more while at Ibrox.

It had cost Rangers in excess of £2million to clinch the transfer. That hefty fee only increased the burden on the shoulders of the Danish international but there were no fears he could not handle it.

He made his debut on 13 August 1994 in that season's Premier Division opener against Motherwell. A deadly accurate cross provided Mark Hateley with Rangers' first goal but the game was heading for a 1-1 draw before the new boy's second intervention of the afternoon. A trademark crossfield dart, wrapping defenders up in a whirlwind, unzipped the Steelmen in the dying seconds to tee up Duncan Ferguson for the winner in a 2-1 success. Laudrup took his arrival in uncharted territory in his stride and inside 90 minutes was a fully fledged Rangers man fit to wear the shirt and to accept the ovations of a fan base who had just had their wish for a new hero granted.

Not only could Laudrup ghost past defenders, equipped with deceptive pace and a neat line in twists and turns, but he could also carve open defences with intelligent passes and catch out goalkeepers with vicious curling crosses. Laudrup also proved to be a composed and reliable finisher. He had the complete package and paired it with the temperament to cope comfortably with the ups and downs of Scottish football and a physique which helped him steer clear of lengthy spells on the sidelines – a manager's dream and obvious target for the affections of the fans.

Laudrup found himself in possession of the No.11 shirt of a side three title successes away from nine in a row celebrations. It was not Celtic who threatened to end that run prematurely but a new order in Scottish football. Aberdeen had been runners-up in five of the previous six years, with Hearts the closest challengers on the other occasion.

The fact it was not an Old Firm battle for supremacy had not made it any less nervous. Walter Smith had watched his side win the league by three points in 1994 and was desperate to avoid another close run contest.

In Laudrup he found a provider and goalscorer who could once again create a more comfortable cushion. In 1995 the Dane collected his first Premier Division winner's medal after helping his side romp to league victory, 15 points clear of Motherwell in second place.

He protested time and time again that hitting the net was not his forte, that he was a creator more than an executor, yet in his maiden campaign the winger bagged 13 goals in 36 games to finish behind only Mark Hateley in the scoring chart, just two strikes adrift.

He had won over the Rangers followers at a stroke and Scottish football as a whole. On the back of an impressive first season

Laudrup became the first foreign player ever to win the Scottish Football Writers' Association player of the year award and made it a double when his fellow professionals chose him for their players' player of the year prize.

As soon as he arrived on Scottish shores his electric pace, ability to rifle through the gears at will, deadly use of the ball and bag of tricks earned Laudrup rave reviews. Walter Smith's stark warning was that he was only warming up – and he was right.

Smith said: "He is certainly a very special player. Brian will always make things happen and with us not having his sort of player for quite some time, the fans really appreciate him. We have not had a pacy wide player since Mark Walters – there aren't too many good ones around."

Smith gave Laudrup freedom to switch wings at will, in fact he positively encouraged it. That made for unnerving afternoons for perplexed defenders and opened up a rich source of opportunities for his team to exploit.

The manager added: "Each time he gets the ball you expect something to happen. Brian has it all. He is strong, well balanced and two-footed with quick feet and a breathtaking change of pace. And there's an end product to it all. He is not the sort of player who goes on aimless runs all over the field. He is direct and each burst tends to end with him sending over a dangerous cross or getting a shot on target. Brian is a strong character too. He has come into our team at a time when we have been making a few changes, so he has not had the luxury of easing himself ito a settled side. Instead of him looking tio the team for help, he has been the one who has produced the goods when we have gone through a ropy spell."

His displays in his impressive opening season had Rangers supporters overflowing with praise. On radio phone-ins and in newspaper columns the Light Blue brigade lavished praise on Laudrup, tagging him as the best ever import to grace Scottish football. Some even went as far as to claim he was the best ever player to wear the jersey. Walter Smith described him as the signing who had made the biggest impact during his time on the Ibrox coaching staff.

With seven down and two to go in the championship quest, Celtic were beginning to re-emerge from their slumbers but were no match for their Ibrox rivals. Eight in a row became reality in 1996 and Laudrup made it a hat-trick of trophy triumphs in just two seasons when he masterminded the 1996 Scottish Cup final success. First he devastated semi-final opponents Celtic with a sublime winner, starting the move which ended with him taking the return ball on his chest and clipping it over the keeper with the outside of his boot to make it 2-1 and book a place in the final.

That showdown with Hearts at Hampden was arguably the finest in a Rangers shirt for the Scandinavian import. He scored twice and set up Gordon Durie for each goal in his hat-trick as Rangers breezed past the Gorgie men without a hint of hesitation.

The fans left the national stadium singing the praises of Laudrup and overflowing with confidence on the eve of the defining season in the club's domestic history. All of a sudden nine in a row was appearing on the horizon, casting a giant shadow over the club and everyone attached to it.

Midway through that season, less than 18 months after his arrival, Rangers had moved to shackle their star man to the club for a substantial period. His initial contract was ripped up and Laudrup committed through to 2008. He claimed it was the easiest decision of his life, reasoning: "I enjoy playing for Rangers, the fans have been tremendous towards me and my family has settled in Scotland. What more could I want?"

David Murray hoped the new deal would put an end to a constant stream of speculation about the winger's future in Scotland. It didn't, and within months the sharks began to circle in European football's confined pool.

Laudrup, who had been belittled in some quarters for starring in what critics claimed was an inferior league, proved his doubters wrong when he stole the show for Denmark in Euro 96, scoring three of his country's four goals in the tournament.

Barcelona liked what they saw and a cheque for millions was waved in front of David Murray. The chairman, in an amazing demonstration of willpower, stood firm. Murray said: "Barcelona were talking in terms of £9million but you would have to wonder what Brian would be worth in today's transfer market. We told them simply that he is not for sale. Brian is a fantastic player, a fantastic guy and Rangers aren't interested in selling him."

When Laudrup first checked in at Rangers, the club owner went out of his way to knock down reports the new man would pocket £16,000 per week. He claimed it was less than half that, but whatever Murray spent was worth it.

For his part, Laudrup claimed money was not the motivation for he or his team-mates. He said: "Every single player on the park wants to be a winner. We all contribute in the way we can. The will to win is particularly strong at Rangers. A lot of people say to me that we go along from year to year winning titles and ask how can we go on like that. But I think there is nothing worse than losing and we all know that. That is why we keep on going. We all have the winning mentality. All the players on our side have that and it is more important than anything else."

With his international commitments out of the way and club future settled, Laudrup returned to Glasgow to focus on the imminent nine in a row attempt in the summer of 1996. It was a time for composure and for cool heads. In the No.11 they had the ideal candidate for a leading role and, not for the first time, he did not disappoint.

In 1996/97 he was the main man. Laudrup sat out only three of the 36 league games and scored in 16 of those 33 fixtures, with a double against Motherwell taking his league tally to 17 for the season.

The title was won by five points but one player was responsible for far more than that winning margin. The three points his goal against Dundee United brought to seal the championship are well documented but Laudrup's goals also earned a point against Aberdeen in October, three against Celtic courtesy of a 1-0 win the following month and a 4-3 victory against Hibs in December before the crunch time arrived. Again he stood up and delivered, with his goal earning a 2-2 draw against Aberdeen in March and another 1-0 victory against Celtic later in the same months. Those priceless goals put Rangers on the path to glory as time after time the club's leading scorer that term put pressure to one side to produce the goods.

His form did not go unnoticed in world football, with a procession of clubs once again poring over footage of his Rangers heroics. The familiar summer ritual of trying to fend off suitors was played out in the summer of 1997. With Laudrup entering the final year of his contract, Rangers could choose to cash in on a multi-million asset or risk losing him for nothing. He had just been named Scotland's player of the year for a second time in three years, following John Greig and Sandy Jardine in doing the double, and was a key man. But money is money and a decision had to be made.

The outcome was a bold one, with the cash sacrificed as David Murray chased 10 in a row. The chairman responded with an increased personal package, worth more than any other in the history of the club, as he rebuffed a £4.5million bid from Ajax and strong interest from Manchester United, who went as far as confirming that they had got their man. In fact it was Murray who won the day, keeping him for at least a year and hoping to extend that further after positive summer showdown talks at his Jersey home.

The club, perhaps mindful of the untouchable aura surrounding the nine in a row foot soldiers, showed remarkable solidarity in the face of such a powerful financial argument. The international star was staying right where he was and was primed for another shot at domestic dominance.

The final season proved to be a damp squib, with success deserting Rangers as a team and the goal fest of the previous term failing to materialise for Laudrup on a personal level. Had he forced the issue he could have hot footed it to Ajax 12 months earlier, after all no club wants and an unhappy player on their books, but he had developed a passion for his Glasgow club and an affinity that was strong enough to sway his decision. Despite the lack of honours, Laudrup never expressed regret about his decision to see out his Gers contract. Like a select band of continental players, he took to life in Scotland with enthusiasm and it translated in his performances on the pitch. He was one import who had the heart the Rangers fans expect.

In 1998, with his contract at an end, Laudrup departed. It was a dignified exit, openly admitting he was heading for Chelsea in search of the European honours he craved.

Before he could tackle English football head on he had the World Cup to contend with, helping his country to another dramatic run. It ended in the quarter-finals, when eventual champions Brazil triumphed 3-2, but Laudrup's quality was again evident. He and Michael both won a place in the Fifa All-Stars team from the France 98 tournament, retiring from the top level after 82 caps.

It allowed him to concentrate fully on his new career with Chelsea but life away from Ibrox proved fruitless, with his Stamford Bridge stay punctuated by a loan spell back home with Copenhagen before his £2million move to Ajax in the summer of 1999. An Achilles injury forced his retirement within months of his move to the Netherlands and brought an abrupt end to one of European football's brightest careers.

Laudrup said: "I had the problem from the World Cup in France in 1998. I tried all sorts of tablets and treatments but the problem would not go away. I thought about an operation but specialists could not give me guarantees that the problem would be solved, so I thought it was best to call it a day. It's always disappointing to end your career with an injury but I have to look over the 14 years I had playing, they were tremendous. My time in Scotland is at the top of my list, it was the best time in my career as a player. I have great memories from my time with Rangers."

Now the legendary winger is back home in Denmark, where he combines television commitments with his role as a partner in the Laudrup and Hogh Pro Camp youth coaching initiative, which also boasts a street football league for Denmark's young talents to hone their skills in the type of uninhibited environment that their mentor thrived in. Laudrup puts enjoyment above all else for the kids who fall under his guidance, the experiences of his own youth colouring his attitude. Laudrup, no stranger to being man marked by three players in his schooldays as he adapted to his big brother's star status, briefly quit the game as a teenager because of the pressure his place in Denmark's premier football family placed him under. Within days the lure of the ball became too strong and he returned to playing, wiser and stronger willed.

Every Rangers supporter can be thankful for that. He went on to provide hours of entertainment, moments of joy and memories that still linger on well beyond the confines of Scotland. Four years after his retirement Laudrup was named by Pele in a celebratory list of 125 of the greatest living football players on the planet to mark Fifa's centenary. One of the world's finest, one of Denmark's finest but a part of Laudrup's heart will always belong to Govan and a large chunk of Scottish football history will forever belong to Laudrup. The ultimate nine in a row hero.

**MAGIC MOMENT:** Govan's adopted Geordie scored an exquisite hat-trick to clinch the title in 1996.

# PAUL GASCOIGNE
## *'GAZZA'* 1995-1998

### GERS CAREER: Games 103; Goals 39; Caps 57

THE RANGERS Football Club was founded on the principles of dignity, respect and of unwavering dedication. Bill Struth became the self-appointed enforcer of those values and the upholder of a proud reputation but if the managerial master has been looking down to cast an eye over the recent history of the club he must surely have shuddered when the Paul Gascoigne circus pitched its tent on the south side of Glasgow.

Gazza was everything the heroes of Struth's era were not. He was loud, brash and unpredictable with a dark side that brought shame on himself and on the club with painful regularity. The contradiction was that as a player Paul Gascoigne was adored by the Rangers' supporters, even if Paul Gascoigne the person was unlovable for large swathes of his time in Scotland.

Walter Smith is a man not alien to the heritage of Rangers and a renowed disciplinarian with a reputation as a wolf in sheep's clothing, or enforcer in a sleeveless cardigan, among those who have served under him for club and country. Smith's patience was pushed to the limit as Gazza lurched from crisis to drama and back again, both on and off the field, but he stuck to the task of harnessing a man who was finding it increasingly difficult to stay on the straight and narrow. He persevered because the rewards were rich when the subject could be kept on the right side of the fine line.

Just as Jim Baxter had been classed as a flawed genius there were substantial chinks in Gazza's fragile armour. In fact, there were gaping holes. A man who publicly pleaded for forgiveness for the violence he subjected his wife too, the demons in his life appear immeasurable. They also appeared unbeatable, as the 40th birthday celebrations which ended with the fallen star in hospital in 2007 point towards, but Gascoigne had a legion of supporters willing him to do just that. They wanted so much for him to somehow come back from the brink and return to deliver the promises his talents had made when his star was in the ascendancy.

*Vision is the art of seeing things invisible to others.*

**Jonathan Swift**

The get out clause for the Ibrox faithful who stood accused of encouraging a man who, by his own manager's admission, tarnished the good name of their club was that when the football was on song the countless negatives were supressed. The suppressed psychological Magyars surfaced when he was not able to take advantage of his on-field therapy.

The midfielder knew it himself, claiming Rangers had saved him, prophetically telling Walter Smith at the end of his honour-laden first season in Glasgow: "Thanks for giving me my life back, my life is football."

It showed on the field with his virtuoso performances and full blooded, unyielding approach. The downside was that it also showed when he was sidelined, whether through the horrendous run of injuries he endured before and during his Rangers career or the familiar suspensions that curtailed his involvement so often.

Taking him to Govan was a gamble in no uncertain terms and the stakes were high. Walter Smith dipped into David Murray's pocket to lay £4.3million on the table not knowing exactly what hand he would be dealt. The punt was on a player who had come through 14 operations on a catalogue of injuries in the three years prior to his move to the Premier Division in 1995.

He still had two years of his Lazio contract to run when it became clear his days in Serie A were numbered. Despite his injury woes an orderly queue formed at his agent's door, with no shortage of foolhardy coaches convinced they held the key to unlocking the secret to Gazza's success.

Aston Villa were keen, Manchester United had been alerted, Chelsea were prepared to throw money at the Geordie and Leeds United also thought they could win the chase. But Rangers came up the blind side and nipped in ahead of the English trio to cross the line first and get their hands on the prize they all wanted – PG's initials on a playing contract.

If ever a player was in desperate need of a father figure then the English international was that man. In Walter Smith he felt he had discovered the mentor who could put his faltering career back on track and it was the manager's influence that played a huge part in the decision to venture into the unknown.

Thousands of fans had turned out at Ibrox to see the bleached-blond star roll up, with chants of 'Only One Paul Gascoigne' almost drowning out the words of the man himself inside at a packed press conference, but it was a bigger audience inside the famous old ground that he craved most.

As he settled into the Blue Room on his first day at work, Gascoigne said: "I met Walter for talks and it took me only minutes to decide I wanted to come here. He strikes me that he will be very like Terry Venables as a manager. You don't mess him around. I considered other clubs who were interested but I know how passionate the people here are about Rangers. It's a massive club.It was the size of the club which swung it for me – the ambition of the two men in charge, Walter Smith and David Murray."

Murray was at the height of his ambition, before the harsh financial realities of football at the turn of the millennium began to bite. The club were even prepared to raise the roof to accommodate their new arrival, quite literally.

Murray crowed: "This deal is just a continuation of our policy that has created the monster called Rangers. We already sell out the ground and next season we will have around 40,000 season ticket holders. Capacity is going up to 51,000 and if it has to go up to 61,000 then it will go up to 61,000. If the ground was looking like going all season ticket I wouldn't hesitate to put another tier on to a stand"

The midfield maestro wanted passion and had gone looking for it in the right place. The player was unmoved by warnings that his life would go under a microscope, claiming: "I've had no hiding place for the past 10 years. I come from Gateshead, so I'm not worried about anything I might face."

His team-mates were used to Glasgow's intense football life but even they were stunned by the furore that surrounded Gascoigne's every cough and splutter. Ally McCoist said: "It has been hard for him with the attention which surrounds him. The eyes of the nation were on him coming to Ibrox and I honestly don't know how he has handled it. I think Paul has not only been the addition of a truly world class player on the park but a huge influence off it. He is great in terms of morale in the dressing room. You have to have a happy dressing room. Paul is a very likeable lad and he is popular with the players."

He was also popular with the supporters from day one, with passionate displays in the pre-season friendlies of 1995 laying the foundations and his willingness to engage with the fans providing the mortar between the bricks. He made his debut in Denmark in a 2-1 win against Brondby, a match not short of incident with the four million pound man nabbing the winner in between stopping a few hearts in the visiting dugout when he went down clutching his right leg and then bawling out Brian Laudrup, a man seen as untouchable by the Rangers' support, for a misplaced pass and enjoying a spot of verbals with opponent Finn Lambek. It was all in a day's work.

The exchanges were not restricted to team-mates and rivals, he would respond to jibes from the stands or lap up the praise, always prepared to inject some humour into the dullest of occasions. That propesnity for on-field comedy so often landed him in hot water. Despite the harsh words that followed his flute mimicking antics during the Ibrox summer tournament of 1995, that infamous incident was an ill-advised piece of banter encouraged by team-mates taking advantage of a new boy's naivety to the Glasgow scene. It would take a foolhardy person to suggest Gascoigne had analysed the finer political nuances of Northern Irish politics and combined that with a social study of Glasgow's relationship to the Ulster troubles before deliberately setting out to stoke the embers of a simmering historic dispute.

This was Paul Gascoigne, he was trying to have a laugh just as he had when he burped in the face of a television reporter in response to a question years previously. Sometimes his humour worked, many more times it fell short of what most people would deem tasteful or respectful. That is the man, like it or lump it.

Not everyone was prepared to turn a blind eye to the comic episodes, particularly the dour Scottish refereeing fraternity. Who could forget official Dougie Smith flashing a card at Gascoigne after the player had administered the yellow to the ref, who had dropped it from his pocket. Another infamous incident, the difference on that occasion was that sympathy rather than over-hyped moral outrage was the overwhelming public response. Soon the SFA's referees' representative George Cumming launched a staunch defence of the whistlers, insisting Gascoigne was not being singled out despite Walter Smith's assertion that nine bookings inside six months was ludicrous. The Rangers manager claimed the harsh treatment was in danger of derailing his side's championship challenge as the suspensions began to mount up but Cummings turned it back on Rangers, claiming: "There is no way they (referees) favour or victimise any player or team – they just give decisions as they see them. It would be very unfair if people thought referees did that. The game would beneft from more honesty on the part of the managers and players who have a major responsibility as role models for young people."

The player was no stranger to bizarre takes on his treatment or on the antics which so often fuelled such great debate. Within months of landing in Scotland he was the subject of an SFA investigation after an over-zealous member of the public had reported the Rangers star for a crime the amateur sleuth considered outrageous and totally unacceptable. Gazza had been pictured pinching the bottom of Hearts striker Alan Lawrence and for that he deserved never to kick a ball again, apparently. Surprisingly commonsene prevailed and the SFA opted against taking action, just as Rangers did when commentator and newspaper columnist Gerry McNee lodged an official complaint that the player who had been the subject of his fiercest criticism had launched a football in his direction.

The police also had their say on Gascoigne during his honeymoon period with the Light Blues, called in to judge on his behaviour in a stormy encounter with Aberdeen in which he stood accused of elbowing Dons pair Stewart McKimmie and Paul Bernard, who also claimed to have been spat at by the England midfielder in the heat of battle at Ibrox. Team-mates John Brown and Alan McLaren were also investigated, along with the then Aberdeen striker Billy Dodds, but after a month's deliberation the procurator fiscal's office in

Glasgow decided against legal action. Coming in the wake of Duncan Ferguson's imprisonment for an on-field headbutt, the headline grabbing saga centred on Gazza once again brought the issue of self-policing in football to the fore. Donald Findlay, still on the Gers board at that stage, argued: "I think football or any sport which has disciplined rules where there is physical contact must police itself. If the law is going to intervene in any sport it is helpful and right that it does it uniformly. If it doesn't do it uniformly that does not seem fair." Was Gazza being singled out for unfair treatment? He couldn't be, the SFA said so.

Enough of that, back to the football. Gascoigne's debut season was as spectacular as the maiden campaign of almost any Rangers player before or after when it comes to sheer impact. Almost any – let's face it, a certain Marco Negri is probably in his rocking chair on his porch sunning himself in Italy thinking his 33 league goals in 28 Premier Division appearances in 1997/98 earn himself a place on the list.

For a midfielder, Gazza's own contribution to the 'goals for' column was not too shoddy in his first term in Ibrox office with 14 strikes in 28 appearances in the top flight and another four to his credit in seven domestic cup games.

The only disappointment came in Europe, where Gascoigne claimed his report card read "must do better" after a Champions League adventure which ended in disappointment as group rivals Juventus and Borussia Dortmund progressed. Gascoigne, who had been sent off against the Germans on the continent for dissent to earn a stinging rebuke from his manager during the campaign, had spelt out his ambitions when he arrived at the club. Conquering Europe was at the top of his list but it proved to be a bridge too far, even for a man of his ability.

He did at least have domestic joy to console himself in. The Gascoigne era kicked of in inauspicious fashion, with a comfortable 3-0 win over Morton at Ibrox in the league cup and continued apace as Rangers chased eight in a row. Gazza was on target on his debut but his first league goal was far more important, coming in a 2-0 victory against Celtic at Parkhead inside the first two months of the campaign.

He continued to score vital goals to help his side to a four-point title victory, including a match-winning double against Partick and the decisive strikes in a 1-0 victory over Aberdeen and 3-2 triumph against Falkirk.

Rangers entertained Aberdeen on the penultimate weekend of the 1995/96 season needing a victory to spark the Premier Division celebrations. Gascoigne did not let his fan club down and produced a virtuoso performance that lives long in the memory of everyone who witnessed it.

The result was Paul Gascoigne 3, Aberdeen 1. He bagged a hat-trick in a game in which Rangers had just five shots on target. It was a sensational performance, vintage Gazza as he rolled back the years and once again showed the type of vitality he had as youngster with Newcastle and Spurs. Brian Irvine had stunned Rangers by giving Aberdeen the lead in 20 minutes but within 90 seconds Gazza took control, collecting a Brian Laudrup corner on the edge of the box before ghosting past three Dons defenders and equalising with the cutest of chips from the outside of his right boot. The match went the distance and the main man lasted the pace, producing a scintillating lung-burster of a run in the 82nd minute which left Aberdeen defenders trailing in the whirlwind his darting run created before producing a curling 18-yard shot to make it 2-1. A penalty six minutes later rounded off the hat-trick and won the coveted league trophy. The Rangers players paraded the silverware resplendent in T-shirts bearing the No.8 in tribute to their run of consecutive titles but as it turned out they would have been justified in lauding their own No.8 in the same way after his one-man demolition act.

Three weeks later a Gordon Durie hat-trick and double from Brian Laudrup, with Gascoigne pulling the strings in midfield, gave Rangers a 5-2 win in the Scottish Cup final against Hearts and allowed the Geordie to exorcise the ghosts of his last appearance on the big stage, when his career was left hanging in the balance after his horrendous injury in Tottenham's 1991 FA Cup showdown with Nottingham Forest.

The rebirth of a hero was complete. Gascoigne had imposed his own media blackout after being branded a football thug and having his private life, including his on-off engagement to future wife Sheryl and a health scare involving new born son Regan, chewed up and spat out during his first year with the club.

He broke that blanket ban on speaking publicly in the wake of a momentous season which also saw him crowned as Scotland's player of the year by his peers to say: "I have had three and a half years of injuries, broken legs, knee caps and cheekbones. I have had them all and I thought my career was going away from me. I wasn't getting anywhere and I was so depressed and down. I would just like to say thanks to the manager, Archie Knox and the rest of the Rangers staff for what they have done. I am enjoying my football again and I am sure you can all see that by how happy I am. I have thoroughly enjoyed this season. It was hard at the start because I had a lot to prove to the fans and the media and I think I have done that. I'm now pleased it's all over – but I would like to add that I am no thug. I was really upset by that comment. I am a nice guy who wants to do well in football under enormous pressure. My main aim in football is to make people happy. I wasn't the most popular player when I first came to Rangers but I have worked hard during the last four months to get back to peak fitness to try and give the fans full value for money. I hope some of the things I have done have given pleasure to all fans, not just the Rangers ones. The game is all about enjoying yourself, win or lose."

Gascoigne often had a troubled relationship with the press but in his first season he was crowned the Scottish Football Writers' Association's player of the year. That prize, as much as the one from his fellow professionals, meant a lot to a man who could never hide his insecurities. He said: "If you lap up the good stuff said and written about you, then you have to accept the bad as well. I have had problems with the press wherever I have been. There were many reporters hoping I would do badly when I first came to Ibrox. Winning their award seems to suggest I have won them over with my ability on the park."

Those words were spoken in the summer of 1996, just before his starring role for England in Euro 96 and when it looked as though there were only clear blue skies where the dark clouds had previously hovered. There were omens however, with the player caught downing vodka in a dentist's chair during the England squad's warm-up tour in the Far East and snared in the controversy of damage to the team plan on their return journey.

A year later Gascoigne should have been revelling in the role of nine in a row hero, part of the dream team after a season peppered with important goals in the landmark title win and a double in the the 4-3 League Cup final success to complete his set of domestic medals.

Whereas football had done the talking the previous season, the shine was taken off what should have been a momentous campaign for Gascoigne by off-field troubles. In October of 1996 the story began to break of the Rangers star's violent attack on wife Sheryl during a stay at the Gleneagles Hotel. He darted away from the media frenzy to play in a Champions League game against Ajax in Amsterdam, where he was sent off, but returned to the sight of 400 supporters who had formed an anti-Gazza protest. The fans who had once adored him had turned and he has nobody to blame but himself, although some remained able to separate the man from the player and continued to back him.

The club, in the midst of the most important league season in its history, faced a huge dilemma. The instant reaction filtering out from the Ibrox corridors of power was that Gascoigne had played his final game in the famous jersey, that there could be no way back. Then came the change in direction, with Gazza back in harness.

Nobody will ever truly know the reasons, whether football or otherwise, behind the decision to give him another chance but Smith, in the aftermath of the reckless tackle that led to the dismissal in the Netherlands, did question his player's mental state and admitted: "There has to be a limit to anybody's patience. Understanding can only go so far." Donald Findlay took it a step further, claiming: "We will give him help if he needs it. Everyone at Rangers takes Gazza as he is. Despite what he has been doing off the park, the guy can play football. We would like him to be left to do that for Rangers."

He did go on to do that, part of the team that won the league at Dundee United and that collected the trophy for the ninth consecutive season at Ibrox the following week.

The couple's reconciliation, and Gascoigne's public apologies and claims counselling had reformed him, made the situation less uneasy as the great healer of time passed. The situation made Gascoigne a natural target for opposition fans, perhaps helping to galvanise support for him from within the Rangers fan base at a time when the jury was out on his merits as a hero.

The 1997/98 season proved trophyless, Walter Smith was on his way out of the club and there would be no room for the increasingly unpredictable midfielder in the new regime. At the turn of 1998 he was fined for a repeat of his flute-playing mime, this time lighting the touch paper in an Old Firm derby, and the relationship was beginning to show signs of strain.

The potential troubles and baggage did not deter a string of English admirers, with Aston Villa leading the chase before

Middlesborough stepped in to clinch a £3million deal to take him back closer to his north-east roots in the summer of 1998.

With Newcastle, Spurs, Lazio and Rangers to his credit this was a different prospect as the Teesiders chased promotion to the top tier of the English game rather than the European honours Gascoigne craved. He played his part in Boro's return to the Premiership before being reunited with Walter Smith, at Everton by that time, in 2000.

A short attempt at prolonging his playing days with Burnley and then the lonely outpost of Gansu Tianma in China came to an end in 2003, as Gascoigne's personal troubles began to take over from his football achievements. His dalliance with management, launched with a short coaching stint with Boston and continued fleetingly as boss of Kettering Town, brought the curtain down on his career in the game that had been his life.

What followed was a trail of difficulties, from dabbling with cocaine to his ongoing battle against alcoholism and everything in between from bulimia, obsessive compulsive disorders and even bipolar disease. It is only post-football that the public has really had an insight into the afflictions that impinged on his activities on the park, revealing there was far more to the man than just a Geordie joker who could pull a few tricks with a ball at his feet.

Now a shadow of the bustling athlete who graced Ibrox, Gascoigne lurches from one incident to the next. His life saving surgery to rectify a burst stomach ulcer in 2007 did not prevent him from slipping back into his old ways of drinking and smoking, leading to warnings that yet another football genius is playing with his life. For a man who once claimed playing was his reason for living, the stark prophecies are unlikely to make a dent. In 2010 a Newcastle car crash, in which the fallen star was hospitalised, was the latest in a string of headline-grabbing incidents. Where next in the world of Paul Gascoigne is anyone's guess. For Rangers' supporters whatever follows will never eclipse or erase the memories of his finest hours with the club crest on his chest.

**MAGIC MOMENT:** The Hammer struck in the first Old Firm derby of 1997 to demonstrate the dead ball ability that became his trademark.

# JÖRG ALBERTZ
## *'THE HAMMER'* 1996-2001

### GERS CAREER: Games 182; Goals 82; Caps 3

I N FOOTBALL it is generally accepted that nice guys win nothing but Jorg Albertz provided the exception to the rule as a Rangers player. The likeable German won the admiration and affection of his club's supporters and an array of silverware during five years at Ibrox. More than anything, he managed to persuade the fans that he had blue blood coursing through his veins and for a man from Monchengladbach rather than Milngavie that was no mean feat,

There were two key tools in the locker for the powerfully built midfielder. The first was a deadly left foot, the second was a killer delivery of some tartan-tinged dialect. Just as Jan Molby turned from Dane to Scouser while with Liverpool, Albertz became the most Scottish German in the history of football.

He was passionate about his new life, swapping Rhineland for Clydeside and all that entailed. Albertz soaked up the Scottish countryside, the culture and the people while in return he was accepted in a way very few overseas players had done before .

John Macmillan, general secretary of the Rangers Supporters Clubs, recalls with fondness the way the German reached out and touched the Light Blue legions. Macmillan said: "You never felt that Jorg Albertz was ill at ease, no matter how many people surrounded him. The fact he spoke such good English was a major bonus – mind you, it was more Scottish than English he spoke. Some of the words he came out with and the accent meant that if you closed your eyes you would think you were in the room with a Scotsman born and bred."

Despite a tremendous pedigree in the Bundesliga, he arrived as a virtual unknown in 1996 but left in 2001 as an honorary Scotsman and a Rangers man through and through. Unlike so many foreign imports, Albertz came equipped with a sponge-like capacity for soaking up his surroundings. It paid off in grand style with instant acceptance and, in time, hero status.

Macmillan said: "From day one the fans seemed to go for Jorg, he was a player everyone appreciated. A big factor in that was the fact he gave 100% every time he played, he wasn't one of the mercenaries who came over and took the money without caring about the club. With Jorg you felt as though he took Rangers to heart. Certainly when it came to leaving he didn't want to go and I don't think I know any fan who wanted him to go either. It's very rare that you get a player who does not divide opinion in some way but he was one of those men.

"He was a great servant at Ibrox, on and off the pitch. I attended many supporters' functions that Jorg was a guest at and he was always happy to be there. He would spend the night chatting with fans, signing autographs and posing for pictures. That might not sound a big deal, but so many players turn up when it is obvious they don't want to be there. Jorg was always aware that the fans turned up every week to give their support and he wanted to give something back.

"Above all he was a fantastic player, one of the best ball strikers in the game. When he stood over the ball for a free-kick there was a real sense of anticipation among the supporters, you expected him to do something spectacular. He scored so many spectacular goals that it's not surprising the supporters took to him."

The relationship was reciprocal, with the expensive import always at pains to stress the importance of the Bears in the stands. The big German, who stood at 6ft 1in and tipped the scales at almost thirteen and a half stone, was an imposing figure on the pitch, only Lorenzo

Amoruso was more powerful, but even he needed a little help from his friends. He said: "It doesn't matter which game you are playing in, with the supporters behind you making noise, it is always easier to play."

Albertz oozed confidence and efficiency in everything he did and his performances won instant approval. Macmillan recalls: "I remember being away from home when Albertz signed and my son phoning to tell me. He was someone I'd never heard of but the papers were dragging up the fact he was a Catholic, which we couldn't understand. It was if they were trying to stir something up when really it shouldn't be a story whether a player is catholic or not. It certainly didn't make any difference to the way he was received because Albertz was an instant success.

"Sometimes you get players who are nice guys but don't quite cut it on the pitch. Albertz had both, and that type of player is rare. The Hammer was such a fitting nickname. I don't know who came up with it, but it describes his left foot perfectly."

Re-runs of the collection of Albertz piledrivers are still popular on internet clip sites. Watch them in detail and what becomes clear is that his scoring touch was as much about precision as it was power, with some subtle finishes mixed in among the net shredding efforts that became the big German's trademark. His shots regularly measured well in excess of 80mph, putting him among world football's big hitters.

*Good left feet are like bricks of gold.* **Jimmy Greaves**

Accused of laziness more than once, the relaxed style of the distinctive flame haired midfielder proved hard for some to accept but his effectiveness put paid to any long term doubts about his ability to make a useful contribution. Some players would run and run for the cause but Albertz did not need to, he had an intelligence that allowed him to make the game look easy and provided him with time and space to do so much damage.

In all competitions he netted 82 goals in 182 games, a remarkable ration that puts him up there with the finest attacking midfielders Rangers have ever had. His best individual tally came in the 1999/2000 season when he scored 20 across the SPL, Scottish Cup and Champions League. It eclipsed Alex MacDonald's bag of 18 in the European Cup Winners' Cup season of 1971/72 and Andy Penman's haul of 19 in 1968/69 and put him alongside the modern equivalents of Barry Ferguson, Paul Gascoigne and Brian Laudrup.

There was far more to Albertz than a goalscoring threat. He cost £4million in 1996, a decent rate for a man who went on to be capped three times by his country after moving to what was far from Europe's most glamorous league. Albertz emerged as a youngster with Fortuna Dusseldorf but it was with SV Hamburg that he really blossomed, appointed captain and labelled with The Hammer tag as his spectacular shots from distance began to be noticed. He was idolised by the Hamburg fans and that worship translated when he moved to Britain.

Albertz made an inconspicuous start to his Rangers career, filling in for the injured David Robertson at the start of the 1996/97 season. After three months he was liberated by Robertson's return, sent forward to the midfield berth he preferred to put teams to the sword.

He eased into Ibrox life with a Teutonic efficiency but soon the shackles flew off and the goals flowed. Bang, Albertz opened his account in front of a home crowd in a 3-1 League Cup win against Ayr United on September 4. Two weeks later, in the next round, he scored in the 4-0 quarter final win against Hibs and five days later bagged the sixth in the 6-1 semi-final win against Dunfermline. Doubles from Ally McCoist and Paul Gascoigne earned the 4-3 victory against Hearts at Celtic park and the medal chase had begun for the new man.

The first of three league championship gongs followed that season, the year of nine in a row. He had contributed a goal in every three games in the Premier Division as part of a free scoring midfield with several attacking thorns. Brian Laudrup bagged 17, Paul Gascoigne had 13 to his name.

The Champions League experience was the sour point, with six group games yielding just a solitary victory against Grasshopper and five defeats at the hands of the Swiss side in the return leg as well as Ajax twice and Auxerre twice.

Season two ended trophyless, with further disappointment on the continent as the Light Blues failed to reach the group stages of the Champions League and fell at the first hurdle in the Uefa Cup.

Albertz hit double figures again in the league, despite his side's run of disappointing form, and hoped to endear himself to incoming manager Dick Advocaat.

He did that, at least to begin with, and was a mainstay for the Dutch coach as the league crown was reclaimed in style as part of a stunning treble. Every competition had the mark of Albertz stamped all over it, not least the League Cup when he scored the winner in the 2-1 triumph against St Johnstone at Celtic Park. His haul of league goals included a hat-trick against hapless Dundee, part of a 6-1 win, and six penalties. He created countless others with his arrowed passes and sharp thinking as the Advocaat party moved into full swing. In Europe Albertz had helped propel his side on a decent Uefa Cup run, ended by Parma, and chipped in with goals against the Italians as well as Shelbourne and Beitar Jerusalem.

The best was yet to come, with Albertz unstoppable in the 1999/2000 campaign. The margin of victory in the Premier Division was an astonishing 21 points from shell-shocked Celtic, with 96 goals scored and 17 coming from the German conductor. He shared the Ibrox golden boot, level pegging with Rod Wallace in the league and the two sharpshooters tied on one apiece in the Scottish Cup for the goal race to end in an honourable draw at 18-18 on domestic terms. Albertz levelled the series with the last strike of the season as he capped the 4-0 Scottish Cup final victory against Hearts with his crowning contribution to the offensive effort of a satisfying season. The midfielder had missed the 1998 Scottish Cup final through suspension but made up for it the following year. Asked if he would shoulder the responsibility for a spot kick if it moved into a dead ball contest he responded: "A penalty shoot out? I'll take all five of them!" In the end, it didn't even come close as Hearts were steamrollered into the turf.

Wallace and Albertz were inseparable in Europe too, each claiming two goals in the Champions League and Uefa Cup. Albertz had the edge in terms of effectiveness, scoring the only goal of the game against Bayern Munich in a 1-1 group draw and the winner in the 1-0 victory at PSV Eindhoven in the next group game.

Off the field, 1999/2000 proved to be an eye-opener. He was an honorary Scotsman in attitude as well as accent but found himself, briefly, in the unusual position of having to issue a public apology to the Tartan Army in 2000. When the German was brought down by Paul Lambert during a 4-2 Old Firm victory his trailing leg struck the grounded Scotland midfielder, causing serious facial injuries and concussion. The result was a penalty to Rangers, converted by Albertz, but he was wracked with guilt despite having no blame apportioned to him. The injury ruled his Celtic opponent out of Scotland's two Euro 2000 play-off matches against England and Albertz said at the time: "I was so sorry to hear that Paul Lambert is missing the two play-off matches because I'd love to see this country beat England. I feel really guilty and I'd like to apologise to the Tartan Army even though there was nothing I could do about the incident. I'll be supporting Scotland because I've become really attached to the country and everyone knows what these matches mean to those involved." The apology was heartfelt but not universally accepted, with a window at his Helensbugh home bricked in the aftermath of the incident.

Albertz loved almost everything about Scotland, not just the football. He took to hillwalking, with Ben Lomond one of his favourite spots in the world, yet he struggled to come to terms with the bitterness surrounding Glasgow football life. He said: "I do love Old Firm games, but it should stop after 90 minutes when we shake hands. I know the importance of the game here, and I respect people who are Protestant or Catholic. If someone gets stabbed or shot during fights after a game I just don't accept it. I just don't understand people fighting over a bad result or a good result or an argument about football. That is beyond me. Old Firm games always have tension around them, that's part of the build up. If there is a bad tackle and the crowd goes up and the players argue on the pitch, that is normal. It is not chess we are playing. I can't be blamed if someone goes out and stabs someone after the game. It has nothing to do with us – or should have nothing to do with us. If it is that way we'd be better to play cards or whatever."

That placid approach did not manifest itself on the pitch when it came to Glasgow contests. All in all, Albertz netted eight times against Celtic in the space of just five seasons. He had the Indian sign over the Hoops.

On the back of his most profitable season for Rangers, the only way was up for a player flying high as the 2000/2001 season arrived. Or was it? With Giovanni van Bronckhorst hitting form, Arthur Numan bedded in and Neil McCann on the books the German was being edged out. Barry Ferguson was blossoming, Claudio Reyna was an international captain and Tugay sparkled. Whether in defence or midfield, the doors were slamming in the face of a crowd favourite.

As early as 1999, Advocaat made it clear that Albertz had no right to expect automatic selection and that was never going to be enough for a proud exponent of football's fine arts. The relationship became tense as the Dutch coach began to increase competition for midfield places, although Albertz never let his professional standards slip and was determined to retain his dignity. Amid the well publicised fall-outs he managed to clock up 20 appearances, and 10 goals, before his tearful farewell at the end of a barren season for the club.

Even when he was at loggerheads with Advocaat, the midfielder never once threw his toys from the pram and was fierce in defence of claims that he was trying to engineer a move away from Glasgow. He said: "I never said I wanted to leave the club. The question was if Rangers came to me now and offered to extend my contract, what would I do? I said that was two and a half years away, which is a long time, and I would have to see the situation then. I said if it is the same situation as it is now after that time, then there would no future for me at Ibrox – but there has never been any intention for me to look for another club to join. It is true for every player that they want to play. Nobody wants to sit on the bench, but everybody knows what Dick Advocaat wants to do and that is to bring good players into the squad. That is the way football is. Not even Manchester United can have the same starting eleven every game. I don't like it but I have to accept it. I try to convince the gaffer every training session that I should be in the starting 11, but the other players are trying as well and we have got good players here."

Advocaat suggested Albertz should have been happy to pocket his pay without breaking sweat, claiming: "Manchester United have four or five top players sitting on the bench and that is a strength of ours at the moment. We can have Jorg Albertz, Colin Hendry, Lorenzo Amoruso or Craig Moore sitting on the bench and, for that amount of money, I would be happy to sit on the bench as well." But Albertz wasn't happy, he wanted to justify his wage.

Before he left. Albertz played his part in a notable first Rangers, one of the 11 men who took to the field against St Johnstone on 4 March 2000 when for the first time in the club's history a team without a single Scotsman was sent out. Albertz was joined by compatriot Stefan Klos, American skipper Claudio Reyna, Italian star Lorenzo Amoruso, Australia's Tony Vidmar, Dutch duo Arthur Numan and Giovanni Van Bronckhorst, Russian winger Andrei Kanchelskis, Turkish international Tugay Kerimoglu, English striker Rod Wallace and Chilean import Seb Rozental. It brought much wailing and gnashing of teeth among representatives of Scotland's pro players, who warned Scottish football was staring into a black hole and would be buried by the relentless succession of imports.

The difference with Albertz was that few would argue he was keeping homegrown talent out of the team under false pretences. Scotland had no player to match his unique talents.

While Advocaat was not a fully fledged fan of the Albertz style, those who played alongside him in the Rangers team were in no doubt about his talents. Brian Laudrup, an expert in attacking midfield play, led the calls for an international recall for Albertz as the World Cup of 1998 loomed. Laudrup said: "Without a doubt Jorg has been sensational. The German squad is immense with some fantastic players, but I'd recommend him to be there in France this summer. I'd certainly have him in my side for the World Cup. Jorg has just signed a long-term deal keeping him at Ibrox well into the next millennium, in the next few seasons I think we could see one of the finest players at Ibrox for a while. I really believe Jorg can surprise us even more and that has to be good news for Rangers."

Laudrup had not bargained on the input of the Little General, who did not share the Danish winger's generous assessment of the German master. It became a battle of wills on the training ground, with Advocaat almost gloating as he admitted: "Everybody knows that I told him at the start of the season that if everyone was fit, it would be difficult for him to get in the team – just the same as I told Colin Hendry. We had a big fight, that is all – and I won." He did win in the short term, yet it is Albertz and not Advocaat who remains held in highest regard in Govan.

Albertz was never flavour of the month with Advocaat, never indispensable, but he remained a valuable asset. It cost Hamburg £3million to reclaim their hero when he returned to Germany in 2001, a record for the club. It was a testing time for the player, who had settled on the west coast of Scotland. He said: "It is not an easy decision for me – it was one of the hardest I have had to make in my life so far. It has been very emotional but I have never said I want to leave the club because I don't like the club any longer. Other things were going on behind the scenes I can't and won't accept because I'm 30 years of age and I'm not a wee boy. I don't want to talk about these things because I'm not the sort of person who wants to make bad stories about other people. I have made up my mind and hopefully everyone will accept it. I had a great relationship with everyone in the team. I also have a proper relationship with Dick Advocaat."

A relationship break-up and his father's ill-health were both cited as reasons for the player's eventual departure in 2001 but he was at pains to deny either of those factors influenced him. Instead, football led his decision to part with the club he loved. He said: "Every player who leaves Rangers will have some regrets, but I have to look forward now. I don't know now if it is the right decision to leave. I will only know that in a couple of months or maybe a couple of years. It is very hard to leave, but you have to make decisions in your life and these decisions have to be for yourself."

Albertz was privately believed to be growing increasingly frustrated by Advocaat's reliance on a burgeoning Dutch colony, with 10 players and coaches from the Netherlands on the Ibrox staff by the time of his departure, but publicly retained a dignified silence. When it was time to go, the club was acutely aware of the potential damage the loss of a fans' favourite could do. Chairman David Murray sprang into action with a charm attack, claiming: "We are categorically not promoting the sale of Jorg Albertz. Jorg spoke to me about a week ago and intimated that eventually he would like to return to Germany, which is understandable all things taken into consideration. There is absolutely no way we are trying to force Jorg out of the door. I fully understand how the supporters feel about Jorg Albertz, but when he eventually does leave, hopefully in the long term rather than the short term, he will know that his application and commitment to the club was greatly appreciated."

In the years that followed the extent of the fall-out became clear, with Albertz revealing: "My time at Rangers was almost perfect. I came and had no problems getting integrated. I got along well with the players and media, I liked the directors and the whole atmosphere at the club. To be honest, I got along very well with everybody, except Dick Advocaat. Advocaat was the reason why I had to leave. I just couldn't cope with him, and then along came Hamburg, and they offered me a return to the Bundesliga."

Albertz, alongside Blackburn-bound Tugay, took part in an emotional lap of honour around Ibrox after making his farewell appearance in a 4-0 thumping of Hibs on the final day of the 2000/01 season. An Albertz penalty opened the scoring and sealed his departure with a goal. Early in 2003, with budget constraints hitting hard, Hamburg took the decision to part company with a player reputed to be collecting £1.5million in wages annually and who had fallen out of favour with both the coach and the fans.

Birmingham and Fulham were both reported to be interested and mischief makers suggested Celtic could offer the perfect chance for a return to his beloved west coast. Almost perfect, with Albertz claiming: "Celtic could offer me all the money in the world, I'd never play for them, I simply wouldn't do that to Rangers, my fans and to myself. Although I am a Catholic I never had any problems with them being the Protestant club. Among the foreign players it is first of all the performance which counts. As I played really well right from the start, I was accepted by the fans. This relationship turned into something like love – I have never had a better relation with the fans than I had with the Rangers' loyals. It doesn't get better than that and wherever I'll go in the future, I'll miss that special feeling."

Aged 32 by that stage, a short spell with Chinese side Shenua was followed by a re-introduction to German football with Greuther Furth before finding his way home to Fortuna Dusseldorf in 2005. A brief flirtation with Scottish football, during a short-term return to action with Clyde in 2008, brought him back into focus before he returned home to enjoy his retirement. The player has gone but the love lingers on in the blue half of Glasgow.

MAGIC MOMENT: Super Mo became the latest
Old Firm hero with his match winner to
help bring the 2009/10 title flag to Ibrox.

# MAURICE EDU
### 'MO' 2008 – present

**GERS CAREER:** Games 37; Goals 4; Caps 16
(up to summer 2010)

I N THE days of David Meiklejohn and company the Glasgow
grapevine was what brought the Rangers heroes closer to the
rank and file supporters. The pub gossip and street corner
chatter was the lifeblood of football's great soap opera in a city that
provided the greatest sporting stage of all.
Almost a century later, the world has changed
and dragged the game with it. Now Twitter
and Facebook are king and a new breed of
stars are being embraced in a way the
founding fathers of Ibrox could never have
dreamt.

Never has the world been so small or quite
so inquisitive thanks to the booming social
networking scene that has brought like
minded souls together from the farthest flung
corners of the globe. At the forefront of the
digital drive is Maurice Edu, the cult hero in
the Rangers pack who has become an
internet sensation off the park as well as a
sterling servant on the pitch. The man from Fontana has brought a
slice of Californian free spirit to Scotland's west coast and has been
welcomed with open arms by a set of supporters bowled over by his

zest for life and passion for the game that has made him an international star. He's young, enthusiastic and enjoying life to the full as he plays the part of a Light Blue idol to perfection. He arrived as a stranger in a strange land but quickly become engrained in Glasgow life and won a place in the collective heart of the Rangers faithful with his energetic performances and bubbly personality.

*It's not called social change or heavy debate, it's called twitter. I mean the clue is in the name.*

**Stephen Fry**

We know about his bubbly personality not because he is particularly prolific in the traditional media but because we can follow his every move and chart his inner thoughts through the medium of Twitter, Edu's vehicle of choice as he bids to keep his growing fan base abreast of the latest developments in his life story. Edu's propensity for posting his movements on the internet have become part of the fabric of football and with every day his list of followers on Twitter is growing. At the time of writing the American midfielder boasts more than 360,000 aficionados on his Twitter page, with each and every one getting good value as their star man throws his heart and soul into his online existence. Everything from photographs from the Rangers pre-season tour of Australia in the summer of 2010 to written updates on every aspect of his day to day existence.

'Morning ppl! On my way to training listening to The Miseducation of Lauryn Hill! One of my fav cds, bringing back some good memories!'

'1st game of the season today vs Kilmarnock! Let's start the season off with 3 pts! Wish us luck, let's go!'

'My Friday night: Nip Tuck box set, sleep. 1st game of the season tomorrow so gotta rest up for it! U guys enjoy your night/day n b safe!'

'Don't u hate when u leave the car wash and it starts raining or u drive through dust/dirt?'

'Sushi time! Love it'

Mundane, maybe. Minutiae, definitely. Interesting, undoubtedly. The very essence of Twitter is to enable anyone and everyone to let the world know about their life. The fact Maurice Edu is better known than the average Twitterer just adds to the intrigue as thousands of Rangers fans, USA fans, football fans and Edu fans converge on his Twitter page every day for their fix.

Endorsed and used by celebrities and Joe Public alike, Twitter has become a phenomenon. Created in 2006 by a trio of American technology innovators, it has taken off in a short period of time at an astonishing rate. The concept is simple, with Twitterers able to post messages, or Tweets, of no more than 140 characters. Frequency is entirely up to the user, with Edu among the more habitual users.

He is far from alone. By the start of 2010 the service boasted more than 75million users across the globe. At its peak, during the summer months of 2009, more than 7.8million new Twitterers were signing up each month. Users are getting younger, with the average age now lower than those getting their social networking fix on Facebook, Myspace and other similar sites.

In many ways Edu is the stereotypical Twitterer, with youth on his side and plenty to shout about on a daily basis as he gets to grips with Glasgow life and all of its eccentricities. The drawback of microblogging from within the Old Firm goldfish bowl is the media attention that Edu's Tweets have attracted and the subsequent tabloid headlines the tales of the SPL's best known Twitterer have attracted.

Even taking that press interest into account, Edu's access all areas approach to life makes him a marketing man's dream. Far from discouraging their American hero's enthusiasm for reaching out to the supporters, Rangers sensibly piggybacked onto his personable spirit with their own slice of the Maurice pie. The neat line in Edu T-shirts, emblazoned with the slogan 'It ain't what Edu, it's the way that Edu it' captured the mood perfectly on the back of his most important contribution in a Light Blue shirt so far – the 92nd minute winner against Celtic at Ibrox as the 2009/10 championship race drew towards a nerve jangling conclusion. Edu struck from all of three yards but it was the importance rather than the style of the goal that counted. That February victory edged Rangers closer to the big prize and ensured Edu's status as a true cult hero was guaranteed. Supporters, players and coaching staff joined the celebrations on the hallowed turf as the likeable American basked in his role as the star of the show.

Success did come at a price though, with Edu quickly learning that sometimes, just sometimes, a low profile is advisable in the wake of an Old Firm battle. Speaking in the aftermath of the match winning performance, Edu said: "I have been trying to stay low key ever since. I haven't been out and about much at all. But when I do bump into fans there has been a big difference in their reaction. They always want to talk about the goal against Celtic. It's the highlight of my time at Rangers – the best goal of my career. When I'm old and grey I can look back and say I scored a last-minute winner in an Old Firm game for Rangers. That's pretty special. I have watched it again a few times and it's brilliant to see the manager and coaches' reaction. I didn't see any of this because I had half the team lying on me."

The worship was not a new thing for Edu, who had been given the warmest of welcomes from virtually the first minute he stepped onto Scottish soil. His first appearance as a substitute warming up in front of the Rangers supporters was greeted by the now familiar Edu chant and from then on he was part of the family.

Not that it has all been a bed of roses in Scotland. Edu admitted in a newspaper interview: "You get a lot of attention being a Rangers player. I suppose being a 6ft-plus black guy in Glasgow does make me stand out a bit more. There are good points and a few bad ones. I try to operate under the radar. There might be some negatives but I'm doing the job I love so who am I to complain? I love playing at such a massive club. There is fame and stuff that comes with it which can be good as well but that's not too important. Playing in big stadiums and the Champions League, that's why I do this. When I stop playing I want to be able to show people my medals. That's why I'm at Rangers."

Mo Edu had a helping hand along the way from Mo Jo, having played under Maurice Johnston at Toronto during his formative years in the MLS. He was rookie of the year in the American league in 2007 and the following summer was snapped up by Walter Smith in a £2.6million deal.

Johnston once described Edu as 'easily the best young player in the United States' and the youngster arrived in Scotland with the weight of expectation on his shoulders. Although he played 12 matches in the 2008/09 championship campaign, his first term at Ibrox was ruined by injury. He was back in time for the second half of the 2009/10 league winning season and by the time the 2010/11 term began he was firmly entrenched in Walter Smith's starting eleven.

He was 22 when he was recruited from Toronto but his powerful performances belied those tender years, with his wholehearted displays in midfield adding steel to the core of Smith's team. With a five year contract in place when he jetted into Scotland, Edu is in it for the long haul.

He was already a US international by the time he arrived, having made his debut in 2007, and featured in three matches during the 2010 World Cup in South Africa to keep the Light Blue flag flying high on the world stage.

Edu, the globetrotting techno fan, is far removed from the traditional view of a Rangers hero as is possible to imagine but he has filled the role in grand style as a surrogate son of the Bears.

The heartland of Rangers has changed beyond all recognition since the days when Davie Meiklejohn patrolled the beat as captain yet the supporters have remained constant in their demands and expectations of the stars in Light Blue through the twists and turns history has plotted for Glasgow's south side. In Meek's era the Bears wanted lion hearted commitment, blue blood coursing through the veins of the chosen few who could leap the boundaries from terracing to pitch, and a passion for the Rangers. Today, fans crave nothing more and nothing less. Edu is one of the imported players able to give that type of commitment to an increasingly diverse band of supporters.

In the 1920s, as Rangers players began to establish themselves as personalities as well as performers, they played to a crowd drawn primarily from Govan and its overspill. Today they come by car, coach, train, boat and plane to catch sight of their favourites and hail from North America, Australia and every global outpost in between.

Perhaps not surprisingly, the heroes have become just as cosmopolitan. Edu is the latest in a proud line of overseas players to have succeeded in weaving their way into the fabric of Ibrox.

Where Edu differs is that he is more steel than silk, whereas the bulk of imported idols have been creators rather than destroyers. Goal scorers in particular have found a path to cult status, with Dado Prso a case in point.

The latter day Mark Hateley breezed into Glasgow in 2004 wearing his pedigree as an experienced Croatian international as a badge of honour. He arrived from Monaco, swapping Monte Carlo for Govan in a move that proved to be an Alex McLeish masterstroke.

Prso proved to be strong, courageous and eager to impress. He scored 21 goals in his first season, winning league and League Cup winner's medals, as his 6ft 2in frame and impeccable technique proved too much for the majority of SPL defences to handle. In the run to the last sixteen of the 2005/06 Champions League he was a key man as he established himself as a firm favourite with the Ibrox supporters before retiring from the game in 2007.

He was outlasted at Rangers by another goal-scoring hero from foreign shores. When Nacho Novo wandered off into the sunset to return to his Spanish homeland with Sporting Gijon in the summer of 2010 it represented the end of a love affair between the diminutive striker and the Light Blue legions.

It had begun when he was lured to Ibrox in 2004 in a £450,000 deal, signed by Alex McLeish after impressing during two years with Dundee. He had first landed in Scotland in 2001 and was given his big break by Raith Rovers. Up to that point he had been an unremarkable player in Spain with lowly SD Huesca. With Raith he scored 20 times in 33 First Division fixtures and was soon bought by Dundee for £100,000.

He wound up at Rangers as a 25-year-old and was leading scorer in his first season, winning the league and League Cup in 2004/05 alongside Prso. With the two together, little and large, there was not a more potent strike force in the country. His goal on Helicopter Sunday at Hibs, to clinch the SPL, became the stuff of legend and put him up there among the modern day icons.

Novo suffered his share of frustration under a succession of managers, dropped and recalled with monotonous regularity, but never lost the spark and determination that made him such an endearing player for the supporters to latch onto.

He was a standout performer in the 2007/08 campaign, when he scored the decisive Uefa Cup semi-final penalty to take Rangers past Fiorentina and into the final, and went on to win a league and cup double in 2008/09 when he scored a stunning Scottish Cup final volley against Falkirk to clinch the prize.

The icing on the cake came in May 2010, just weeks before his departure from the club was confirmed, when Novo launched his memoirs. The title was simple but effective: *I Said No Thanks*. It pointed to Novo's curt and decisive response when he was invited to join Celtic rather than Rangers in 2004, a decision he would never regret after embarking on a long and passionate partnership with the Bears.

Novo's six year stint in club colours made him one of the longest serving players of his era.

American actor Will Rogers famously claimed that 'heroing is one of the shortest-lived professions there is' and he appeared to have a point. The most loved players at Ibrox in recent years have come and gone, with Kris Boyd's departure for Middlesbrough in 2010 marking the departure of another cult figure.

Siege mentality had a big part to play in Boyd's popularity. Pilloried in so many quarters for a perceived lack of effort and application, the former Kilmarnock man had the all-important knack of scoring goals. Anything else he did, or didn't do, on the park seemed something of an irrelevance. By the end of 2009/10 his record stood at 127 goals in 152 starts, the type of form that tempted Boro boss Gordon Strachan to return to Scotland to plunder the land for the finest scoring talent.

There were fears that Kirk Broadfoot would follow Novo and Boyd down Edmiston Drive and into the sunset when his contract ran down in the summer of 2010. With the club in financial flux, there was the very real fear that another cult figure was destined to be consigned to the history books.

While Novo and Boyd, with their goals and glory, were natural icons for the supporters to pin their hopes on, defender Broadfoot is a more unlikely hero. Yet he has won cult status, not to mention a collection of medals and the beginnings of a Scotland cap collection, thanks to his hard work and good old fashioned honest endeavour. His promotion to the Scotland side was met with cynicism by those outside of Ibrox in 2008 – but he responded by becoming an instant hero, scoring on his debut against Iceland to prove the doubters wrong. You can't keep a good Bear down.

The days when the burgh of Govan was on the up and up are gone but through a swathe of agencies and organisations there is hope on the horizon of major regeneration, with one beacon of the glorious past still towering proudly above the skyline. Ibrox remains the proud throwback to the area's glorious past. The Archibald Leitch façade will forever be preserved, even if the giant stadium it now fronts has been transformed beyond all recognition from the 10,500 capacity grandstand Meiklejohn and his team-mates plied their trade in front of. The surroundings may have changed but the Ibrox loyal still crave a west coast working class hero to call their own – and Broadfoot fits that bill, fulfilling the role of the fan on the pitch long after the likes of Barry Ferguson and Kris Boyd have been tempted away by the lure of bumper wage packets elsewhere.

He was the St Mirren captain, and a Love Street hero, when he became an unexpected target for Walter Smith in 2007. He joined in time for the 2007/08 season and was an ever-present in the run to the Uefa Cup final in 2008, a League Cup winner in the 2007/08 campaign and collected an SPL badge in 2009 and 2010 as a valuable member of the title winning squads despite misfortune with injury. That bad luck included the curious case of the exploding egg, when the Ayrshire lad was hospitalised after an accident whilst microwaving a snack for himself at home. It is all part of the rich tapestry of life with Broadfoot on board.

The defender committed himself to a three-year contract in 2010 to end the uncertainty about his future. Despite links to Premier League newcomers Blackpool and to other English sides, home is very much where the heart is for the wholehearted stopper. Broadfoot and Edu look set to entertain the Ibrox crowd for years to come. The big question is who will follow them into the ranks of Ibrox cult heroes. The stage is set and the audience awaits as the latest band of players make their pitch in front of a crowd with a proud history of embracing its stars with warmth and affection that is difficult to match.

# Bibliography

*My Story*
John Greig
Headline, 2006

*Rangers: The Complete Record*
Bob Ferrier and Robert McElroy
Breedon, 2006

*To Barcelona and Beyond*
Paul Smith
Breedon, 2006

*Captain of Scotland*
George Young
Stanley Paul, 1951

*Legend: Sixty Years at Ibrox*
Bob McPhail and Allan Herron
Mainstream, 1988

*Rangers: The Waddell Years*
Stephen Halliday
Chameleon, 1999

*Rangers: An Illustrated History*
Rab MacWilliam
Aurum, 2002

*Rangers: The Official Illustrated History*
Stephen Halliday
Arthur Barker, 1989

*A Scottish Soccer Internationalists Who's Who*
Douglas Lamming
Hutton Press, 1987

Additional archive sources:

The Herald
Evening Times
The Scotsman
Sunday Mail
BBC Radio Scotland
Daily Telegraph
Aberdeen Press and Journal
www.rangersfc.co.uk
www.daviecooper.com